Algorithmic Reason

Algorithmic Reason

The New Government of Self and Other

CLAUDIA ARADAU
TOBIAS BLANKE

OXFORD
UNIVERSITY PRESS

OXFORD
UNIVERSITY PRESS

Great Clarendon Street, Oxford, OX2 6DP,
United Kingdom

Oxford University Press is a department of the University of Oxford.
It furthers the University's objective of excellence in research, scholarship,
and education by publishing worldwide. Oxford is a registered trade mark of
Oxford University Press in the UK and in certain other countries

Published in the United States of America by Oxford University Press
198 Madison Avenue, New York, NY 10016, United States of America

British Library Cataloguing in Publication Data
Data available

Library of Congress Control Number: 2021949806

ISBN 978-0-19-285962-4

DOI: 10.1093/oso/9780192859624.001.0001

Printed and bound by
CPI Group (UK) Ltd, Croydon, CR0 4YY

Links to third party websites are provided by Oxford in good faith and
for information only. Oxford disclaims any responsibility for the materials
contained in any third party website referenced in this work.

Contents

Acknowledgements

This book has been a journey of several years, which has spanned multiple disciplines in the social sciences, humanities, and computing. It took us several years to make sense of how disciplines and approaches diverge in their diagnoses of what is at stake with big data, algorithms, machine learning, or artificial intelligence. Tracing the sinuous contours of different debates across disciplines has been an arduous, at times disorienting, but also rewarding task. It has required getting to grips with varied concepts and methods and attending to how words carry not just different meanings but work differently across disciplinary and intradisciplinary practices. This journey was partly made possible by the fact that both of us had previously traversed disciplines and worked with the ambiguities and tensions between these: Claudia from English and French to political science and then international relations; Tobias from political philosophy to computer science and then digital humanities. Our rather eclectic trajectories can perhaps explain the theoretical and methodological eclecticism of the book. Yet, this is not an eclecticism of 'anything goes', but one that has been fostered by controversies and contestations we have followed and by the commitment to take seriously actors who enter these dissensual scenes, whether engineers or activists, scientists or workers.

This journey among and between disciplines would not have possible without the generosity and critical engagement of many friends and colleagues across different fields and institutions. Several friends have read and commented on different aspects of the book. Special thanks to Martina Tazzioli for discussions on knowledge and Michel Foucault, Elisa Oreglia on accountability and China, Jef Huysmans on enemies and anomalies, and Anna Leander on ethics and politics. Several chapters of the book have benefited from being aired at conferences, workshops, and invited lectures at universities in the US, UK, Brazil, France, Germany, Nepal, Switzerland, and South Korea. We would like to thank Jonathan Austin, Didier Bigo, Mercedes Bunz, Werner Distler, Jonathan Gray, Mireille Hildebrandt, Andy Hom, Alexandra Homolar, Anna Leander, João P. Nogueira, Sven Opitz, Martina Tazzioli, and Tommaso Venturini for invitations to present various aspects of this work. The panels on 'Data Worlds? Public Imagination and Public Experimentation with

Data Infrastructures', at the EASST 2018 Conference, provided a source of inspiration and motivation to continue work with digital methods. Friday's writing sprints with Jonathan Gray and Liliana Bounegru have brightened the final path towards completion.

We are especially grateful to the three anonymous reviewers for their generous support and insightful comments on a draft of the book. As their reports arrived at different times through the long COVID-19 pandemic, the book has gone through several instantiations, and it will probably look quite different if they were to see it again. Any errors, omissions, or misinterpretations remain ours alone. We would like to thank Dominic Byatt at Oxford University Press for his support for this project throughout its journey.

<u>From Claudia</u>: I would like to thank the participants of the Technology and Global Politics reading group. Reading a different book every month has been such a joy of collective thinking, transdisciplinarity, and the work of critique. The discussions greatly helped to trace a path that is neither determinist nor undetermined but what we have come to call in this book technological underdetermination. Thank you to everyone who has joined the group along the way and persisted through Zoom fatigue and all the other demands on their time. I am grateful to Amanda Chisholm for introducing me to the idea and practice of 'writing sprints', which have offered so many moments of motivation through the writing and rewriting process. The editorial collective of *Radical Philosophy* has been a source of reflection on untimely critique and the politics of working against disciplinary boundaries.

Over these years, my work on the book was made possible by support from the European Research Council Consolidator grant SECURITY FLOWS ('Enacting Border Security in the Digital Age: Political Worlds of Data forms, Flows and Frictions', Grant 819213) and the Economic Social and Research Council-funded project GUARDINT under the Open Research Area ('Oversight and Intelligence Networks: Who Guards the Guardians?', Grant ES/S015132/1). Many conversations with Ana Valdivia, Sarah Perret, Lucrezia Canzutti, and Emma Mc Cluskey have shaped my thinking and offered occasions for reflection on different disciplines and approaches. Special thanks to Ana Valdivia for bringing the Access Now/Spotify controversy to my attention and many inspiring discussions about technology. Study leave at King's College London had earlier offered the time to imagine this work as a book project. I am grateful to Vivienne Jabri for many conversations and friendship.

<u>From Tobias:</u> I would like to thank my colleagues at the various critical artificial intelligence (AI) communities in Amsterdam. There are too many to be all named here, but special thanks to Giovanni Colavizza, Ivana Išgum, Eelke

Heemskerk, Natali Helberger, Stefania Milan, Julia Noordegraaf, Thomas Poell, Maarten de Rijke, Sonja Smets, and Claes de Vreese. Each one of them comes from a different discipline and academic background, which makes Amsterdam so unique in a field that is too often dominated by either fatalist or technicist discourses. Without the knowledge and support from peers, this book could not exist.

The University of Amsterdam has provided me with the privilege of a research university chair, which meant I could spend much of my time on this book. Otherwise, my contributions have been made possible through several grants and collaborations over the years, which have mainly shown how difficult but also enjoyable it is to develop something interdisciplinary together. The work on digital methods with colleagues from the Public Data Lab and various Digital Humanities and Computational Social Science communities in Europe, Asia, and the US, which seem to only be growing in research strength and depth, deserves special mention, as does the work on critical tools and methodologies for the mobile ecosystem with Mark Coté, Giles Greenway, and Jennifer Pybus in several grants from the Arts and Humanities Research Council: 'Our Data Ourselves' (Grant AH/L007770/1), 'Zones of Data Translation' (Grant AH/R008477/1), and the ongoing European Commission-funded SoBigData collaborations (Grant Agreements 654024 and 871042).

Chapter 3 draws on some material published in 'Governing Others: Anomaly and the Algorithmic Subject of Security' in the *European Journal of International Security* (2018), particularly the third section on networks. Chapter 2 discusses some of the empirical material on the 'hacking' app published in 'Acts of Digital Parasitism: Hacking, Humanitarian Apps and Platformisation', *New Media & Society* (2019).

The image for the book cover was generated with the help of Daniel Chávez Heras, who researches computational spectatorship and how machines see at King's College London. It started as a collaborative exploration of a model developed by OpenAI using natural language phrases to generate images. We used several combinations of the book title and sentences from the book and ultimately settled on a combination of 'algorithms, self, and other'. OpenAI has not published how it created the model and exactly how its training data was collected, beyond mentioning that publicly available text–image pairs on the Internet were used (https://openai.com/blog/clip/). We have created several versions of the image and discarded the many that interpreted 'self' and 'other' as gendered male shapes. We also made many choices about style, and the one we settled for was inspired by 'glitch art'. The hard work of training the algorithm was done by Daniel. In the process, we could also see that the algorithm could not tackle abstract concepts well. The final image called for human estimation, approximation, and simple guesswork. It was more work than creativity. Producing the image additionally required infrastructure credits from Google. The book cover therefore is an expression of one of the key ideas in this book: that we need to understand algorithmic operations and AI from the perspective of work.

List of Figures

Introduction

From the hidden entrails of the National Security Agency to Silicon Valley, algorithms appear to hold the key to insidious transformations of social, political, and economic relations. "'Ad-tech" has become "Natsec-tech." Potential adversaries will recognize what every advertiser and social media company knows: AI is a powerful targeting tool', announced the Final Report by the United States (US) National Security Commission on Artificial Intelligence (AI).[1] Chaired by Eric Schmidt, former CEO of Google, and published at the end of the Trump administration in the US, the report captures a feeling of inevitability of AI for national security. National security will be defined not only by AI—understood as a constellation of digital technologies—but by a particular use of these technologies for marketing and targeted advertising. The comparison with advertising technology is not new for national security applications. It has become a staple of public understandings of digital technologies in an age where we are exposed to AI through our everyday online and social media experiences. We have become used to being targeted as part of our digital lives, while data insidiously travels between security and advertising, public and commercial actors.

Security agencies like GCHQ, the UK's signals intelligence agency, and big tech companies such as Facebook appear connected through the transformation of ourselves into data. Yet, these connections are less than seamless, as companies claim to protect privacy against mass surveillance and intrusion by security agencies, while the agencies in turn assert that they are the only ones to conduct legitimate surveillance. An exhibition at the Science Museum in London, which was dedicated to the centenary of GCHQ, prominently displayed a photo from an anti-Facebook demonstration.[2] Mass surveillance, the image seemed to suggest, is what companies like Facebook do, not GCHQ. This apparent confrontation between GCHQ and Facebook obscures the long-standing entwinement of state and commercial surveillance.

---

[1] NSCAI, 'Final Report'.
[2] Science Museum, 'Top Secret'.

Algorithmic Reason. Claudia Aradau and Tobias Blanke, Oxford University Press.
© Claudia Aradau and Tobias Blanke (2022). DOI: 10.1093/oso/9780192859624.003.0001

In the wake of the Snowden disclosures, a coalition of nongovernmental organizations (NGOs) challenged mass surveillance by UK intelligence agencies in a case brought before the European Court of Human Rights. They point out how state and commercial surveillance have been intermingled via direct collaborations as well as through infrastructures and techniques of data analysis: 'Facebook or WhatsApp messages, or emails, between two Londoners may be routed via California servers and are thus likely to be intercepted by the UK's bulk surveillance techniques and/or accessible via the intelligence sharing arrangements with the US, and subjected to automated profiling and analysis'.[3] However, according to the US National Security Commission on AI, security agencies risk missing out on the technological cutting edge. They are not guiding how state and commercial intelligence work together and are rather 'lagging behind' the commercial actors in their use of 'new and disruptive technologies such as AI'. A new competition with commercial surveillance demands that AI is integrated into more and more security practices.[4]

We can find such faith in algorithms, data, and AI almost everywhere in public and private spaces. It is not only security agencies and big tech companies that deploy similar technologies, extol their prowess, and embrace their inevitability. The NGO Save the Children set up a collaboration with a consulting firm, Boston Consulting Group, to develop predictive analytics technologies for their work on displacement. They were present at an exhibition on big data, which we attended, where their collaboration was heralded as the future of humanitarian action.[5] The prototype technology Save the Children developed was meant to predict the duration and scale of forced displacement and thereby transform humanitarian action by answering urgent questions: 'With limited resources and capacity, should they prioritise the delivery of water in trucks or construct a water pipeline? Distribute food vouchers or offer agricultural support? Build camps or move people into longer-term housing and support them to work in the community?'[6] The distinction as to what designates a long-term versus short-term crisis has become relegated to predictive algorithms, which promise to anticipate crises and their temporalities, as well as to reconfigure humanitarian action.

What do these algorithmic reconfigurations mean? How did algorithms—and the cognate technologies of big data and AI—come to inform so many

---

[3] Big Brother Watch, 10 Human Rights Organisations, and Bureau of Investigative Journalism and Others, 'Applicants' Written Observations', §19.

[4] NSCAI, 'Final Report', 63.

[5] Big Data & AI World London, 2019.

[6] Kaplan and Morgan, 'Predicting Displacement', 9.

social and political practices? How did they become an inevitable answer to problems of governing globally? The promise of algorithms traverses social and political fields globally, ranging from the politics of security to that of humanitarian action. This book proposes to understand the conditions of possibility of their production and circulation, which we call 'algorithmic reason'. Crime, displacement, terrorism, border control, democratic governance, security, and humanitarianism are increasingly reconfigured through new algorithms borrowed from other fields and massive amounts of data.

While there has been a lot of attention to differences in how digital technologies and algorithmic governance materialize across disparate sites, there is still a question about how algorithms and associated digital technologies have become the common answer to such heterogeneous and globally dispersed problems. We use algorithmic reason to render the rationalities that hold together proliferating and dispersing practices. The concept goes beyond algorithms as mere instruments for governing and emphasizes how a relatively new political rationality is ascendant. Through algorithmic reason, we can understand how national security questions find a link to Facebook's methods and how humanitarian action to govern precarious lives is entangled with big tech companies and start-ups. These are only two of the transformations that this book investigates. Across different social, political, and economic transformations, we show how algorithmic reason 'holds together' a new government of self and other, reshapes power relations between the governing and the governed, and unblocks the impasses of knowledge about individuals and populations.

Algorithmic reason

Algorithmic reason renders the conditions of possibility of rolling out algorithms for governing the conduct of individuals and populations, of friends and enemies, of normality and abnormality across social worlds and political boundaries. Following Michel Foucault, we attend to 'how forms of rationality inscribe themselves in practices or systems of practices, and what role they play within them'.[7] In her analysis of 'neoliberal reason', political theorist Wendy Brown has formulated it as 'a distinctive mode of reason, of the production of subjects, a "conduct of conduct," and a scheme of valuation'.[8] Similarly, we argue that algorithmic reason is a distinctive rationality, which

---

[7] Foucault, 'Questions of Method', 79.
[8] Brown, *Undoing the Demos*, 21.

makes possible governing practices and the production of datafied subjects through the promise of more precise knowledge and more efficient decision-making. Algorithmic reason has up to now been sparsely used, but we could trace its first mention in the work of legal scholar Antoinette Rouvroy to render the rationalities of algorithmic governmentality as 'data behaviourism', which does not require hypotheses, tests, and even subjects to help bureaucracies anticipate the behaviour of people.[9]

In arguing for a relatively novel algorithmic reason, we propose to analyse a distinctive, but not radically rupturing transformation. Social and political researchers tend to emphasize revolutionary epistemic and political rup-tures, and identify digital technologies—whether big data, algorithms, or more recently AI—as exceptional, leading to a mutation of democracy, the disap-pearance of reflexive subjects, and even the 'end' of politics.[10] Some go as far as claiming that algorithms threaten the mutation of democracy into a differ-ent mode of government altogether: 'algocracy' or the rule by algorithms.[11] Increasingly deployed in different spheres of social and political life, algo-rithms intensify oppression, inequality, and discrimination, which gives rise to the fear of a new algocracy.[12] They endanger collective action, human rights, political claims, and democratic imaginaries. Algorithms also dissolve norms and rules of international interaction, including the conditions of violence, as echoed in the infamous claim by General Hayden from the NSA that '[w]e kill people based on metadata'.[13] In these analyses, algorithms often acquire excep-tional and spectacular capabilities, which are intensified through the power of machine learning and the insatiable collection of big data.

While most observers are preoccupied with ruptures and dramatic trans-formations, critical scholars across the humanities and social sciences have cautioned that the focus on disruption effaces persistent continuities of so-cial and political inequality and exclusion. Science and technology studies (STS) scholar Ruha Benjamin has argued that algorithms continue to 'am-plify hierarchies', 'ignore and thus replicate social divisions', even when they purport to address discrimination and racial bias.[14] As she aptly points out, algorithmic discrimination is not just the result of a lack of diversity among engineers and data scientists or the effect of bias in the data. The racializing

[9] Rouvroy, 'The End(s) of Critique'.
[10] Kitchin, 'Big Data, New Epistemologies and Paradigm Shifts'; Rouvroy and Berns, 'Gouverne-mentalité algorithmique'.
[11] Danaher, 'The Threat of Algocracy'.
[12] Seminal contributions to these debates include Noble, *Algorithms of Oppression*; Benjamin, *Race after Technology*; Atanasoski and Vora, *Surrogate Humanity*; Apprich et al., *Pattern Discrimination*.
[13] Cole, '"We Kill People Based on Metadata"'.
[14] Benjamin, *Race after Technology*, 160.

effects of algorithms need to be analysed through wider socio-technical and political processes. Thus, Benjamin is careful to attend to what is distinctive about algorithmic discrimination and inequality by inviting us to 'decode … the racial dimensions of technology and the way in which different genres of humanity are constructed in the process'.[15] Given the ways in which algorithms amplify inequality and exploitation, critical scholars have coined 'technoprecarity' as a 'contemporary expression of long-extant forms of violence under racial capitalism'.[16]

Diagnoses of rupture and continuity undergird both public and academic discussions of the power of algorithms. We propose to understand these transformations without overemphasizing either continuity or discontinuity. Firstly, the conceptualization of algorithmic reason allows us to trace the entanglements of continuity and discontinuity in these practices of governing. Secondly, algorithmic reason offers a prism through which we can understand how the workings of algorithms are held together despite their apparent heterogeneity in practice. Therefore, we are concerned not to overstate ruptures but to attend carefully to Benjamin's warning not to ignore continuities of domination and oppression. In her work on imperial formations, anthropologist Ann Laura Stoler has invited us to think of continuity as simultaneous to reconfigurations and displacements, without falling back upon the extremes of 'too smooth continuities' or 'too abrupt epochal breaks'.[17] Stoler focuses on how colonialism endures, which requires attention to reactivations, reconfigurations, displacements as well as dispersions, and fragmenting processes. This also means working with concepts as not stable but fragile apparatuses. We trace the emergence of algorithmic reason and its materialization through conceptual apparatuses that are simultaneously stable and fragile, enduring and emergent.

Algorithmic reason names the conditions of possibility for what are multiple, mundane, and messy operations deployed to conduct the conduct of individuals and populations, self and other. Algorithms did not have an entry in mathematical dictionaries in the mid-nineteenth century and became central to the formalization and economic rationalization of behaviour only later, after the end of the Second World War.[18] We aim to understand how algorithmic reason emerges out of the obduracies of power relations and the asymmetries that sustain these. Through algorithmic reason as rationality, we

---

[15] Ibid., 32.
[16] The Precarity Lab, *Technoprecarious*, 2.
[17] Stoler, *Duress*, 6.
[18] Erickson et al., *How Reason Almost Lost Its Mind*, 30.

offer an account of what 'holds together' the heterogeneity of practices in their proliferation and dispersal.

In theoretical computer science, algorithms are understood as a sequence of instructions so that a computer can implement an activity on data. Communication science scholar Tarleton Gillespie succinctly renders algorithms when noting that they 'need not be software: in the broadest sense, they are encoded procedures for transforming input data into a desired output, based on specified calculations.'[19] In computing, algorithms are studied to design more efficient computational procedures with the final aim of automating certain activities as much as possible. In the 1970s, Donald Knuth, one of the most famous precursors of modern computer science, argued that computing is about the tension between automating processes and sometimes failing at it, and that 'the process of going from an art to a science means that we learn how to automate something.'[20] Algorithms are attempts to integrate automation and human skill. Machine learning algorithms, which are key to the transformations this book discusses, can be defined as automating the production of algorithms through learning from data or as algorithms learning to produce algorithms.

While the theory of algorithms has not changed much since Knuth's days, the practice of algorithms has developed into a global system of production and reproduction. Algorithms are often used as a stand-in for a variety of practices, to render the novelty, secrecy, and unintelligibility of alignments, tensions, struggles, ruptures, and power relations. Algorithms are socially managed and form the basis of a new view on social organizations. They consist of parts that are generally independently produced, often in a distributed fashion. Especially once algorithms materialize as code, they are less a single definable whole but consist of bits and pieces of reusable parts shared across the Internet and embedded in thousands of systems. Codes and algorithms are thus hardly ever the product of a single originator, be it an individual or organization. Their work is global, is distributed, is taken in small steps, and employs workflows that assemble fragments into products through human labour. In choosing 'algorithms' for the coinage of 'algorithmic reason', we attend to the conditions of possibility of practice as well as their messy and dispersed materializations. As anthropologist Nick Seaver cautions, we should not award algorithms 'a homogeneity and coherence that is elusive in practice.'[21]

---

[19] Gillespie, 'The Relevance of Algorithms', 167.
[20] Knuth, 'Computer Programming as an Art', 668.
[21] Seaver, 'What Should an Anthropology of Algorithms Do?', 381.

Like anthropologists, STS, and media scholars, we understand algorithms as multiple, entangled in complex socio-technical systems.[22] At the same time, we argue that we should not grant too much messiness and contingency to algorithms so that it becomes difficult to diagnose how algorithms are taken up, promoted, and circulate across the conduct of warfare, practices of security, the policing of populations, and the commercialization of individual behaviours. Questions of homogeneity and heterogeneity are not specific to algorithms, data, or technology, but have undergirded research on capitalism and governmentality more broadly. Tensions between the 'drive to economize all features of existence, from democratic institutions to subjectivity'[23] and 'actually existing neoliberalism'[24] are underpinned by these questions of what holds together and what distinguishes practices in their heterogeneity. However, it is possible to account for both homogeneity and heterogeneity, as political theorists Sandro Mezzadra and Brett Neilson have shown in their analysis of the extractive operations of capital as 'a systemic logic that both exploits discontinuities between existing social differences and produces new forms of spatial and temporal heterogeneity'.[25]

Rather than the spectacular, sovereign, or decisionist politics implied in algocracy, we trace the emergence of algorithmic reason through controversy and dissensus over the knowledge and power of algorithms and then unpack its materializations across mundane workflows of data gathering, cleaning, processing, and analysing that are often distributed globally and bound together through new infrastructures. Algorithms appear much more mundane, a matter of professional expertise, everyday work than what we often hear in the media. The more precise knowledge that algorithmic reason promises is one of decomposing and recomposing small and large data and processing these through various computational systems. The more efficient decision-making that algorithmic operations are supposed to entail can be split up into workflows of small steps of data representations and transformations. None of this is exceptional, but still transformative for how individuals and populations, self and other are to be governed.

---

[22] Bucher, *If ... Then*; Seaver, 'What Should an Anthropology of Algorithms Do?'; Ziewitz, 'Governing Algorithms'.

[23] Brown, *In the Ruins of Neoliberalism*, 11.

[24] Peck, Brenner, and Theodore, 'Actually Existing Neoliberalism', 3.

[25] Mezzadra and Neilson, *The Politics of Operations*, 19.

Governing self and other

As algorithms permeate practices of governing, they raise political questions about human–machine relations and 'the power to structure possibilities'.[26] In this book, we focus on how algorithmic reason reconfigures the lines between self and other, normal and abnormal, them and us. We analyse it from the perspective of government understood as the 'technique which permits people to conduct the life of other people'.[27] In this sense, government refers to a whole range of practices, actors, and devices to act upon the behaviour of self and others. The terminology of government and governing is oriented to asymmetric power relations between the governing and governed, techniques of shaping the conduct of others, and the relations of those who govern to themselves or what Foucault calls 'techniques of the self'.[28]

Algorithmic reason redraws the boundaries among those to be brought within the remit of government: the part and the whole, the individual and the population, self and other. What had in the past required strong narratives of difference about cultures, ethnicities, gender, or race is now produced and reproduced through permanent algorithmic practices that reconfigure lines of difference. For example, a predictive policing algorithm continuously and in real-time reconfigures a city space into suspicious and non-suspicious places, at the same time creating non-surveilled places and areas of interest. Facial recognition targets everybody in a crowd to find the one suspicious 'needle in the haystack' that stands out. It can only know how the needle is different from the haystack by comparing everybody with everybody else and producing modulations of the norm and regularity. Not only does algorithmic reason promise to find new others, but it invites 'techniques of the self' through a regime of datafication and efficiency. As we discussed earlier, NGOs like Save the Children discover how to integrate predictive analytics into their humanitarian actions. Digital platforms learn to decompose themselves into microparts to project their global power more efficiently. Similarly, AI organizations produce accountability and remake themselves as auditing organizations to be able to claim public 'trust' in their algorithms.

This book's orientation towards the government of self and other shares an interest in diagnosing the social and political effects of algorithms across social sciences and humanities. However, we have a different focus from the literature on algorithmic governance, which traces a form of 'social ordering

---

[26] Ananny, 'Toward an Ethics of Algorithms', 97.
[27] Foucault, *About the Beginning of the Hermeneutics of the Self*, 103.
[28] Ibid.,

that relies on coordination between actors, is based on rules and incorporates particularly complex computer-based epistemic procedures.'[29] Research on algorithmic governance has been broadly concerned with the 'automation of governance' and how to ensure its legitimacy, efficiency, and fairness.[30] Scholars have questioned the role of algorithmic sovereigns that act as 'mighty administrator[s]'—either in the way that algorithms work and seem to provide new solutions or in the failures they create.[31]

Algorithmic governance entails analyses of how algorithms become tools of governance, how they create problems of legitimacy, and how these problems can be addressed through a different regime of governance. The algorithmic power of social 'steering' and 'shaping' is often assumed, while algorithms themselves remain stable objects across time and place.[32] Moreover, as political theorist William Walters has noted, studies of governance tend to work with an irenic view of politics, which 'imagines a world in which nearly all the major problems can be solved by cooperation, networking, stakeholding, etc.'[33] By attending to how self/other relations are imbricated with algorithmic operations, we start from an understanding of governing practices as fraught and contested. Rather than depoliticizing, neutralizing, or apolitical, the materializations of algorithmic reason are deeply political.

When investigating the social effects of algorithms, there is an ambiguity in the literature about whether algorithms work a little too well, thereby ushering in algocracies, or whether they do not work so well and therefore fall short of discourses of efficiency, legitimacy, accuracy, and objectivity. For instance, reports on the Chicago police predictive policing software concluded that 'it didn't work.'[34] While the predictive policing software used by the Chicago police was among the most problematic, as it focused on personal and risk profiling, this diagnosis of failure has been replicated across several predictive policing programmes. And yet, the sale and production of predictive policing software continues apace. Not only have big players continued to expand their offerings, but new private actors have entered the fold. How can we account for the sustained production and circulation of these technologies when algorithms are publicly diagnosed as not working that well?

We argue that it is important to understand how algorithms underpin governing practices by destabilizing distinctions between what works and what

---

[29] Katzenbach and Ulbricht, 'Algorithmic Governance', 2.
[30] Danaher et al., 'Algorithmic Governance'.
[31] König, 'Dissecting the Algorithmic Leviathan', 477.
[32] Ibid.,
[33] Walters, *Governmentality*, 66.
[34] See Saunders, Hunt, and Hollywood, 'Predictions Put into Practice'.

does not work. Critical data scientist Cathy O'Neil also asks about the implications of how we define 'working' algorithms and unpacks it into three related questions: '[A]re the algorithms that we deploy going to improve the human processes that they are replacing?', 'for whom is the algorithm failing?', and 'is this working for society?'[35] However, O'Neil's analysis ultimately relies on the distinction between working and failing and thus leaves little room for contingent or emergent effects. We propose to attend to the operations of algorithms even when they appear not to work and when their promises do not seem to go together with their performative effects. We use 'operations' here in the etymological sense of workings, activities that are productive rather than activity in a general sense.[36] We are inspired by Mezzadra and Neilson's use of operations to render the interval that separates input from outcome.[37] Understanding how algorithms operate entails attention to the work that takes place in the interval or the production details and workflows to move from an input to an output.

Algorithmic operations cannot be separated from the data work that happens in-between in terms of big data processing, datafication, metadata work, machine learning, deep learning, and AI, which have come to infuse public and governmental vocabularies. Each of these terms is underpinned by specific modes of knowledge, practice, and politics. For instance, analyses of (big) data have tended to focus on activities of data collection. They have also attended to relations between citizens and state, as citizens have been made processable through the practices of data collection and processing. According to Didier Bigo, Engin Isin, and Evelyn Ruppert, data has become 'generative of new forms of power relations and politics at different and interconnected scales'.[38] Media theorist José van Dijck has emphasized the imagined objectivity of data that produces an ideology of 'dataism', where computational expressions of cultural and social relations are taken as the truth of these relationships.[39] 'We are data', cautioned cultural theorist John Cheney-Lippold in his analysis of how individual and collective subjectivities are transformed and unformed.[40] As data orients attention to the relations between state and citizens, it can also become an engine of activist politics. Scholars have proposed agendas around 'data activism' and 'data justice'.[41] Sociologists Davide

[35] Upchurch, 'Interview with Cathy O'Neil'.
[36] Oxford English Dictionary, '"Operation"'.
[37] Mezzadra and Neilson, The Politics of Operations, 67.
[38] Bigo, Isin, and Ruppert, 'Data Politics', 4.
[39] Van Dijck, 'Datafication, Dataism and Dataveillance'.
[40] Cheney-Lippold, We Are Data.
[41] Gutiérrez, Data Activism; Dencik et al., 'Exploring Data Justice'.

Beraldo and Stefania Milan have argued that we need to supplement 'data politics' with a 'contentious politics of data' to understand how data is effective at
every political level and 're-mediates activism'.[42] According to the critical data
scholar Jonathan Gray, 'data witnessing' renders another mode of attending
to 'the systemic character of injustices across space and time, beyond isolated
incidents'.[43]

Unlike data, the language of machine learning and AI as another in-between
of algorithmic operations has directed political attention towards the transformations of what legal scholar Frank Pasquale has called the 'black box society'.[44] Machine-learning algorithms and related AI technologies can quickly
appear as both secret and opaque, even to their designers. As such they can
intensify questions of discrimination, accountability, and control and reacti-
vate anxieties about human–machine relations as 'an insensate and affectless
system [that] seems to violate some fundamental notion of human dignity and
autonomy'.[45] As critical AI researcher Kate Crawford has pithily put it, AI is a
'registry of power', because 'AI systems are ultimately designed to serve existing dominant interests.'[46] Unlike the contentious politics of data, algorithms
and machine learning seem to more drastically restrict the space of political
contestation.

Therefore, critical analyses of algorithms and AI have been largely oriented
towards questions of power as domination. For Rouvroy and Berns, algorithmic governmentality is highly depoliticizing. It eschews the reflexive human
subjects by producing modes of supra-individual behaviour, which do not require subjects to give an account of themselves.[47] If the statistical government
of populations focused on producing aggregates, categorizing risk groups, and
assessing abnormalities, algorithmic governmentality is no longer concentrated on either individuals or populations, but on their relations. Beyond
shared norms and normativities, algorithms challenge political projects of the
common and emancipatory possibilities of action. Even when algorithms are
thought to produce publics, these are often seen as de-democratizing subjects,
a 'calculated public' as the network of subjects and objects linked together
through the digital.[48] Becoming 'algorithmically recognizable' creates the

[42] Beraldo and Milan, 'From Data Politics to the Contentious Politics of Data', 3.
[43] Gray, 'Data Witnessing: Attending to Injustice with Data in Amnesty International's Decoders Project', 985.
[44] Pasquale, *The Black Box Society*.
[45] Burrell and Fourcade, 'The Society of Algorithms', 14.
[46] Crawford, *The Atlas of AI*, 8.
[47] Rouvroy and Berns, 'Gouvernementalité algorithmique', 8.
[48] Gillespie, 'The Relevance of Algorithms', 168.

illusion of community, as algorithms are thought to produce echo chambers and filter bubbles.[49]

By analysing algorithms within the government of self and other, we attend to how algorithms are both productive and contested, how they encounter frictions, refusals, and resistance. Therefore, we aim to avoid narratives of loss, corruption, and depoliticization. Rather, as media theorist Bernhard Rieder has pointedly observed, 'the "politics" of an algorithm can depend on small variations that lead to radically different outcomes'.[50] We unpack these small variations through what we call a methodology of the scene.

Methodology of the scene

We approach algorithmic reason through the methodological device of the 'scene', as developed in the work of philosopher Jacques Rancière. For Rancière, the scene is the site of an encounter, which exposes the various ways in which a thing can be perceived.[51] We mobilize scenes as particular arrangements, which bring together algorithmic rationalities, make them temporally visible, and rearrange them. Scenes cannot be fully 'curated', as they unfold over time and can lead to unexpected actions and events. A scene reconfigures what is visible and knowable, what is accountable and unaccountable, what is particular and general. Scenes combine durability and contingency, homogeneity and heterogeneity, contestation and connection.

On the one hand, scenes are not just about arrangements of people and things, they are about litigious situations, controversies, debates, disputes, and even scandals. A scene can be dissensual or polemical, as the language of 'making a scene' captures. On the other hand, scenes require subjects as well as objects and cannot be imagined or staged outside processes of subjectivation and materialization. For Rancière, a scene draws together bodies, gestures, ways of seeing, words, and meanings. In so doing, it reconfigures a field of experience.[52] The idea of co-appearance has been central to understandings of a theatrical scene. A scene connects a multiplicity of things and not just people. Although scenes are often associated with theatre, a scene is not an institution, but it can be an everyday, mundane occurrence, as the language of 'scenes of everyday life' indicates.

---

[49] Ibid., 184.
[50] Rieder, *Engines of Order*, 19.
[51] Rancière and Jdey, *La méthode de la scène*, 30-1.
[52] Ibid., 29-31.

The methodology of the scene means that we do not start with presuppositions about which subjects and objects count, or which actors with which equipment should be considered important. People, technologies, devices, knowledge, and actions are drawn together in a scene. They appear, fade, or disappear as the scene unfolds. A scene can be a technology expo, the Snowden leaks, a parliamentary inquiry into the role of Cambridge Analytica, or an educational scene of 'hacking' algorithms. Scenes unfold in different directions, as they draw in a multitude of people, discourses, and things. For instance, Facebook became the object of public attention and controversy after it emerged that a lot of false information promoted by alt-right groups had circulated via the social network at the time of the US 2016 presidential election and the Brexit referendum in the UK.[53] This scene of controversy over machine learning and disinformation might have started in the media, but it has unfolded in a multitude of directions. It developed from the US Congress inquiry, an investigation led by journalists and the whistle-blower Chris Wylie, to Facebook acquiring AI start-ups in order to step up its fight against 'fake news'.

Approaching algorithmic reason through scenes allows us to attend to both their dispersed and distributed operations and the regime of rationality that holds these operations together. Feminist and information studies scholar Leopoldina Fortunati invites us to analyse the Internet as 'a terrain of confrontation, struggle, negotiation and mediation between social groups or political movements and even individuals with different interests'.[54] As a methodological device, the scene alerts us to internal differences and contestations over how algorithmic reason unfolds. A scene entails a hierarchy of spaces and a temporality of action. This asymmetry is central to a scene. All that is required is a movement of elevation: a step, a podium, or a threshold is sufficient.[55] These asymmetries also mean that a scene orients analysis to power asymmetries rather than assumptions of flatness and symmetry that have been often associated with related ideas such as assemblages.[56]

Our empirical analyses combine a wide range of materials, from analysing online and offline documents across fields of expertise to observing the justifications that actors offer of their practices at professional exhibitions, talks, and industry conferences, as well as in patents and online media. We have also used digital methods to follow algorithmic operations or to 'hack' apps developed by humanitarian actors. Developing the methodology of the scene

[53] O'Hear, 'Facebook Is Buying UK's Bloomsbury AI'.
[54] Fortunati, 'For a Dynamic and Post-Digital History of the Internet', 182.
[55] Duguy, 'Poétique de la scène', 148 (translation ours).
[56] Bennett, *Vibrant Matter*; Latour, *Reassembling the Social*.

required eclectic analytical vocabularies and methods that cut across the qualitative/quantitative binaries. This would not have been possible without our backgrounds in different disciplines, and the aim to speak across the computational and social sciences, and the humanities. For us, eclecticism has been an epistemic and political commitment to work beyond and against disciplinary boundaries.

Our different disciplinary backgrounds meant that we could not take analytical vocabularies for granted or make assumptions about what algorithms do. Much of the literature on algorithms, digital technologies, and AI has focused on processes of de-democratization and depoliticization, as these technologies are entwined with practices of domination, oppression, colonialism, deprivation of freedom, and debilitation of political agency. In this book, through the methodology of the scene, we offer a different political diagnosis of algorithmic reason. The scenes we attend to are all scenes of dissensus and controversy. Therefore, they allow us to trace how algorithmic variations inflect and hold together heterogeneous practices of governing across time and space. Moreover, in Part III of the book we argue that scenes of dissensus and controversy can become democratic scenes, in the sense of the opposition between processes of 'de-democratization' and 'democratization of democracy'.[57]

Structure of the book

The book is structured around three elements of algorithmic reason: rationalities (Part I), materializations (Part II), and interventions (Part III). The first two chapters unpack algorithmic reason as a political rationality that produces knowledge about individuals and populations to conduct their conduct and enables decisions that draw lines between self and other. In Part II, we investigate across three chapters how these rationalities are materialized in practice: the construction of potentially dangerous others, the power of platforms, and the production of economic value. The final three chapters unpack social and political interventions that aim to render algorithms governable by making them ethical, institutionalizing accountability, and reinscribing borders between the national and the international. Each chapter traces these transformations by following how particular scenes unfold through controversies and dissensus.

In the first chapter, we analyse the forms of knowledge that are produced through algorithmic operations on big data. Big data has generated much

---

[57] Balibar, *Citizenship*, 6.

anxiety about the ways in which traditional modes of knowledge have been unsettled by its ability to expand, given the increase in storage capacities and cloud technologies. We start from the scene of the Cambridge Analytica scandal, as the main actors claimed to have been effective in using large amounts of data to achieve substantial changes in the political behaviour of individuals and groups. While much of the controversy concerned the possibility of manipulating elections, we show that a different political rationality of governing individuals and their actions is at stake here. We argue that it is the decomposition and recomposition of the small and the large that constitutes the political rationality of governing individuals and populations. This logic of recomposition also recasts the distinction between speech and action so that a new mode of 'truth-doing' is established as constitutive of algorithmic reason.

Chapter 2 turns to algorithmic decisions and difficult political questions about algorithms making life and death decisions. We place algorithmic judgements within the controversial scene of predictive policing and use the method of 'following an algorithm' to understand the operations of an algorithm developed by CivicScape, a predictive policing company. Theoretically, we connect algorithmic decision-making with decisions as enabled by work relations, drawing on the lesser-known critical theory of Günther Anders. By following a predictive policing algorithm, we show how it operates through workflows and small shifts in data representations where each of the elements might influence the overall outcome. A second element of algorithmic reason emerges through the partitioning of abstract computational spaces or what are called 'feature spaces' in machine learning.

The next three chapters map how these rationalities of algorithmic reason are materialized through processes of othering, platformization, and valorization. Chapter 3 investigates the algorithmic production of suspicious and potentially dangerous 'others' as targets of lethal action. How is the line between the self and other drawn algorithmically, how do figures of the other emerge from the masses of data? Starting from the public scene of the NSA SKYNET programme, which wrongly identified the Al Jazeera journalist Ahmad Zaidan as a suspect terrorist, we show how others are now produced through anomaly detection. We argue that anomaly detection recasts figures of the enemy and of the risky criminal in ways that transform our understanding of racial inequalities and is more aptly understood in terms of what political philosopher Achille Mbembe has called 'nanoracism'.[58] Methodologically, there are numerous limits to analysing the unfolding of this scene, as the work

---

[58] Mbembe, *Politiques de l'inimitié*.

of security algorithms is kept secret. Some details were revealed by Snowden, but these remain partial. We draw on this disclosed material in conjunction with legal cases which challenged the targeting of Zaidan and another journalist, Bilal Abdul Kareem, as well as computer science literature and funded projects that expound the importance and techniques of anomaly detection.

Chapter 4 explores the materialization of algorithmic reason through the power of infrastructures. While the literature on digital platforms often focuses on data extraction, the building of monopolies, and the modes of enclosure that platforms bring about, we argue that the power of platforms emerges from the work of decomposing and recomposing. They simultaneously split up their components and recompose them into a globally integrated, but dispersed workflow. Platforms transform the Web of protocols and standards to become programmable and micro-serviced. Platform power makes the digital world programmable from a decomposed centre. We trace the materialization of platform power through the scene of digital humanitarianism and controversies over what algorithms and predictive analytics do to humanitarian action. Using the digital method of 'hacking' apps produced by humanitarian actors for refugees, we show how humanitarianism becomes 'platformized'. Humanitarian actors are increasingly entangled with big tech companies creating dependencies that shape the future of humanitarian action.

The third materialization of algorithmic reason we explore is that of value. How do algorithms generate and enhance economic value? Research on the value of data and the extractive dynamics of digital economies has supplemented work on digital practices of global exploitation and labour-centric analysis of value. Moreover, recent controversies about 'surveillance capitalism' and 'platform capitalism' have brought to public attention how value is produced differently as behavioural surplus and network value. We supplement these analyses with another form of valorization based on the rationality of decomposing the large and recomposing the small as analysed in Chapter 1. We take a scene of controversy around Spotify as an inquiry into the conjunction of digital production and surveillance. Expanding this scene through an analysis of Spotify patents, we show how value materializes not just through the global exploitation of human labour and the extraction of data at the multiple frontiers of capitalism, but also by augmenting limited music products with the expanding datafication of small and very small lived experiences.

The final three chapters discuss three 'interventions' to render algorithmic operations governable. We move here from being governed by algorithms to making algorithms governable. Vocabularies of ethics, accountability, and law have increasingly informed calls to restrict the power of algorithms and big tech companies. In Chapter 6, we analyse a series of initiatives by state, supra-state, tech industry, and civil society actors to deploy ethical principles and guidelines as a way of 'conducting the conduct' of developers, engineers, and companies. We argue that ethicizing algorithms has become a form of pre-empting dissensus. In contrast to this ethics of consensus, we analyse scenes of friction that turn algorithms and AI into 'public things'. We approach ethics as socio-material practices that are entangled with—rather than sepa-rate from—politics. 'Scenes of friction' can be both mundane events—such as the petition by the 4,000 Google employees against Google's involvement in the development of AI for military purposes—and experiments in frictional subjectivation—such as 'hacking' events where motley collectives of coders and non-coders are assembled.

Chapter 7 unpacks the facets of accountability as it emerged in the global scenes to render facial recognition algorithms controllable. It addresses po-litical calls across the world to make algorithms accountable and commit to explainable AI. An algorithmic accountability and auditing industry is de-veloping to answer growing concerns that humans cannot trust algorithms anymore. Facial recognition in particular has attracted wide public atten-tion and controversy. As facial recognition systems are increasingly deployed around the world, from the US to China, civil liberties activists and demo-cratic actors have underscored the high error rates and privacy invasions of facial recognition algorithms. The chapter shows how calls to render algo-rithms accountable have relied on producing accounts of algorithmic error and giving trustworthy explanations of what algorithms do. However, the implied translation of bias eschews the ways in which error enables the op-timization of algorithms, as error rates are just another means of ensuring that computers learn. Explainable AI makes algorithms accountable not through more equal understanding, but by demanding trust in algorithms and experts. Drawing on scenes of contestation of facial recognition in China, we offer a conceptualization of accountability through refusal. Attending to refusal as a form of accountability expands the political scene of algorithmic interventions and challenges Cold War political imaginaries that allocate 'good' and 'bad' algorithms as well as liberal and authoritarian approaches to technology to different parts of the world.

We close this book by turning to how algorithms have reactivated questions of borders between the domestic and international, between state power and the global power of big tech companies. The capabilities of big tech companies to extend their operations across the globe are by now almost taken for granted. At other times, the international emerges in the guise of warlike or colonial continuities: Google attempting to access the Chinese market, Facebook providing asymmetric digital infrastructures in India. Starting from the problem of drawing borders and boundaries as constitutive of the international, we analyse how states attempt to render algorithms governable by redrawing sovereign boundaries and by creating legal regulations of the content which social media companies have and circulate. In response to the reactivation of sovereign borders, social media companies have prioritized a different mode of governing that works through thresholds rather than geopolitical borders. Following a controversy over the governance of hate speech in Germany, we trace how states, companies, and workers reshape the contours of the international in several scenes that focus on Facebook. We show how workers disturb these renditions of the international by resisting both the companies and their discourses of AI-led content moderation as well as state claims to protect generic citizens.

In the Conclusion, we bring together the range of practices of contestation to develop a conceptualization of the relation between democracy, dispute, and de-democratization. While different theoretical approaches have prioritized specific dimensions of contestation, such as struggle, controversy, or dissensus, we argue that these need to be understood as a continuum. We discuss the implications of friction, refusal, and resistance for the politics of algorithmic reason.

PART I

RATIONALITIES

1

Knowledge

Algorithms embody reasoning.
—N. Katherine Hayles, *How We Think: Digital Media and
Contemporary Technogenesis* (2012), 49

Since the Snowden disclosures in summer 2013, no metaphor has circulated
more widely between defenders and critics of digital surveillance by intelligence agencies than the 'needle in a haystack'. Infamously used by Keith
Alexander, former director of the National Security Agency (NSA), to justify
mass surveillance, it has been invoked by the members of the UK's Intelligence
and Security Committee to make sense of the practices of GCHQ, the UK
signals intelligence agency; it is employed by the United Nations High Commissioner on Human Rights in reports on privacy, and by journalists to render
what is at stake in the practices of intelligence agencies concerning big data. It
has also become one of the most used analogies in the public discourse of big
data, artificial intelligence (AI) algorithms, and their capabilities.

The metaphor of the 'needle in a haystack' is not new. It goes back at least to
the discourses of security agencies post-9/11. Then it supplemented the mantra
of 'connecting the dots' that justified post-9/11 developments in counterterrorism, data mining, and algorithmic governance. In his critique of the Total
Information Awareness Act of the United States government back in 2003, security technologist Bruce Schneier agreed that '[d]ata mining is like searching
for a needle in a haystack'.[1] Yet, data mining for counterterrorism was inevitably flawed as 'throwing more hay on the pile doesn't make that problem
any easier'.[2] A mere decade later, such concerns had all but disappeared.

The 'needle in a haystack' metaphor continues to permeate public discourses
of knowledge production through big data and imaginaries of an epistemic
big data 'revolution'.[3] The report by the National Security Commission on AI,

---

[1] Schneier, 'Why Data Mining Won't Stop Terror'.
[2] Ibid.,
[3] Mayer-Schönberger and Cukier, *Big Data*.

Algorithmic Reason. Claudia Aradau and Tobias Blanke, Oxford University Press.
© Claudia Aradau and Tobias Blanke (2022). DOI: 10.1093/oso/9780192859624.003.0002

with which we started this book, sees AI as seamlessly helping intelligence professionals 'find needles in haystacks, connect the dots, and disrupt dangerous plots by discerning trends and discovering previously hidden or masked indications and warnings'.[4] For intelligence professionals, the 'needle in a haystack' captures a vision of globality and global threat and epistemic assumptions of visibility and invisibility, of uncovering secrets and accessing that which is hidden and concealed. It buttresses an epistemology of security that proceeds through 'small displaced fragments of information, establishing the investigation of links between subjects of interest, understanding patterns of behaviour and communication methods, and looking at pieces of information that are acquired through new and varying sources'.[5] It is also reassuring in its bucolic resonance and 'comforting pastoral imagery of data agriculture'.[6]

More than an associational epistemology of 'connecting the dots', the 'needle in a haystack' captures the epistemic shift in relation to the algorithmic processing of big data, away from problems of data size and scale towards seeing opportunities in fragments of digital data everywhere. This shift is not limited to the worlds of security professionals, as it is also present in the idea of long-tail economies that have driven algorithmic rationalities and big data analytics for the past decade.[7] Popularized by the former *Wired* editor Chris Anderson, known for his prediction of the 'end of theory' in the age of big data, long-tail economies render the move from economies based on a few 'hit' products to the increased number of 'niche' products. The promise of long-tail economies is that of 'infinite choice' and—implicitly—of profit from even the smallest products. The niche products of long-tail economies are the unknown needles in the haystack of interest to security professionals. This epistemological promise of small fragments, unknown 'needles', and the long tail has also travelled to political concerns about democracy and publics. Fears of so-called 'microtargeting' are translated into anxieties about how algorithmic knowledge can thwart or even undo democratic processes.

What is at stake in these concerns across security, economic, and political worlds is the relation between the large and small. Initial concerns about volume and scale of big data have given rise to inquiries into the small, the granular, and the micro. It is in this sense that the philosopher of information Luciano Floridi sees the value of big data in the 'small patterns' that it can

---

[4] NSCAI, 'Final Report', 111.
[5] House of Commons, 'Investigatory Power Bill', Column 1087.
[6] Crawford, *The Atlas of AI*, 207.
[7] Anderson, *The Long Tail*.

reveal.[8] Louise Amoore and Volka Piotukh have highlighted the 'little analytics' which turn big data into 'a series of possible chains of associations', while computer scientists speak about 'information granularity' and 'data granules'.[9] Big data connects the epistemological promise of capturing everything—collecting and storing all data records seems within humanity's reach—and of capturing the smallest, even insignificant details. The small, banal, and apparently insignificant detail simultaneously harbours the promise of personalized medicine, atomized marketing, granular knowledge of individuals, and security governance of unknown dangers. In a world of data, nothing is too small, trivial, or insignificant.

Long before big data, the small and the large, the whole and its parts, the general and the particular had been part of the great epistemic 'divides' in natural and social sciences, requiring distinct instruments that would render them accessible as well as separate methods and infrastructures of knowledge production. For instance, statistical reasoning in the social sciences, which prioritized the generality of groups and aggregates, was criticized for effacing individual complexity and specific detail. Historian of statistics Alain Desrosières challenges such a strong line of separation in arguing that statistics, understood in its institutional and not just scientific role, has been a mediator between state activities focused on the individual (such as courts) and on the general population (such as economic policy or insurance).[10] Statisticians had to connect small and disparate elements to produce aggregates. The gap between the small and the large and attempts to transcend it are not unique to statistics and can be understood in relation to the government of individuals and populations.

Algorithmic reason promises to transcend the methodological and ontological distinctions between small and large, minuscule and massive, part and whole. As the languages of macro-scale and micro-scale or holistic and individualistic methods indicate, the small and the large have historically required different material apparatuses and analytical vocabularies. Transcending the gap between them has been a partial and difficult endeavour. Yet, with big data, '[t]he largest mass goes along with the greatest differentiation', as historian of

---

[8] Floridi, *The Fourth Revolution*, 16.

[9] Amoore and Piotukh, 'Life Beyond Big Data'; Pedrycz and Chen, *Information Granularity*.

[10] Desrosières, 'Du singulier au général'. Desrosières offers examples where statistical reasoning does not exclude individual cases. He argues that the traditional dichotomy between individual and aggregate cases can be surpassed (271). However, this move seems unidirectional, as it proceeds from singular pieces of information to aggregates or adds aggregate statistics to make decisions on individual cases.

risk and insurance François Ewald has aptly put it.[11] The theorist of networks Bruno Latour and his colleagues have also argued that, with big data, '[i]nstead of being a structure more complex than its individual components, [the whole] has become a simpler set of attributes whose inner composition is constantly changing.'[12] In their pithy formulation, the whole has become smaller than the sum of its parts. While social sciences have grappled with the problems of the great divides and have attempted to dissolve, blur, or resist these dichotomies, these tensions in knowledge production have been reconfigured through big data.[13]

We argue that, rather than privileging the small over the large, the part over the whole or vice versa, algorithmic reason entails the continuous decomposition of the large into the small and the recomposition of the small into the large.[14] This epistemic transformation, which combines previously exclusive methods, instruments, and approaches, is transforming the government of individuals and populations. What can be known and what becomes unknowable? What becomes governable and what is ungovernable? To trace the elements of algorithmic reason, we start from the Cambridge Analytica scandal and its use of digital data in elections around the world. The initial public denunciation of Cambridge Analytica's use of data and machine learning algorithms problematizes the relation between populations and individuals, large and small, significant and insignificant both epistemologically and politically. What could be known about individuals and groups through the masses of data extracted by Cambridge Analytica from Facebook and other digital platforms? Was the large too large to be comprehensible and the small too small to be consequential? How is such knowledge mobilized in the government of populations and individuals? These controversies that burst into the public show how algorithmic reason transcends the binaries between the small and the large, the individual and collective, telling and doing, which have shaped both social sciences and the government of individual and collective conduct.

---

[11] Ewald, 'Omnes et singulatim', 85.

[12] Latour et al., '"The Whole Is Always Smaller Than Its Parts"', 607.

[13] Latour gives the example of Tarde's sociology as an attempt to transcend such divides. Latour, 'The End of the Social'.

[14] We use variations of 'composition' to understand algorithmic reason, as the terminology of composition combines heterogeneity and some coherence by putting different objects together. As Latour notes, composition becomes a question of what is well or badly composed rather than what is constructed or not. What is composed can also be decomposed. Latour, 'An Attempt at a "Compositionist Manifesto"', 474. Moreover, as Jonathan Austin has argued about security compositions, a composition is a 'symbiotic combination or compounding in which relationally linked objects become, quite literally, more than the sum of their parts'. Austin, 'Security Compositions', 259; see also Bellanova and González Fuster, 'Composting and Computing', and Leander, 'Sticky Security'.

Cambridge Analytica large and small

The former British company Cambridge Analytica erupted into public light following media revelations that it had worked with Donald Trump in the 2016 US election campaign.[15] The ensuing controversy, which has unfolded across the pages of newspapers, parliamentary inquiries, and academic journals, has seen journalists, activists, politicians, and social scientists split over whether Cambridge Analytica's techniques of data collection and algorithmic processing were simply another form of propaganda or whether they were able to manipulate elections by changing the views and behaviour of significant numbers of individuals. This debate was then folded into a wider controversy that unravelled transnationally—from the UK and Germany to the US and Canada—and which refocused on the role of social media companies and particularly Facebook in political campaigning.[16] Much of the controversy concerned the harvesting of user data and breaches of privacy by Facebook, from whom Cambridge Analytica initially collected the data. The $5 billion settlement between Facebook and the US Federal Trade Commission highlighted the new privacy obligations and the privacy regime that Facebook would need to set in place.[17] Mark Zuckerberg reacted to the scrutiny of Facebook after Cambridge Analytica in a long blog post where he reiterated a 'pivot towards privacy' within Facebook and promised extensive machine-learning capacities to remove 'harmful content'.[18]

Initially centred on the 2016 presidential elections in the US and the Brexit referendum in the UK, the Cambridge Analytica revelations showed wide-ranging interventions in elections around the world, from India to Kenya. However, it soon became clear that, unlike traditional polls or surveys companies employed in political campaigns, Cambridge Analytica had used large sets of third-party data combined with survey data of US populations. 'This is publicly available data, this is client data, this is an aggregated third-party data. All sorts of data. In fact, we're always acquiring more. Every day we have teams looking for new data sets', explained Alexander Nix, former CEO of Cambridge Analytica.[19] Such public statements and the subsequent

---

[15] Cadwalladr and Graham-Harrison, 'Revealed: 50 Million Facebook Profiles Harvested for Cambridge Analytica'; Rosenberg, Confessore, and Cadwalladr, 'The Facebook Data of Millions'.
[16] The final report by the Digital, Media, Culture, and Sport Committee of the UK House of Commons outlines these transnational elements of the controversy. DCMS, 'Disinformation and "Fake News": Final Report'.
[17] Federal Trade Commission, 'Statement of Chairman and Commissioners'.
[18] Zuckerberg, 'Facebook Post'.
[19] Butcher, 'Cambridge Analytica CEO Talks to Techcrunch about Trump, Hillary and the Future'.

journalistic emphasis on the volume and variety of data collected by the company focused public attention on the legal uses of data by Cambridge Analytica, which included questions of informed consent, privacy, and data protection. Much of the debate in the wake of reporting by the UK's the *Guardian*, the *Observer*, and Channel 4 addressed privacy and the effects of psychological profiling on the US 2016 presidential election. But wider questions of the social and political effects of big data also emerged.

The public life of big data extracted by Cambridge Analytica started with an app designed by psychologist and former Cambridge University research associate Aleksandr Kogan. The app 'thisisyourdigitallife' contained a survey that promised to give participants insights into their psychological profile. The app also gained access to the participants' network of friends, likes, and, according to former Cambridge Analytica employee and whistle-blower Chris Wylie, even private messages.[20] Paul Grewal, Facebook former Vice President and Deputy General Counsel, claimed that the 270,000 people who downloaded the app 'gave their consent for Kogan to access information such as the city they set on their profile, or content they had liked, as well as more limited information about friends who had their privacy settings set to allow it'.[21] Given that the app could access not only the information of the people who downloaded it, but also of their friends, Facebook estimated that Kogan had data from 87 million Facebook users.[22]

What did Cambridge Analytica know with the data it had acquired and how did it know from the data? The distinction between the small and the large, individuals and populations has been central to these questions. While the media has placed emphasis on the 87 million social media users whose personal data has been extracted, others have focused on the intimate details that can be garnered from apparently insignificant data. For many of the media reporters and social scientists involved in the debate, big data afforded access to large numbers of individual profiles. Yet, the practices of Cambridge Analytica were indicative of a shift in how political campaigns used voter data: 'The capture and consolidation of these data permit the construction of detailed profiles on individual voters and the "micro-targeting" of increasingly precise messages to increasingly refined segments of the electorate, especially in marginal constituencies.'[23] In his memoirs, Wylie also credits the knowledge of Cambridge Analytica as reaching to the micro-level and the individual: 'Behind

[20] Wylie, *Mindf*ck*.
[21] Grewal, 'Suspending Cambridge Analytica'.
[22] Information Commission Office, 'Facebook Ireland Ltd. Monetary Penalty Notice'.
[23] Bennett, 'Voter Databases, Micro-Targeting, and Data Protection Law', 261.

the campaign was the emerging practice of *microtargeting*, where machine-learning algorithms ingest large amounts of voter data to divide the electorate into narrow segments and predict which *individual voters* are the best targets to persuade or turn out in an election.'[24]

Not everyone agreed that the prediction of individual behaviour and electoral propensities was so successful. For critics, Cambridge Analytica sold a big data myth and had neither the data nor the microtargeting capacities it was allegedly wielding. It was doubtful that Cambridge Analytica had the data to develop psychographic profiles or that their algorithms could 'yield subtler information than classic marketing'.[25] Moreover, microtargeting could only over-promise macro-results for large population groups in society.[26]

The two positions can be understood along opposite epistemic lines. The first one emphasizes the volume of data and therefore access to exhaustive knowledge about large numbers of individuals. According to critical theorist Bernard Harcourt, this knowledge is 'far richer' than the knowledge of biopower, as it 'extends into every crevice and every dimension of everyday living of every single one of us in our individuality'.[27] In this approach, it is either the large or the small that gains epistemic priority. The large translates into exhaustive knowledge about the general population, while the small renders granular knowledge about various facets of individuals' lives. The opposite position critiques continuing difficulties as well as the impossibility of ascending from the small to the large and of descending from the large to the small. Here, the gap between the small and the large is unsurpassable. Neither access to psychological profiling nor the quality of data justifies the knowledge of individuals that Cambridge Analytica advertised.

On both sides of this controversy, big data is indicative of a novel epistemic promise. With big data, algorithmic operations ascend from the small to the large or descend from the large to the small, thereby transcending the limits of statistics, which traditionally used induction, averages, and summaries. The mobilization of statistics to govern populations has often been equated to a shift from individuals and individualizing power to populations and massifying techniques of biopower. As statistics aimed to develop a 'macrosocial

[24] Wylie, *Mindf*ck*, 22(emphasis added).
[25] Venturini, 'From Fake to Junk News', 124.
[26] Resnick, 'Cambridge Analytica's "Psychographic Microtargeting"'. The mathematician Hannah Fry has also pointed out that the effects of microtargeting or micro-manipulation can be marginal. As she puts it, 'even with the best, most deviously micro-profiled campaigns, only a small amount of influence will leak to the target'. At the same time, she acknowledges that 'those tiny slivers of influence might be all you need to swing the balance' (Fry, *Hello World*, 37).
[27] Harcourt, *Exposed*, 103.

order superior to contingent individuals', it enacted a displacement from the level of the individual to the level of the mass.[28] Therefore, in moving from the singular individual to the general population of aggregates and averages, statistical methods do generally not address 'the desire to be more accurate in the individualized case'.[29]

Statistics gave rise to a distinct political rationality of governing populations. It aimed to stabilize and govern collective objects by using large numbers. As Desrosières has put it,

> [t]he aim of statistical work is to make *a priori* separate things hold together, thus lending reality and consistency to larger, more complex objects. Purged of the unlimited abundance of the tangible manifestations of individual cases, these objects can then find a place in other constructs, be they cognitive or political.[30]

Unlike statistics, algorithmic operations do not purge 'the tangible manifestations of individual cases' but thrive on their multiplication and proliferation. We can understand the need for big data analytics to address the statistical limitations of governing populations. With data analytics and the recent explosion of digital data, we see a 'back and forth between individuals and their respective regroupings'.[31]

For one of the most prominent practitioners of big data in the social sciences and advocate of a new 'social physics', Sandy Pentland from the MIT Media Lab, 'a mathematical, predictive science of society that includes both individual differences and relationships between individuals has the potential to dramatically change the way government officials, industry managers, and citizens think and act'.[32] If statistics enacts stable collective objects and relations between these, it has often been accussed of sacrificing individuality and complexity in the general aggregates and averages. The individual could only be derived from the characteristics of the group to which it had been subsumed.[33] Big data, however, promises to return to the individual and even infra-individual details, while not losing the population, the whole, or the large in the masses of data.

---

[28] Desrosières, 'Masses, Individus, Moyennes'.
[29] Harcourt, *Against Prediction*, 32.
[30] Desrosières, *The Politics of Large Numbers*, 236.
[31] Desrosières, 'Mapping the Social World'.
[32] Pentland, *Social Physics*, 165.
[33] Bernard Harcourt argues that, in the early twentieth century, an actuarial logic 'reoriented thought ... toward the *group* and *classification*' (Harcourt, *Exposed*, 147 (emphasis in text)).

The reconfiguration of key dichotomies of social and political life and the return to the individual have given rise to a discourse of fear about the uses of what Wylie has called in the earlier quote 'microtargeting' for political campaign purposes and the fate of democracy. Microtargeting has become the political equivalent of security practitioners' 'needle in a haystack'. Researchers have debated its underlying epistemic effects and particularly what a UK parliamentary inquiry into 'Disinformation and "fake news"' labelled as a 'risk to democracy'.[34] The report goes as far as to assume that the knowledge produced through big data amounts to a new form of propaganda, as 'this activity has taken on new forms and has been hugely magnified by information technology and the ubiquity of social media'.[35] In addressing concerns about echo chambers and filter bubbles, Internet studies researcher Axel Bruns, however, cautions that such alarmist arguments are often based on 'technological determinism and algorithmic inevitability'.[36] Rather, we need to ask what is distinctive about the knowledge produced through algorithmic operations upon big data and what is specific about algorithmic microtargeting.

At first sight, the political techniques advertised by Cambridge Analytica resonate with older techniques of targeted communication: audience segmentation and targeted advertising. Yet, epistemically, it is the 'micro' in the 'targeting' that has raised most questions and concerns about lasting risks to democracy. What is produced as 'micro' with data? Surveys, polls, and questionnaires have long relied on statistical classifications of populations, but they summarized and represented groups, developing expectations of behaviour based on different versions of the 'average'. 'Average' behaviour stands for a 'macro' expectation we might have of everybody's behaviour. Traditionally, statistics produced and relied on macro-ensembles of national, ethnic, or class categorizations.

In an inquiry into the uses of social media and Facebook in the UK, Nix gave a lengthy outline of the key elements of microtargeting as deployed by Cambridge Analytica, while acknowledging that specific strategies and techniques depend on different legislative environments around the world. According to Nix, the most important element of their work was the collection of diverse data, taking in everything they could possibly find:

In a country such as the United States, we are able to commercially acquire large datasets on citizens across the United States—on adults across

---

[34] DCMS, 'Disinformation and "Fake News": Final Report', 15.
[35] Ibid., 5.
[36] Bruns, *Are Filter Bubbles Real?*, 19.

the United States—that comprise of consumer and lifestyle data points. This could include anything from their hobbies to what cars they drive to what magazines they read, what media they consume, what transactions they make in shops and so forth. These data are provided by data aggregators as well as by the big brands themselves, such as supermarkets and other retailers. We are able to match these data with first-party research, being large, quantitative research instruments, not dissimilar to a poll. We can go out and ask audiences about their preferences, their preference for a particular purchase—whether they prefer an automobile over another one—or indeed we can also start to probe questions about personality and other drivers that might be relevant to understanding their behaviour and purchasing decisions.[37]

Once assembled from diverse sources, Nix's big data can be used to create associations that enable the segmentation of smaller and smaller groups, as well as the creation of dynamic categories beyond averages. In the quote, these are 'personality and other drivers', which categorize behaviour and decisions. Such work requires ever more data, with Facebook being only one source among many. Nix cites mainly commercially available data in the US, which can be employed to build profiles for social media microtargeting. The US data broker Acxiom, for instance, claims to have files on 10% of the world's population.[38] It offers 'comprehensive models and data' on consumer behaviours and interests.[39]

Big data is used to produce continually emergent and changing composites among populations to be targeted. To make clear how effective this operation can be, Nix uses the comparison with advertising to account for the power of Cambridge Analytica's data and algorithms. In the inquiry, he compares their work with 'tailoring' and 'communicating' products like 'cars' so that 'you can talk about, in the case of somebody who cares about the performance of a vehicle, how it handles and its metrics for speeding up and braking and torque and all those other things'.[40] Different aspects of a vehicle are assumed to speak to different groups, so that marketing communication could selectively target these fragments of an imagined whole. Nix seems to be suggesting that Cambridge Analytica approaches targeting as a division of the whole into parts—the whole of the message is split into parts like the whole of a car can be split in fragments; the population

---

[37] Nix, 'Oral Evidence', 14.
[38] Office of Oversight and Investigations, 'A Review of the Data Broker Industry'.
[39] Acxiom, 'Consumer Insights Packages'.
[40] Nix, 'Oral Evidence', 14.

is divided into micro-groups, which are then correlated with other data fragments.

In Nix's vision, the accumulation of more and more data is simultaneous with the greatest fragmentation. It is perhaps even only interesting because of that. The promise of Cambridge Analytica's microtargeting is the ability to decompose the largest population into the smallest data and to recompose the smallest part in the largest possible data. How is the epistemic conundrum of the large and the small solved? The large and the small are quantities upon which Cambridge Analytica and other data analytics companies apply different techniques of composition and decomposition. In the section 'Composing and decomposing data', we show how algorithmic reason can appear so politically attractive, as it transcends the binaries of part and whole, populations and individuals by composing the smallest details and decomposing the largest multiplicities.

Composing and decomposing data

As Nix's comments in the section 'Cambridge Analytica large and small' outline, what is at stake in the public controversy around Cambridge Analytica and Facebook data is the epistemic tension between the large and the small, the micro and macro, the individual and the population. The decomposition of the whole into the smallest possible data and its recomposition is not simply a mathematical operation of division and addition. By decomposing and recomposing the large and the small, algorithmic reason has produced not just an epistemic transformation, but also a political rationality of governing individuals and populations.

For many, it was the massive data, the collection and algorithmic processing of vast amounts of data that might have changed the fate of the 2016 elections in the US or the Brexit referendum in the UK. Massive data has many fans in many areas of digital analysis. Peter Norvig, Director of Research at Google, has claimed that Google does not necessarily have better algorithms than everybody else, but more data.[41] Marissa Mayer, Google's former Vice President of Search Products and User Experience, had also noted 'that having access to large amounts of data is in many instances more important than creating great algorithms'.[42] Many algorithms had not fundamentally changed, and there was

---

[41] Quoted in Schutt and O'Neil, *Doing Data Science*, 338.
[42] Quoted in Perez, 'Google Wants Your Phonemes'.

'no single scientific breakthrough behind big data', as 'the methods used have been well known and established for quite some time'.[43]

The concept of 'datafication' has particular significance in this context, since it suggests that everything can be data. As Mayer-Schönberger and Cukier have put it, 'to datafy a phenomenon is to put it in a quantified format so that it can be tabulated and analysed'.[44] They use the example of the Google Ngram Viewer to show how the larger data of a whole book can be further datafied by splitting it in smaller parts or N-grams.[45] N-grams are here simply a number 'n' of characters in a word joined together. The word 'data', for instance, contains two 3-grams: 'dat' and 'ata'. N-grams might not help us understand texts better, but they provide computers with a way to parse vast amounts of heterogeneous texts.

If books can become computer-readable data, then everything can be data. Mayer-Schönberger and Cukier have argued that big data unravels existing epistemologies and methodologies of knowledge production by providing us with N = all, where 'N' is the common letter used to describe samples in statistics, while 'all' stands for the totality of data.[46] In N = all, N does not stand for the number that cannot be expanded upon anymore. It is the moment the sample becomes everything so that the distinction between part and whole can be transcended. Statistics appears revolutionized not through scientific breakthroughs and new models, but through the exhaustiveness of data. In 2009, Microsoft researchers proclaimed the emergence of a fourth paradigm of data-intensive research in science.[47] With massive data, science moves from the idea that 'the model is king' to 'data is king'.[48]

Yet, big data is not only problematic in its empiricist promise of capturing reality, but in the capacity of turning it into knowledge for the government of individuals and populations.[49] Deemed 'too big to know', big data challenges existing analytical and methodological capacities to transform it into something workable. This is the challenge that computer scientists and engineers identified in big data when arguing that '[t]he pathologies of big data are primarily those of analysis'.[50] Big data always goes beyond what can currently be processed. This paradox has been starkly expressed in the wake of the Snowden disclosures about intelligence practices. Documents released by the Intercept

[43] Lehikoinen and Koistinen, 'In Big Data We Trust?', 39.
[44] Mayer-Schönberger and Cukier, *Big Data*, 78.
[45] Ibid., 85.
[46] Ibid., 26.
[47] Hey, Tansley, and Tolle, *The Fourth Paradigm*.
[48] Abbott, *Applied Predictive Analytics*, 11.
[49] Rob Kitchin has offered one of the most lucid criticisms of big data empiricism. Kitchin, 'Big Data, New Epistemologies and Paradigm Shifts'.
[50] Jacobs, 'The Pathologies of Big Data', 20.

note the 'imbalance between collection and exploitation capabilities, resulting in a failure to make effective use of some of the intelligence collected today'.[51] The problem here is not the bigness of data, but the computational capabilities and algorithmic operations to analyse data.

This epistemic concern behind the 'big data revolution' is repeated with either optimism or regret about the capabilities of acceding to minuscule and granular details, which could be detected within the large collectives or the whole of data. As Wylie argues in his memoirs, 'data-driven microtargeting allowed campaigns to match a myriad of granular narratives to granular universes of voters—your neighbour might receive a wholly different message than you did, with neither of you being the wiser'.[52] As discussed earlier, critics of Cambridge Analytica's discourse challenged this epistemic optimism and argued that the company neither had the knowledge of the electorates it purported to have nor could it be directly effective and manipulative of large numbers of voters.[53] The small details remained insignificant and could not be translated into governing the conduct of large populations.

The initial denunciation of Cambridge Analytica's practices turned into an epistemic controversy over large-scale or small-scale inquiry and their specific instruments. The conjunction of the small and the large, the individual and the population has never been straightforward or even feasible. With statistics, the production of aggregates, averages, and classifications relied on but subsequently effaced individual details. With big data, as Latour and his colleagues have astutely pointed out, the shift from the small to the large, from the part to the whole and back has become possible.[54] Algorithms can decompose big data into smaller and smaller units and recompose them again into bigger data. Book content can be split up into N-grams and reassembled again. This ontology of small and big data entails the promise to seamlessly move in any direction and only ever find data—whether small or large. With data, one can move from the very large, the massive data that would ultimately capture everything and record everyone on the planet, as well as the small, the insignificant, or even infinitesimal detail that might hold the clue to an election win, the next terrorist attack, pandemic, or smallest socio-economic advantage. While data work is never seamless, the algorithmic decompositions and recompositions of big data undo the dichotomies that have structured methodological and epistemological debates about the small and large. They also transcend the tensions in the government of *omnes et singulatim*, of all and

---

[51] The Intercept, 'Digint Imbalance'.
[52] Wylie, *Mindf*ck*, 14.
[53] Karpf, 'On Digital Disinformation and Democratic Myths'.
[54] Latour et al., '"The Whole Is Always Smaller Than Its Parts"'.

each, namely the rationalities and techniques directed towards individuals and those oriented towards populations.[55]

The practices of Cambridge Analytica have also appeared to be much less exceptional than Nix's grand announcements might have suggested. The company deployed rather mundane algorithmic operations on data. Their banality was highlighted in the investigation conducted by the Information Commissioner Elizabeth Denham (ICO) in the UK. It concluded that Cambridge Analytica and its parent company SCL Group were not exceptional in their practices, as their methods relied on 'widely used algorithms for data visualisation, analysis and predictive modelling'. Rather than new algorithms,

> [i]t was these third-party libraries which formed the majority of SCL's data science activities which were observed by the ICO. Using these libraries, SCL tested multiple different machine learning model architectures, activation functions and optimisers ... to determine which combinations produced the most accurate predictions on any given dataset.[56]

Denham's letter to the UK Parliament explains that, instead of developing complex new algorithms, Cambridge Analytica's emphasis was on collecting all possible data, small and large:

> SCL/CA were purchasing significant volumes of commercially available personal data (at one estimate over 130 billion data points), in the main about millions of US voters, to combine it with the Facebook derived insight information they had obtained from an academic at Cambridge University, Dr Aleksandr Kogan, and elsewhere.[57]

This large volume and variety of data points allowed Cambridge Analytica to build computational models that clustered not the whole population, but individuals who could be targeted by advertising. Wylie had concurred that the company's work required a permanent focus on data and finding 'extra data sets, such as commercial data about a voter's mortgage, subscriptions, or car model, to provide more context to each voter'.[58]

Decompositions and recompositions of the small and the large produce not just larger clusters and groups, but the individuals themselves. The singular

[55] Foucault, 'Omnes et singulatim'; Foucault, Security, Territory, Population.
[56] ICO, 'Letter to UK Parliament', 16.
[57] Ibid., 2.
[58] Wylie, Mindf*ck, 24.

individual has now been replaced by a big data composite. Individuals have become the staging points of big data strategies, abundant multiplicities of data rather than reductive statistical averages.[59] As one practitioner has put it: 'Big Data seems primarily concerned with individual data points. Given that this specific user liked this specific movie, what other specific movie might he [sic] like?'[60] The epistemic specificity of big data resides not in the details of individual actions or massive data about social groups and populations. Algorithmic reason is not simply recasting the relation between masses and individuals, between part and whole, making possible their continual modulation. It affords infinite recompositions of reality, where small and insignificant differentials become datafied and inserted in infinitely growing data. Data is without limits at both the macro-scale and micro-scale, and it allows the conjunction of scales in ways that are unexpected for both social and natural sciences. As Ewald has remarked, '[e]ach element of data is unique, but unique within a whole, as compared to the rest'.[61]

Algorithmic reason conjoins *omnes et singulatim*, the particular and the general, the part and whole, the individual and the population and transcends limitations of epistemic and governing practices.[62] Its distinctive promise is not that of endless correlation or infinite association, but that of surmounting the epistemic separation of large-N/small-n through relations that are endlessly decomposable and recomposable. Yet, these algorithmic compositions and decompositions are not necessarily truthful. Which data compositions gain credibility and which ones should undergird governmental interventions? If nothing is too small or insignificant to produce knowledge, what will count as truthful knowledge? Although less reverberating than the Cambridge Analytica scandal, a related professional controversy about speech and action simmered in the worlds of big data. It became no less tumultuous, as it moved from the world of social and computer sciences to that of a public debate.

Truth-telling, truth-doing

In his lecture series on *Wrong-Doing, Truth-Telling*, Michel Foucault traces a specific mode of the production of truth—truth-telling about oneself or

---

[59] The concept of dividual was coined by Gilles Deleuze and is widely used to render the quantified or datafied self. Deleuze, 'Postscript on the Societies of Control'. On the quantified self, see Lupton, *The Quantified Self*.

[60] Janert, *Data Analysis with Open Source Tools*, 7.

[61] Ewald, 'Omnes et singulatim', 85.

[62] Foucault, 'Omnes et singulatim'.

avowal. Avowal, Foucault argues, was 'the decisive element of the therapeutic operation' in the nineteenth century and became increasingly central to the fields of psychiatry, medicine, and law.[63] For instance, the therapeutic practice required the patient to speak the truth about oneself. Law also demanded avowal as confession, truth-telling about oneself. For Foucault, avowal is a verbal act through which a subject 'binds himself [*sic*] to this truth, places himself in a relation of dependence with regard to another.'[64] Avowal as a form of truth-telling about oneself is different from other modes of knowledge production—for instance, the demonstrative knowledge of mathematics or the inductive production of factual knowledge. Avowal is situated in a 're-lationship of dependence with regard to another', relying on and reproducing asymmetric power relations.[65] Truth-telling about oneself would appear to be a strange intruder in the world of computer science and datafied relations. And yet, questions of what is truthful in the masses of data, whether small details should count or not, are entwined with the problematization of truth-telling about oneself.

The extension of algorithmic operations to the smallest and least significant element has problematized what counts as truthful knowledge about individuals and collectives. Which elements of the datafied individual should feed the algorithms? 'You are what you click', announced an article in *The Nation* in 2013.[66] 'You are what you resemble', states controversial computer scientist Pedro Domingos in his book, *The Master Algorithm*.[67] In their complaint against Cambridge Analytica, the Federal Trade Commission describe this production of subjectivity through 'likes':

> For example, liking Facebook pages related to How to Lose a Guy in 10 Days, George W. Bush, and rap and hip-hop could be linked with a conservative and conventional personality. The researchers argued that their algorithm, which was more accurate for individuals who had more public Facebook page 'likes', could potentially predict an individual's personality better than the person's co-workers, friends, family, and even spouse.[68]

Clicking and liking are the elements that enable the algorithmic production of 'truth' from what otherwise appear to be unconnected actions. How do these

---

[63] Foucault, *Wrong-Doing, Truth-Telling*, 12.
[64] Ibid., 17.
[65] Foucault, *Wrong-Doing, Truth-Telling*, 17.
[66] Auerbach, 'You Are What You Click'.
[67] Domingos, *The Master Algorithm*, 177.
[68] Federal Trade Commission, 'Complaint against Cambridge Analytica', 3.

different actions compose the small and the large and what happens with truth-telling about oneself in the process?

Sandy Pentland, former MIT Media Lab director and one of the most influential data scientists, articulates the difference between what he calls 'honest signals' beyond raw data and the implicitly dishonest sense of language.[69] He draws a sharp distinction between social media big data and behavioural big data. The former is about language, while the latter is about traces of actions. If for Foucault truth-telling about oneself entailed a verbal act in the form of avowal, Pentland appears to discard the truth of language in favour of the truth of action. In this sense, big data is not only about quantification or even mathematization, but it is about reconfiguring relations between speech and action, undoing distinctions between saying and doing.

While discarding social media 'likes', Pentland acknowledges the significance of language by recasting it as 'signals' of action. Language is not significant for what people say, but for the signals that reveal the nonconscious actions accompanying speech: 'How much variability was in the speech of the presenter? How active were they physically? How many back-and-forth gestures such as smiles and head nods occurred between the presenter and the listeners?'[70] Pentland proposes to build 'socioscopes', which are the combined big data equivalent of the 'telescope' and the 'microscope', as they can compute the complexity of social life in rich and minute detail.[71] His socioscopes become the basis of a renewed science of 'social physics'.[72] The data of interest to Pentland is what individuals do rather than what they say: 'Who we actually are is more accurately determined by where we spend our time and which things we buy, not just by what we say and do'.[73]

Former Google data scientist and author of the *New York Times* bestseller and the *Economist* Book of the Year *Everybody Lies*, Seth Stephens-Davidowitz joins Pentland in the indictment of the truthfulness of what we say. To avoid the problem of deception through language, big data promises access to the 'truth' of behaviour by recording banal, seemingly insignificant actions: 'Big Data allows us to finally see what people really want and really do, not what they say they want and say they do'.[74] If Pentland focuses on

---

[69] Pentland, *Honest Signals*.

[70] Ibid., vii–viii.

[71] Pentland, *Social Physics*, 10.

[72] Pentland is interestingly oblivious to the genealogy of social physics and Adolphe Quetelet's nineteenth-century proposals for a new science of the social. Quetelet's social physics was based on the probabilistic law of large numbers and ideas of the average man. Desrosières, *The Politics of Large Numbers*.

[73] Pentland, *Social Physics*, 8.

[74] Stephens-Davidowitz, *Everybody Lies*, 44.

digital traces collected or leaked on mobile phones, Stephens-Davidowitz takes Google searches as indicators of truthfulness. He translates Google queries into truthful actions rather than deceptive speech. Queries become acts or doings, as they are not uttered in a social context defined by collective normative and ethical constraints. In his general pathologization of behaviour, Stephens-Davidwitz effaces the distinction between normative constraint and construction. Assuming that we are generally alone when searching online, he proceeds to explain that Google users dare to ask questions such as 'Why are black people rude?' or 'Why are Jews evil?'.[75] The conditions of production of racist and anti-Semitic content on the Web are discarded in favour of reading them as truthful 'signals' of subjective behaviour.

Algorithmic reason promises to undo another great divide in the history of knowledge production between the social and natural sciences, that between speech and action. Rather than shifting from speech to action or recasting speech as action, both speech and action are decomposed in order to descend into the minuscule details of 'truth-doing about oneself'. In this reasoning, it is the small, banal acts that become valuable data as the proxies that can be computed and composed to produce truth. For Stephens-Davidowitz, big data about ourselves does not 'lie' because Google search engine data does not filter cultural and ethical constraints. We can zoom into the hidden details of lives free of constraint or social construction. Big search data produces a granular and at the same time 'true' understanding beyond the supposed lies of everyday human communication. Pentland's 'socioscopes' similarly put their trust into the smallest digital traces, the data our devices, bodies, and transactions 'leak', often without our awareness.

When Pentland argues for a shift from social media and speech to digital traces of action, he is justifying not just the truth of doing, of conduct and behaviour but a particular type of doing. It is the involuntary in the body, the nonconscious action and speech that become the harbingers of truth. The subject's speech and action are produced as truthful insofar as they have become 'noncognizers', to use literary critic Katherine Hayles's terminology. For Hayles, noncognizers are part of a distributed cognitive ecology of human and nonhumans, which destabilizes the dichotomy of conscious/unconscious by adding a further form of 'nonconscious cognition'.[76] Unlike cognizers, noncognizers cannot make choices and produce interpretations. The concept is particularly helpful here, as it draws attention to another

---

[75] Ibid., 219.
[76] Hayles, *Unthought*.

decomposition of dichotomies, this time not by multiplying relations but by inserting a supplementary term. As Sun-ha Hong has aptly noted, technologies of self-surveillance such as tracking devices are 'technologies of and for the nonconscious'.[77] Cognizers and noncognizers are not distinguished along human/nonhuman lines, but the human subject is enacted in a hierarchy of conscious and nonconscious cognition, speech and action, truth and nontruth.

Avowal was one governmental technique of connecting language and action, saying and doing, conscious action and choice. Foucault outlines this technique in the hypothetical speech of a judge: 'Let us say that the judge essentially told the accused: "Don't simply tell me what you did without telling me, at the same time and through this, who you are".'[78] Big data continues such questioning of subjectivity, but differently. If instead of a judge, we take Mark Zuckerberg and his hypothetical speech, then we would have variations of: 'Do tell me what you like and at the same time and through this, you tell me who you are' or 'Do click and at the same time and through this, you tell me who you are'. Unlike Zuckerberg, Pentland's socioscope would insert a subtle variation: 'Don't tell me what you did but keep doing what you did'.

To form connections between speech and action, material devices are needed to render a multitude of acts into computable data. These devices that record clicks, how much of a movie we watched on Netflix, whether we have 'liked' a page on Facebook, at what time a search was performed or from which location do not just render our lives measurable and quantifiable. These devices—from social media platforms to different sensors—create new regimes of knowledge and truth. They turn minuscule actions and nonconscious gestures into signals and finally 'structured data'. In so doing, they avoid the complexities and ambiguities of language and replace them with something that digital devices can better compute. They also eschew the limits of truth-telling, which was underpinned by both moral and civic assumptions that presupposed 'a reciprocal and prior recognition of the group by the individual and the individual by the group' and made truth-telling an impossibility in, for instance, the colonial context.[79] Deception and sincerity cannot be separated from the social and political context of dependence or domination.

Yet, algorithmic reason transcends such moral and political limits of truthtelling by recasting both saying and doing as nonconscious actions, which take the form of structured data. As computer scientists know well, computers

---

[77] Hong, *Technologies of Speculation*, 165.
[78] Foucault, *Wrong-Doing, Truth-Telling*, 215.
[79] Fanon, 'Conduits of Confession in North Africa (2)', 304. For a discussion of confession in Foucault and Fanon, see Lorenzini and Tazzioli, 'Confessional Subjects and Conducts of Non-Truth'.

prefer structured and semantically defined data for their processing. In times of messy and varied big data, smaller structured data has become ever more valuable, as it can be more easily computed. Thus, truthful knowledge is produced in a digital economy, where 'nonconscious' actions are more readily datafied. For instance, a tweet contains a limited number of characters and has become well known for its pithy communication. However, the structured data linked to it can be much larger than the content of any one tweet.[80] This is what the *Economist* called the 'digital verbosity' of a tweet that can reveal a lot both about the author of a tweet and their social network.[81] Here, this additional structured data stands for the algorithmic relevance of small details that are structured enough to be 'actionable' by computers. While media scholars have rightly argued that 'raw data' is an oxymoron,[82] what is produced as computable structured data is what becomes truthful. Truthful knowledge is what can be easily datafied and made algorithmically actionable as structured data.

As we saw in the Introduction, big data has been criticized for its 'generalized digital behaviourism' that avoids any confrontation with the human subject, either physically or legally.[83] We have argued that neither generalized empiricism nor behaviourism can account for the production of algorithmic knowledge. Algorithmic reason transcends dichotomies of speech and action through a reconfiguration of doing as nonconscious actions rather than willed acts, either individual or collective. Truth-telling about oneself has entered computer science through the mediation of digital devices that extract data at the smallest level as digital traces. Testimony, speech, evidence do not disappear, but are decomposed as both conscious saying and nonconscious doing. For Stephens-Davidowitz, queries using the Google search engine are not just significant semantically, but also as signs that are indicative of doings. Algorithmic reason decomposes speech and action and reconfigures their relation to truth by rendering them as nonconscious acts.[84]

Decomposing the large and recomposing the small, reconfiguring language and action hold together the intelligence professionals' desire to find the 'needle in a haystack', the marketing and advertising professionals' dream to access consumers' desires and the politicians' quest for a granular representation of

---

[80] Stoker-Walker, 'Twitter's Vast Metadata Haul'.

[81] *The Economist*, 'Digital Verbosity'.

[82] Gitelman, *Raw Data Is an Oxymoron*.

[83] Rouvroy, 'The End(s) of Critique'; Rouvroy and Berns, 'Gouvernementalité algorithmique'.

[84] This decomposition of saying and doing cannot be understood in the terms of 'signals' and 'traces', the former carrying meaning and the latter simply recording behaviours. Dominique Cardon has conceptualized a 'radical behaviourism' in order to render the growing relevance of digital traces for algorithms (Cardon, *À quoi rêvent les algorithmes*, 66–71).

electorates. Algorithmic reason binds these varied 'wills to knowledge' by transcending the great divides of natural and social sciences. Part and whole, small and large, individual and mass, language and action are no longer produced with different devices and deployed in different regimes of knowledge. Big data does not discard one in favour of the other and it does not prioritize the mass, the population, and the group at the expense of individual differences. It also does not simply rely on our 'curated' information and exposure as a basis for correlations. Through big data's moves of composition and recomposition of the small and the large, the singular individual and the general population are inextricably entwined and infinitely extricable.

The small and the large, the individual and the collective are continuously composed and decomposed, from focus groups to Facebook 'likes', and from clicks to debt information. What is at stake here is not to uphold an ahistorical discourse of scientificity, rigour, causality, or demonstrative truth against the imagined algorithmic 'undoing' of knowledge, but to understand how algorithmic reason responds to the epistemic cleavage between the small and the large and the gap between the government of individuals and populations. As new rationalities appear to simultaneously transcend the great divides and dichotomies of the social sciences and the impasses of governing *omnes et singulatim*, they also encounter the question of difference. How are governmental lines to be drawn? In Chapter 2, we turn to this other element of algorithmic reason: the problematization and government of difference.

2

Decision

To decide is to cut.

—Michel Serres, *The Parasite* (1982), 23

Algorithms shape not only what we see, how we are taught, how books are written, how party manifestos are put together, but also what urban areas are policed, who is surveilled, and even who might be targeted by drones. As most explicitly put by the US whistle-blower Chelsea Manning, '[w]e were using algorithms to catch and kill'.[1] In Foucault's terms, algorithms appear to 'let live and make die', thus resuscitating the arbitrariness of sovereign decisions.[2] Algorithmic decision-making carries the spectre of sovereign exceptionalism through the verdict on the figure of the enemy and the constitution of a new normal.[3] Unlike the knowledge of individuals and populations, algorithmic decision-making is about the 'cut', which induces perceptions of the splitting of self and other, of the delimiting, confinement, and management of zones of suspicion, risk, and danger.

In 2016, two data scientists, Kristian Lum and William Isaac, published a paper that simulated the use of PredPol, a predictive policing software deployed by many police forces in the US and beyond, to a large urban area in the US.[4] They compared the number of drug arrests based on data from the Oakland Police Department with public health data on drug use. Using the PredPol algorithm, they could show that, 'rather than correcting for the apparent biases in the police data, the model reinforces these biases'.[5] Initially developed by the anthropologist Jeffrey Brantingham at UCLA and the mathematician George

[1] Woods, '"We Were Using Algorithms to Catch and Kill"'.
[2] Foucault, *The Birth of Biopolitics*.
[3] Algorithmic decision-making can be seen as more akin to administrative discretion than the decisionism that Carl Schmitt saw as defining sovereignty. According to Bonnie Honig, 'within the rule-of-law settings that Schmitt *contrasts* with decisionism, something like the decisionism that Schmitt approvingly identifies with a dictator goes by the name of discretion and is identified (approvingly or disapprovingly) with administrators and with administrative governance' (Honig, *Emergency Politics*, 67).
[4] Lum and Isaac, 'To Predict and Serve?'.
[5] Ibid., 18.

Algorithmic Reason. Claudia Aradau and Tobias Blanke, Oxford University Press.
© Claudia Aradau and Tobias Blanke (2022). DOI: 10.1093/oso/9780192859624.003.0003

Mohler at Santa Clara University in California in collaboration with US police forces, PredPol had quickly come to stand in for the new technologies of
predictive policing. But it has equally become one of its most controversial
technologies, despite claims of not using personal data and reliance on criminological theories. Activists, data scientists, and other scholars then entered
the fray.

Brantigham responded to these denunciations of bias and discrimination
with a paper of his own.[6] His arguments were largely shaped by the distinction of human/nonhuman decision-making and the problems of algorithmic
opacity/legibility. For the proponents of data-driven, predictive policing, algorithmic decision and crime models were imagined as 'augmenting' and
'supporting' human decisions. Algorithms remained devices of objectivity—
rather than subjectivity—and increased accuracy—rather than bias and stereo-
typing. For critics, algorithms wrested the power of decision and discretion
from humans, as they increasingly decided not just what we should pay attention to, but who becomes the target of governmental control.[7] Rather than
reducing power asymmetries and racialized suspicion, algorithmic decision-
making produced intensified bias, worked upon racialized data, and amplified discrimination.[8] Ruha Benjamin argued the crime prediction algorithms
should be called 'crime *production* algorithms', as they act as 'self-fulfilling
prophecies' in the continuity of institutional racism in the US.[9]

In the debates on predictive policing, algorithmic decisions are also often
criticized as opaque and unintelligible, as they were undoing human styles
of reasoning and democratic accountability. As the Institute of Mathematics
noted in their evidence submitted to a UK House of Commons inquiry into
algorithmic decision-making, 'no human being can say "why" the algorithm
does what it does, nor can predict what it will do on data which are not the
training data'.[10] Critical scholars have highlighted the intensified inscrutability
of algorithms, making 'predictions based solely on algorithm-derived correlations opaque and difficult to interpret (and hence difficult to justify to
stakeholders)'.[11]

---

[6] Brantingham, 'The Logic of Data Bias and Its Impact on Place-Based Predictive Policing'.
[7] Amoore and Raley, 'Securing with Algorithms'.
[8] For instance, Noble, *Algorithms of Oppression*; Benjamin, *Race after Technology*.
[9] Benjamin, *Race after Technology*, 83 (emphasis in text).
[10] Institute of Mathematics and its Applications, 'Written Evidence', 6.
[11] Chan and Bennett Moses, 'Is Big Data Challenging Criminology?', 36. See also Pasquale, *The Black Box Society*; Introna, 'Algorithms, Governance, and Governmentality'; Burrell, 'How the Machine "Thinks"'.

In response to these critiques, governmental and corporate actors have tried to 'tame' the exceptionality of algorithmic practices by submitting them to a 'bureaucratization' of decisions. Rather than decisionist acts, bureaucratization relies on the introduction of norms, rules, and formalities within governance processes.[12] For instance, in the UK, a parliamentary inquiry into algorithmic decision-making recommends accountability tools such as principles and codifications, audits of algorithms, certification of algorithm developers, and ethics boards charged with oversight of algorithmic decisions.[13] Bureaucratization entails the production of norms and standards, as well as a range of instruments for reducing uncertainty such as transparency, trust, or explainability. According to IBM, '[t]rust in AI systems will be earned over time, just as in any personal relationship. Put simply, we trust things that behave as we expect them to.'[14] Trust tames uncertainty about the workings of algorithms. We will address this call for the bureaucratization of algorithms through accountability in Chapter 7. In this chapter, we concentrate on the production of algorithmic decisions.

We propose to understand how heterogeneous algorithmic decisions are constitutive of another element of algorithmic reason and the government of difference. To do so, we 'follow' a predictive policing algorithm in order to unpack its decisions as distributed workflows and unexceptional data transformations. As Kate Crawford has highlighted, understanding algorithms as making sovereign or autocratic decisions 'focuses solely on the moment of where an algorithm "acts" to produce an outcome, [and] forecloses more complex readings of the political spaces in which algorithms function, are produced, and modified'.[15] To develop an understanding of the political rationality of algorithmic decision, we look towards nuclear technologies, as analysed by critical theorist Günther Anders.[16] Algorithms have not produced the amount of destruction that nuclear technologies have, but both are inflection points

---

[12] Béatrice Hibou has proposed the terminology of 'bureaucratization' to understand a 'set of normative and procedural arrangements [that are] diffuse, dispersed and often elusive' (Hibou, *The Bureaucratization of the World*, 11). Bureaucratization is not limited to the state, but it characterizes practices of private and civil society actors as well.
[13] House of Commons Science and Technology Committee, 'Algorithms in Decision-Making', 74.
[14] IBM, 'Written Evidence'.
[15] Crawford, 'Can an Algorithm Be Agonistic?', 3.
[16] Anders, *Burning Conscience*; Anders, *Nous, fils d'Eichmann*. Anders's work has inspired discussions about technology and society largely outside the English-speaking world. The correspondence with Claude Eatherly is one of the few translations available in English. Excerpts from the first volume of *Die Antiquiertheit des Menschen* have recently appeared in English: Müller, *Prometheanism*. An unofficial translation of Anders's *Die Antiquiertheit des Menschen 2* is available online as *The Obsolescence of Man*. We have used quotations from this English translation but have also compared them with the German original. English-language debates of Anders have tended to focus on nuclear weapons and nuclear techno-politics, like van Munster and Sylvest, 'Appetite for Destruction'. The potential

for rejecting binaries of the human/nonhuman brought about by technological developments and transforming the meaning and practice of decisions. Situating algorithmic decisions within the details of production or workflows shows them as unexceptional and yet transformative. We argue that algorithmic decisions are partitions of an abstract space of data features based on calculations of distances. The 'cut' or the partition of so-called feature spaces reconfigures binaries of human/nonhuman, opacity/legibility, and self/other. The rationality of partitioning acquires an infra-sensible character, which recasts political questions of collective sense-making. It is also supra-sensible, as it operates in high-dimensional spaces beyond human perception.

To develop this argument, we start with Anders's diagnosis of the impossibility of decision in the age of nuclear technology. In a second step, we turn to a public scene of controversy over predictive policing and the transformation of police discretion and algorithmic discrimination. Most of the research on predictive policing so far has focused on the policing side, outlining the effects of algorithms on policing practices. Our interdisciplinary collaboration makes it possible to 'follow an algorithm' that CivicScape, a company producing predictive software for policing, has made available on GitHub in a move to render its data and analytics publicly auditable. While most predictive software is shrouded in commercial secrecy, CivicScape responded to public controversies over discrimination by promoting its 'transparent' algorithm. This allows us to show how algorithmic decisions are produced as mundane partitions of data spaces. Thirdly, we retrace algorithmic decision-making through computational geometries of what we term 'betweenness', which are spatialized relations between data points.

Unexceptional decisions in the Nuclear Age

Günther Anders has developed a detailed theory of decisions in the industrial society. His analysis focuses on a highly exceptional moment—the invention and deployment of nuclear weapons. Yet, Anders's analysis starts from the everyday, unexceptional conditions of work and production under capitalism, which lead to an unprecedented transformation. In that sense, Anders offers a different analytical prism through which to approach decision than either exceptionalism or bureaucratization. Exceptionalism has been most closely connected with the work of Carl Schmitt, who has proposed an antidemocratic

of Anders's critical theory for addressing the digital revolution have also been highlighted by Fuchs, 'Günther Anders, Undiscovered Critical Theory'.

theory of decision-making. As international relations scholars Daniel Bessner and Nicolas Guilhot note, '[f]rom the 1920s until today, the decisionist imagination was shaped by a pessimistic sensibility in which liberal democracy was considered an ineffective form of governance whose representatives were incapable of making existential decisions'.[17] Confronted with this antidemocratic penchant, most prominent in Schmitt's rendition of sovereign decision as exceptional and irrevocable, other scholars have turned to bureaucratization as a more democratic view of decision-making. Whether embedded in parliamentary procedures or administrative discretions, decisions are seen as 'frequent and multiple, and they are available to a number of political agents'.[18] The diagnosis of bureaucratization is not only limited in its understanding of dispersed decisions, but it has paid scant attention to questions of technology, even as a key moment of the bureaucratization of decision-making was shaped by the uncertainty of nuclear weapons and war.

Although the invention of nuclear technology was an exceptional moment, which portended the possible annihilation of all humanity, Anders analyses its conditions of possibility within industrial capitalism. His work is little known in the English-speaking world and has generally been less translated in comparison to other Frankfurt School critical theorists. One of the few works available in English is Anders's correspondence with the Hiroshima pilot, Claude Eatherly.[19] In 1959, he sent a letter to Eatherly, of whose psychiatric disorders, inability to live a 'normal' civil life, and internment in a psychiatric ward he had read about in a US magazine. For the critical theorist, Eatherly's malaise speaks to the diagnosis of the technological society that Anders outlines across the two volumes of *The Obsolescence of Man*.[20] He highlights the impossibility of sovereign decision, which emerges in a complex system of redistribution of labour between human and machine, where the pilot both acts and does not act:

For example, the claim that the pilot of the plane that dropped the bomb on Hiroshima 'acted' when he pressed his button, sounds incorrect. In view of the fact that his physical effort, which might have attested to his 'productive

---

[17] Bessner and Guilhot, 'Who Decides?', 19.

[18] Palonen, 'Parliamentary and Electoral Decisions as Political Acts', 85.

[19] While there is a paucity of translation in English, Anders's work has been more widely translated into French, Italian, and Spanish.

[20] In later work, Anders provocatively argues that 'Hiroshima is everywhere', as a manifestation of the transformation of societies in the age of the second and third Industrial Revolutions (Anders, *Hiroshima Ist Überall*).

activity', was entirely insignificant, one might even say that he did not do any-thing at all.... Nor did he see the effect of his 'productive activity', since the mushroom cloud that he saw is not the same as the charred corpses. Nonethe-less, with the help of this 'not doing anything', in a kind of *annihilatio ex nihilo*, he caused two hundred thousand people to pass from life to death.[21]

As Anders explains in the letters to Eatherly, humans have become 'screws in a machine' in this technological world, which are 'used in actions, the effects of which are beyond the horizon of our eyes and imagination'.[22] Yet, it is neither passivity nor simply the Marxist rendition of the alienated worker that An-ders establishes here. Eatherly is caught in a dispersed system, where action as well as decision have changed their meaning, and in an epistemic and ethical conundrum about the effects of his act.

Anders's response to Eatherly's conundrum is underpinned by his analysis of work in industrial capitalism. As workers no longer have the image of the whole product of their labour and thus come to lose the imagination of what the end product of work can be, Anders locates a gap between subject's capac-ities of action and imagination. This disjunction was at the heart of what he saw as the second Industrial Revolution, where we produce more than we can imagine. In distributed and complex work systems, workers cannot visualize what they have become able to produce.[23] The diagnosis of this disjunction was also central to other letters, which Anders sent to the son of Adolf Eichmann. These, however, remained unanswered. Unlike the intense correspondence with Eatherly, Anders only penned two letters to Eichmann's son. In the first letter, he reiterates his view of human decision and agency:

An abyss has opened up between our capacity to manufacture and our capacity to conceptualize, and it is growing every day; our capacity to manufacture—given that technological progress cannot be contained—is un-limited, but our ability to imagine the implications is by its nature limited. To put it more simply, the objects that we are today accustomed to produc-ing with the assistance of our impossible-to-contain technology, as well as the effects we are capable of causing, are so enormous and so powerful that we can no longer comprehend them, much less identify them as our own. And naturally it's not just the excessive magnitude of our achievements that

---

[21] Anders, *The Obsolescence of Man*, 44. In the original, Anders uses 'ungenau' at the end of the first sentence, which is better translated as 'inaccurate' rather than 'incorrect'.
[22] Anders, *Burning Conscience*, 1.
[23] Anders, 'Theses for the Atomic Age', 496.

overwhelms our capacity to imagine their implications, but also the unlimited mediation of our work processes.[24]

According to Anders, the making of productive workers is also a particular disciplining of the senses and cognitive faculties. This is not the production of 'docile bodies' that Foucault has analysed.[25] Rather, our means of manufacturing discipline the ways of creating comprehension, because they limit the capacity for imagination. It is not just the fragmentation of work that ultimately impedes the comprehension of the product of one's labour, but equally the magnitude of what humans can produce. This magnitude needs to be understood as relational, only 'too big' in relation to the production of sensory and cognitive limits, already restricted through the processes of production. Anders coins the terminology of the 'supraliminal' to render this relational magnitude of objects, events, and technologies that humans produce. In a later interview, Anders presents the 'supraliminal' as one of the central conceptual interventions in his work alongside the disjunction between imagination and production.[26] The terminology of the 'supraliminal' parallels that of the 'subliminal' in the physiology of sensation, that which is 'too small' to be open to conscious perception.[27]

The production–imagination disjunction is entwined with a cause–effect disjunction. The cause is so small, so insignificant that there is a new disjunction between the cause and the effects that are attainable through what we can produce. The effects of these apparently insignificant decisions, actions, or gestures can become catastrophic, but they are increasingly reduced to insignificant actions which do not appear to do much at all. This mode of production underpins social practices more broadly, because 'there is no difference between the bombing of Hiroshima in this respect and any button pushing employed in the normal process of production'.[28]

Anders's analysis of industrial capitalism as a condition of possibility for the invention and use of atomic weapons shows that there is no sovereign subject. Both decision and action have become ramifications of apparently insignificant gestures that are only a detail in the chain of production.[29] Anders

---

[24] Anders, *Nous, fils d'Eichmann*. An unofficial translation into English by Jordan Levinson is available at http://anticoncept.phpnet.us/eichmann.htm?i=1. The quote is from this English translation.

[25] Foucault, *Discipline and Punish*.

[26] Anders, *Et si je suis désespéré, que voulez-vous que j'y fasse?*, 71–4.

[27] Anders also associates the subliminal with Leibniz's theory of 'tiny perceptions', the infinitely small perceptions that pass beneath the threshold of consciousness (Anders, *The Obsolescence of Man*).

[28] Ibid., 46.

[29] Anders offers a modification of Ulrich Beck's understanding of the contemporary 'world risk society' as being characterized by 'unseen' risks. If Beck was able to draw a distinction between the

also witnessed the increased computerization of life and labour when he diagnosed a similar disjunction between computational and human capacities. According to him, computers are able to not 'only process a thousand times more data than a thousand workers could process in a thousand hours, but also a thousand times more data than a thousand men could use in a thousand hours'.[30] Although his diagnosis was made decades ago, it resonates with many contemporary critiques of algorithmic operations, which can process big data that largely surpasses human capacities of understanding and use.

If we start from Anders's analysis of work relations, algorithmic decisions and their impact on knowledge production take on different political valence. Let us consider the image of a decision tree algorithm in Figure 2.1, a common way of making algorithmic decisions.[31] There is nothing exceptional about this algorithm as such—either in its representation, which reproduces the contours of a tree and the reassurance of natural forms like trees, or in its content, which follows everyday options. Not only is the content rendered innocuous, but so is the process of decision, which appears banal, a decision on the weather and its suitability for playing tennis. At the end, there is always a decision to be made. It is impossible not to conclude in a 'Yes/No' fashion. Decision trees are

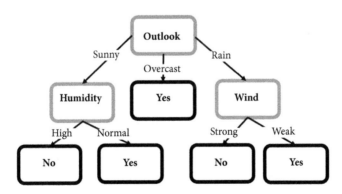

Fig. 2.1 Decision tree algorithm.

instruments of scientists who make such risks visible and the wider public who can come to recognize themselves as part of 'world risk society' only through the scientific explanation of these risks, Anders places less faith in making technologies visible exactly because of their apparent innocuity (Beck, *World at Risk*).
[30] Anders, *The Obsolescence of Man*, 8.
[31] Mitchell, 'Machine Learning'.

both mundane and widely used in computer science. They are imbrications of data, formalisms, language, and reassuring natural metaphors.

If decisions are still traceable in this diagram, many algorithmic decisions have dispersed trajectories, which are both inconspicuous and almost imperceptible. Their workflows of people, systems, and data remain illegible. A good example are random forests, which are illegible as they are built from many different decision trees whose answers are combined. Random forests 'build thousands of smaller trees from random subsections of the data'.[32] Mathematician Hannah Fry explains the use of random forest algorithms in the justice system:

> Then, when presented with a new defendant, you simply ask every tree to vote on whether it thinks awarding bail is a good idea or not. The trees may not all agree, and on their own they might still make weak predictions, but just by taking the average of all their answers, you can dramatically improve the precision of your prediction.[33]

Fry describes an algorithmic decision as unexceptional, a human–machine 'workflow' where the lines between human and nonhuman, legibility and illegibility are uncertain. In the section 'Policing with algorithms', we return to the use of predictive analytics for policing. While a lot of attention has been paid to the future-oriented implications of predictive policing, there has been much more limited engagement with how algorithmic decisions are produced in distributed workflows and how they come to underpin the government of difference.

Policing with algorithms

Predictive policing takes its inspiration from other big data operations and incorporates 'more variables as some departments already have done, and perhaps even other data sources beyond police and government records like social media and news articles'.[34] PredPol, one of the most discussed companies producing predictive policing software, prides itself on not employing personal data, and relying only on the time and location of crimes as recorded by the

---

[32] Fry, *Hello World*, 57.
[33] Ibid., 58.
[34] CTOLabs, 'To Protect and Serve with Big Data', 5.

police.[35] In response to accusations of bias and discrimination made in the 2016 article we mentioned in the chapter's introduction, PredPol researchers have argued that most place-based policing focuses on crimes reported to the police by the public rather than what is called 'victimless crime' data.[36] Because PredPol's algorithmic decision-making is mainly based on locations, its co-founders Brantigham and Mohler claim that it is less discriminatory than police 'best practice'.[37] Against this assumption, the Brennan Center of Justice, which filed a lawsuit for the release of documents on predictive policing trials run by the New York Police Department, reports that predictive policing could reinforce racial biases in the justice system by the over-policing of particular neighbourhoods.[38]

The grassroots organization Stop LAPD Spying Coalition has argued that predictive policing or data-driven politics relies on past data 'to patrol the same streets and neighborhoods, continuing a cycle of criminalization, occupation, and trauma that does not benefit communities and does not make communities more safe'.[39] In 2019, Los Angeles ended its predictive policing efforts because it was not considered to offer additional value in times of tighter public finances.[40] This rollback came in the wake of extensive community activism by the Stop LAPD Spying Coalition, the publication of a report uncovering the predictive programs used by the Los Angeles Police Department, and successful litigation for access to documents.[41] In 2021, PredPol decided to change its name to Geolitica (from 'geographical analytics'), arguing that the word 'predictive' is inadequate and that the software is 'predictionless'.[42]

Given the commercial secrecy and opacity of machine-learning algorithms used in predictive policing, discriminatory and other negative impacts on communities are hard to trace. Organizations contesting predictive policing practices had to rely on documents obtained through Freedom of Information requests or simulations of algorithms and data. Before PredPol relinquished its association with 'prediction', other companies had reacted to public criticisms

---

[35] For a discussion of the different software and types of predictive policing, see Ferguson, *The Rise of Big Data Policing*.

[36] Brantigham, 'The Logic of Data Bias and Its Impact on Place-Based Predictive Policing', 484.

[37] Brantigham, Valasik, and Mohler, 'Does Predictive Policing Lead to Biased Arrests?', 3. Another public controversy emerged around the use of an earthquake model for crime prediction by PredPol, as a result of an intervention by the sociologist Bilel Benbouzid. As the model was developed by a French seismologist, Benbouzid helped set up an exchange between the earth scientist and the PredPol applied mathematician (Benbouzid, 'On Crime and Earthquakes').

[38] Lau, 'Predictive Policing Explained'.

[39] Stop LAPD Spying Coalition and Free Radicals, 'The Algorithmic Ecology'.

[40] Puente, 'LAPD Pioneered Predicting Crime'.

[41] Stop LAPD Spying Coalition, 'Groundbreaking Public Records Lawsuit'.

[42] PredPol, 'Geolitica'.

by activists, scholars, and even some police departments and had begun to share details of their algorithmic decision-making. CivicScape was a company that garnered particular attention for a while, as it had taken the seemingly radical approach of making its algorithms openly available online, so that it could tackle bias and discrimination publicly. The company published their code on GitHub, a community site for sharing code online.[43] Rather than making assumptions about the model and the algorithm, as researchers have had to do for PredPol, we could trace the workflow of predictive policing by following the instructions on CivicScape's GitHub.[44]

CivicScape did not publish sample datasets on its GitHub repository. As machine learning is based on a combination of data and algorithms, this is a severe limitation for the company's self-proclaimed transparency. This exclusion of data from GitHub, however, is part of their business model, as AI companies depend on their strategic data acquisition. In the age of GitHub and global sharing of software, it is increasingly hard to defend the intellectual property rights of code. Upon request, the company pointed us to publicly available datasets from police departments in the US. As the company's founder once worked for the Chicago Police Department, we chose its data portal and the crime data published on it from 2001 to present.[45] The data from the Chicago police includes reported incidents of crime.

By publishing their code on GitHub, CivicScape have turned transparency into a business model. 'Our methodology and code are available here on our GitHub page', they explain, to '[i]nvite discussions about the data we use'.[46] CivicScape's GitHub pages are then also not just technical records but embed code in a set of assurances of social utility. CivicScape promises to work (1) against bias and (2) for transparency by (3) excluding data that is directly linked to vulnerable minorities, and to (4) make classifiers transparent.[47] However, just because we can see code on GitHub does not mean that we know it. There are serious limitations to these imaginaries of making 'black boxes'

---

[43] CivicScape, 'CivicScape Github Repository'. The site is not active anymore, but its static content without the code can still be accessed through the Internet Archive with the last crawl in September 2018, available at https://web.archive.org/web/20180912165306/https://github.com/CivicScape/CivicScape, last accessed 30 January 2021. The CivicScape code and notebooks have been removed from GitHub. Its website (https://www.civicscape.com/) has also been taken down.

[44] At the time of writing this chapter, in 2020, CivicScape is not producing identifiable products anymore. Its founder Brett Goldstein, a former police commander in Chicago, is now at the US Department of Defense, where he has a high-profile role leading the Digital Defense Service (Miller, 'Brett Goldstein Leaves Ekistic'). The Digital Defense Service is a key strategic initiative of the Pentagon to provide Silicon Valley experience to its digital infrastructure (Bur, 'Pentagon's "Rebel Alliance" Gets New Leadership').

[45] City of Chicago, 'Crimes—2001 to Present'.

[46] CivicScape, 'CivicScape Github Repository'.

[47] Ibid.,

visible and the equation of seeing with knowing.[48] The CivicScape code on GitHub was not enough to reproduce all their algorithms fully, but it allowed us to follow the algorithmic workflows.

Even if we could render a predictive system legible, this would not necessarily mean we can make effective use of this knowledge. The CivicSpace code requires setting up a separate infrastructure to process the data and therefore favours those who have the effective means and expertise to do this. A lack of infrastructure and social environment considerations has long been identified as a shortcoming of the open-source transparency agenda. In a critique of early open-source initiatives in India, Michael Gurstein has shown that the opening-up of data in the case of the digitization of land records in Bangalore led to the intensification of inequalities between the rich and the poor, as the necessary expertise 'was available to the wealthy landowners that enabled them to exploit the digitization process'.[49] Without access to expertise and infrastructure, the 'effective use' of open digital material remains elusive. We were only able to follow the CivicSpace algorithm, once we had organized our own infrastructure, downloading the Chicago crime data and setting up an algorithmic decision-making environment in the R and Python programming languages.

To trace algorithmic decision-making in the CivicSpace algorithm, we need to first take a step back and understand the components involved. According to Andrew Ng from Stanford University, who co-founded and led the Google Brain project and was Chief Scientist at Baidu, the most economically relevant algorithmic decision-making is supervised prediction.[50] Here, algorithmic decisions is understood as mappings from an input space A to a target output space B: $A \rightarrow B$, where B is predicted from A. Other machine-learning approaches like reinforcement learning have increasingly attracted public attention, as computers managed to surpass humans at complex games such as Go. Yet, the mundane reality of machine learning generally consists of more banal chains of $A \rightarrow B$ decisions. Examples of such decisions include the recognition of red lights by self-driving cars, the discrimination of benign and malign cell growth in medical imaging, and the development of places of interest for urban policing. A predictive policing algorithm might develop chains of $A \rightarrow B$ mappings to decide on all places in a city and to declare new policing hotspots.

---

[48] Ananny and Crawford, 'Seeing without Knowing'.
[49] Gurstein, 'Open Data'. For a more recent critique of transparency in the open data agenda, see Birchall, *Radical Secrecy*.
[50] Ng, 'The State of Artificial Intelligence'.

The algorithmic reasoning of A → B decisions is created from specific combinations of data representations. Behind the current machine-learning boom is also the definition of a consistent way to datafy the world by generating combinations of so-called 'features'. Decomposing objects into quantifiable features assigns properties to individual data items, which makes them processable by computers. In Figure 2.2, crime data collected by the Chicago police consists of a number of features that distinguish each reported incident from other reported incidents. For instance, the IUCR acronym stands for the Illinois Uniform Crime Reporting code and Primary Type for its description, while Block describes a location, etc. Based on these features, the data can be reordered and prepared so that it can become algorithmically processed. As we can see in Figure 2.3, theft is the most registered crime. Homicide is outside the top ten and does not appear here. Some of the features are more ambiguous than others and it is not clear to what extent these categories of crime datafication are mutually exclusive. For instance, there are many ways to represent areas of a city that are close to each other and might thus be deemed similar from a policing point of view.

Algorithms do not solve such uncertainties in data but reconfigure them into computable forms. The choices for reconfigurations are manifold here, but all need to be based on creating features out of data categories such as city blocks or Chicago's IUCR. Features are measurable algorithmic inputs and are prepared to be processed in abstract spaces called 'feature spaces'. In these spaces, each feature defines one axis, and any object or data item can be represented

```
'data.frame':   25000 obs. of  22 variables:
 $ id                   : num  11023904 11733061 11734352 11169354 11165311 ...
 $ case_number          : chr  "JA354631" "JC318989" "JC320506" "JA537986" ...
 $ date                 : chr  "7/19/2017 13:45" "6/22/2019 19:00" "6/24/2019 19:30" "12/5/2017 16:30" ...
 $ block                : chr  "024XX W LITHUANIAN PLAZA CT" "037XX N HALSTED ST" "022XX E 79TH ST" "048XX N FRANC
ISCO AVE" ...
 $ iucr                 : chr  "143A" "820" "502P" "460" ...
 $ primary_type         : chr  "WEAPONS VIOLATION" "THEFT" "OTHER OFFENSE" "BATTERY" ...
 $ description          : chr  "UNLAWFUL POSS OF HANDGUN" "$500 AND UNDER" "FALSE/STOLEN/ALTERED TRP" "SIMPLE" ...
 $ location_description : chr  "OTHER" "STREET" "STREET" "OTHER" ...
 $ arrest               : logi  TRUE FALSE TRUE TRUE FALSE FALSE ...
 $ domestic             : logi  FALSE FALSE FALSE FALSE FALSE FALSE ...
 $ beat                 : num  832 1923 414 2031 235 ...
 $ district             : num  8 19 4 20 2 2 6 19 11 3 ...
 $ ward                 : num  15 46 7 40 5 5 17 44 28 6 ...
 $ community_area       : num  66 6 46 4 41 41 71 6 26 69 ...
 $ fbi_code             : chr  "15" "6" "26" "08B" ...
 $ x_coordinate         : num  1161120 1170260 1192487 1156348 1187594 ...
 $ y_coordinate         : num  1858829 1924854 1853027 1932071 1868671 ...
 $ year                 : num  2017 2019 2019 2017 2017 ...
 $ updated_on           : chr  "2/10/2018 15:50" "6/30/2019 15:56" "7/1/2019 16:17" "2/10/2018 15:50" ...
 $ latitude             : num  41.8 41.9 41.8 42 41.8 ...
 $ longitude            : num  -87.7 -87.6 -87.6 -87.7 -87.6 ...
 $ location             : chr  "(41.768308395, -87.684976205)" "(41.949292379, -87.649546279)" "(41.751680875, -8
7.570191104)" "(41.96938944, -87.700488807)" ...
```

Fig. 2.2 Features of the Chicago police crime data

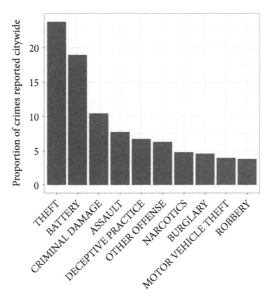

Fig. 2.3 Proportion of reported crimes in Chicago

as a dot/data point or vector through a combination of features.[51] Algorithms then process all data points such as crimes, using the distances between the points. Feature spaces are high-dimensional geometric spaces where 'a notion of "distance" makes sense' computationally.[52] Once crime data is mapped onto a feature space, algorithms can make decisions about crimes using the 'geometry of the space'.[53] Whether observations close to each other in the feature space count as belonging together or as different depends on the method of calculating the distance between these. In the language of data science and machine learning, algorithmic decisions are based on the 'partitioning' of feature spaces using distances between data points. An algorithmic decision needs to be understood quite specifically in the etymological sense of a 'cut'.

The Chicago crime data we used to recreate the CivicScape decisions had twenty-two features overall (called 'variables' in Figure 2.2). In principle, there is no limit to the number of features that can be used to create feature spaces.

[51] Provost and Fawcett, *Data Science for Business.*
[52] Schutt and O'Neil, *Doing Data Science*, 81.
[53] Van Rijsbergen, *The Geometry of Information Retrieval*, 20.

There can be hundreds, thousands, or hundreds of thousands of features and dimensions, depending on how much of this 'curse of dimensionality', as machine-learning practitioners call it, a computer can handle. The abstract geometries of the feature space drive the (big) data needs in machine learning, as noted by a practitioner of predictive analytics:

> How many data points would you need to maintain the same minimum distance to the nearest point as you increase the number of inputs of the data? As the number of inputs increases, the number of data points needed to fill the space comparably increases exponentially, because the number of inputs corresponds to the number of features.[54]

To understand how algorithmic decisions are made, we investigate the workflow of generating features in high-dimensional spaces and calculating distances in these abstract spaces. In the section 'Algorithmic partition and decision boundaries', we trace how the CivicScape algorithm might use feature space geometries to reason about crimes with the aim of generating 'hotspots' for policing intervention.

Algorithmic partition and decision boundaries

> Given a set of data points, partition them into a set of groups which are as similar as possible.
> —Charu Aggarwal and Chandau Reddy, *Data Clustering:*
> *Algorithms and Applications* (2013), 2

Once the Chicago crime data is featurized, predictive policing might target so-called hotspots or locations of interest. Geographies are popular features for predictive policing as they are easily quantifiable and enable further calculations. They follow a globally unique referencing systems such as latitudes and longitudes, which are themselves abstract representations of locations on a globe. Even though they can be 'proxies' of a discriminatory past, geographies are often seen as much less controversial than personal data such as the infamous 'heat list' used by the Chicago police—an index of about 400 people in the city of Chicago supposedly most likely to be involved in violent crime. Despite the confidence of former Chicago Police Commander Steven Caluris,

---

[54] Abbott, *Applied Predictive Analytics*, 127.

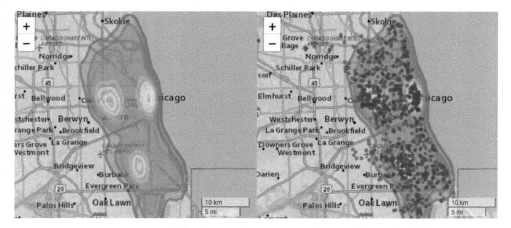

Fig. 2.4 Clustering Chicago police crime data
Map data © 2021 Google.

who believed that '[i]f you end up on that list, there's a reason you're there,'[55] 'heat list' policing was quickly discarded in Chicago for its potential privacy violations.

Using the space abstractions of latitudes and longitudes, we can recreate a workflow and trace how an algorithm might arrive at 'hotspots' of crime within Chicago. In just a few lines of code, existing crime locations can be algorithmically clustered and then heat-mapped on a Google map (Figure 2.4). The clustering assumes crimes to be related if they are co-located and simply counts the number of crimes for any particular geographic location. On the left-hand side of Figure 2.4, which we created with the Leaflet visualization toolkit, we see that there are three hotspots in Chicago. However, on the right-hand side, we show that the visualization of the clusters can be deceptive, as crime locations are very much distributed across the city as a whole. Heatmaps are known to create such visual distortions. In their analysis of predictive policing in Germany and Switzerland, Simon Egbert and Matthias Leese have argued that crime maps were one of the most important elements, as they 'would preconfigure to a large extent how crime risk information would be understood'.[56]

[55] Stroud, 'The Minority Report'.
[56] Egbert and Leese, *Criminal Futures*, 128.

Although latitudes and longitudes can be deployed to create crime clusters and heatmaps, for a more generic predictive policing algorithm such as those employed by CivicScape, they are just two quantifiable features like any others.[57] We can already see this in the Chicago crime data, where locations alone are also encoded in multiple ways as a 'police beat', a 'ward number', etc. For the geographic clustering algorithm behind the heatmap, longitude and latitude do not matter because they can be geographically mapped, but because they can be rendered as numbers with an order that indicates spatial relations. They can thus be used as axes in the abstract feature spaces, which algorithms manipulate in order to create decisions for each crime incident. The geographical maps in Figure 2.4 reconfigure these abstract feature spaces into a visualization that can be read and rendered actionable by the police.

Latitudes and longitudes are easily computable categories that can become input for algorithmic operations, but they are far from simply technical data. They reflect the targets they are supposed to map. In our case, these are types of crimes our algorithm has clustered. Not all crimes are equal. For instance, our list of Chicago crimes did not include white-collar crimes, which are reported differently. If white-collar crimes were to be represented on a map, they would scare away tourists from its Manhattan hotspot in New York.[58] Furthermore, legal scholar Andrew Guthrie Ferguson has shown that heterogeneous types of crime are recorded differently by the police: for instance, a burglary would have a fixed location, while a police choice of a suspect (for a drug-related crime) would have several location possibilities. He explains that the use of location and the more frequent reporting of burglary, car theft, or theft from cars made these crimes the first one to be used in the development of predictive policing.[59] Latitudes and longitudes are the result of histories of inequality and racism in policing, as certain areas have been rendered hyper-visible to police surveillance and intervention.

Decisions on risky or dangerous zones are not new to policing, as neighbourhoods, wards, beats, and hotspots have long underpinned police and military action. The increased availability and collection of data, however, allow the proponents of predictive policing to articulate new governmental

---

[57] According to its GitHub pages, CivicScape includes all kinds of data like, e.g., weather data in its predictions. To keep it simple, we only consider the baseline crime statistics in our rendering of its algorithmic reasoning.

[58] The New Inquiry, 'White Collar Crime Risk Zones'.

[59] Ferguson, *The Rise of Big Data Policing*, 72–75.

interventions that depart from statistically based hotspot policing, which produces maps based on historical data of crime frequency. For data scientist Colleen McCue, policing needs to 'shift from describing the past—counting, reporting, and "chasing" crime—to anticipation and influence in support of prevention, thwarting, mitigation, response, and informed consequence management'.[60] Data-driven predictive policing technologies promise to be proactive rather than reactive, as historical data was thought to replicate the past rather than 'intervening in emerging or future patterns of crime'.[61]

To unpack such predictive decisions, we developed a simple machine-learning algorithm using a wider subset of features in the Chicago crime data. We trained a decision tree algorithm as already introduced in Figure 2.1. Then, we used this algorithm to predict whether every possible location within Chicago might be a crime location—and not just the locations already recorded in the crime statistics. Figure 2.5 shows the result. It visualizes the move from clustering existing crime locations in Figure 2.4 into predicting new ones. The rotated contours of Chicago remain visible, but the algorithmic operations are entirely different. Even if a location has not been listed in the historical crime data, it becomes possible to predict whether a recorded police incident is likely for a specific location (light-grey dots). While the rather simple algorithm struggles with performance of less than 80% accuracy, it manages to identify two of the three hotspots from Figure 2.4, though missing out on the inner city one, where the locations are too close to each other. The algorithm identifies potential new hotspots in the bottom right corner. Even with such a simple algorithm, crime locations are not just reproduced based on past data, but new zones of criminality are generated.[62]

Computers do not need visualizations and crime maps to support algorithmic decisions. The abstraction of the feature space allows algorithms to move beyond 'chasing' existing crimes by clustering what has happened into hotspots and become anticipatory to predict crimes for all places in Chicago. Figure 2.5 is still easily identifiable as Chicago. Algorithmic decisions need the geographies of Chicago only in so far as these help produce feature spaces. Here, hotspots are translated into partitions and cuts, subspaces demarcated by dividing lines. So-called 'decision boundaries' separate some data items in

---

[60] McCue, *Data Mining and Predictive Analysis*, xxiv.

[61] CTOLabs, 'To Protect and Serve with Big Data'.

[62] This is one of the main differences from hotspot policing, which replicates past areas of crime. See also Brayne, Rosenblat, and boyd, 'Predictive Policing'.

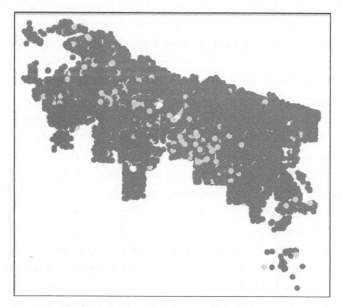

Fig. 2.5 Predicting crime locations for Chicago

the feature space and bring others together.[63] This does not mean that the 'decision' is effaced, but that it is dispersed so that it is difficult to trace it in both its banality and multi-dimensional abstraction.[64] As Michel Serres has put it, geometry gives us the 'theoretical conditions of resemblance', where figures can move without deformation.[65]

Figures 2.6 and 2.7 move away from the human-readable geographical maps to visualize the geometry of feature spaces directly, even if artificially limited to two dimensions in order to make them printable. Both figures represent how a machine-learning algorithm would 'know' and 'see' the Chicago crime data. We used two typical machine-learning algorithms, which can partition the abstract feature space of crime data into two distinct areas and distinguish crimes from non-crimes. The axes are simplified representations of two types of spatial data—latitude and longitude—and the data items are simulated, as otherwise the decision boundaries and data points would become unreadable. The real Chicago crime locations are more overlapping, which makes

[63] Janert, *Data Analysis with Open Source Tools*, 414.

[64] We do not aim to aggregate 'little actions' that connect 'subjective decisions to the reproduction of a sovereign decision to securitize, to make an exception'. Huysmans, 'What's in an Act?', 380.

[65] Serres, *Hermès II*, 100.

boundary drawing even less obvious. Notwithstanding these simplifications, a predictive policing algorithm will work in a similar way, trying to separate an area of low crime (dark dots with light background) from an area of high crime (light dots with dark background). Even with the simulated data, the algorithmic decisions are fragile results of a distributed workflow. The legend indicates the measure of certainty with which the dots are split up. Many data items are wrongly assigned and lie across various levels of certainty in this space.

Figure 2.6 visualizes how a 'decision tree' algorithm works to create boundaries in the two-dimensional feature space.[66] What appeared as an easily traceable decision in Figure 2.1 becomes much opaquer in Figure 2.6. The darker coloured decision subspace is created by what at first sight seem to be random selections of subspaces that are not linked. In Figure 2.7, we show the partition of the feature space using a more advanced neural network algorithm, such as the one referenced by CivicSpace. The different subspaces are connecting, but the dividing line between them is even more complex. We used a single neural network. In the CivicScape system, the decision line would be

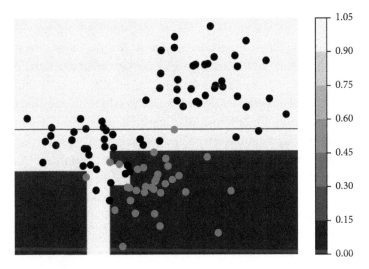

Fig. 2.6 Decision tree algorithm

---

[66] For this example, we have generated a random dataset of 150 observations distributed over three distinct regions the algorithms had to cut.

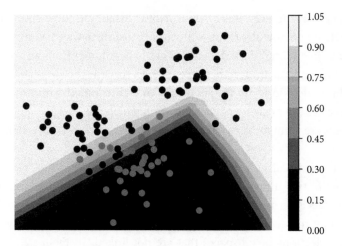

Fig. 2.7 Neural network algorithm

much more complicated, as they employed '100 feed-forward artificial neural networks' for violent crime data in Chicago.[67] In the language of machine
learning, neural networks have more capacity than decision trees and 100 neural networks have even more capacity, thus translating into complex decision
boundaries that 'cut' the feature space.

   In the process of working with different machine-learning algorithms, we
generated over 100 different partitions. Algorithmic decisions turn out to be
continually emergent lines to cut through complex abstract spaces. Not only
are the lines constantly changing, but their positionality cannot be fully justified, even with more traditional algorithms such as decision trees and not only
with neural networks. The emergence of partition lines relies on continuous
shifts in a geometric relation we have called 'betweenness', which is our coinage
for how algorithms make sense of different geometric distances.[68] Betweenness captures the measure of the shortest path between two data points in the
feature space. Decisions can be made only once algorithms partition the feature spaces and calculate the betweenness of data points. Rather than networks
or associations, algorithmic decisions emerge through dynamic workflows of
partitioning an abstract space based on metrics of betweenness. This human–
machine workflow is only possible through the collection and cleaning of
crime data and infrastructures within which machine-learning algorithms can

[67] Goldstein and King, 'Rare Event Forecasting System and Method'.
[68] Aradau and Blanke, 'Politics of Prediction'.

operate. While predictive policing might also mobilize criminological models and theories, algorithmic decisions can work with whichever data is available and easy to use. This workflow is closer to Anders's insight about industrial capitalism that 'You must not refrain from using that which can be used!' than any criminological model.[69]

The feature space is highly dynamic and in a state of permanent recomposition. In our simulations of different partitions, we achieved the best results with two of the currently most popular algorithms. Neural networks were used by CivicScape, while Random Forest algorithms have already been discussed as a second group of high-performing data models, which are commonly employed in predictive policing. Our best performing partition had an accuracy of well over 85%, which is not bad given our limited infrastructure and access to data.[70] In all our experimental configurations, location information and especially latitude and longitude turned out to be among the strongest predictors, which explains their popularity in predictive policing algorithms.

Moving from data-driven hotspot policing in Figure 2.4 to anticipatory predictive policing in Figures 2.6 and 2.7 depends on a workflow of data transformations. Whether these transformations worked with locations on a map or dots in abstract feature spaces, there was nothing exceptional about them. The process of algorithmic decision-making presents itself as banal and continuous data transformations. Like other predictive policing software, CivicScape deployed their algorithms so that they re-partitioned the feature space daily or even hourly in order to develop new betweenness relations all the time. To police officers, algorithmic recommendations materialize as a reorganization of their daily routines rather than anticipations of the future. Many scholars concur with the conclusion of a RAND report that predictive policing is about 'implementing business processes' rather than crime prediction.[71] In that sense, algorithmic decisions are also reconfigured in police work, for instance by tinkering with the number of alerts 'in order to avoid an overload of work tasks for patrols', as Egbert and Leese have observed.[72] Thus, algorithmic reason transforms both the government of 'others' and the government of the 'self'. Not only does it produce suspects to be targeted, but it makes it necessary to transform police practices.

---

[69] Anders, *The Obsolescence of Man*, 8.
[70] The data and visualizations we have developed for this chapter can be found on a GitHub page at https://github.com/goto4711/algorithmic-reason.
[71] Perry et al., *Predictive Policing*, 128.
[72] Egbert and Leese, *Criminal Futures*, 103.

By trying to 'follow' an algorithm working on police data, we did not aim to make its operations transparent. Indeed, the calculations of betweenness and partitions of the feature space still contain many opacities, even when algorithms are made public, given that the threshold between what is perceptible and what is not varies between the police, the engineers, the companies, scholars, and publics. Following the algorithm meant tracing the entanglements of algorithmic operations within human–nonhuman workflows. What is key here is that algorithmic decisions do not just reproduce the existing government of difference, but make differences proliferate. As sociologist Adrian Mackenzie has astutely remarked, algorithms make possible 'assembling differences, sometimes through purifying, sometimes through bending and blurring, and sometimes through multiplying them'.[73] They can only do so through the distribution of human–machine labour. By following the algorithm, we have developed a workflow, which was only partially shaped by our own decisions on what to include, what to select, and what to target. These decisions both appeared 'small' and were simultaneously non-decisions as they depended on the data that could be used. Each of these small details changed what we could perceive as next possible steps, so that it was ultimately less and less clear what we had decided and what algorithmic operations had produced.

Debates about algorithms and AI have tended to emphasize the suprasensible effects of technologies, which always do more than what we imagine, their exceptionalism ultimately leading to catastrophic imaginaries of the future. In our analysis, these effects appeared as the impossibility to represent the precise creation of decision boundaries in very high-dimensional feature spaces. However, from the perspective of human–nonhuman work, algorithmic operations are also mundane workflows, where decisions need to be understood in the etymological sense of cuts, partitions of abstract feature spaces, their power residing at the threshold of perceptibility and legibility.

Following the CivicScape algorithm has drawn attention to an important dimension of algorithmic reason. Algorithmic decision-making is about partitioning. While many of the predictive policing algorithms remain proprietary, CivicScape has decided to make its algorithmic workflows public to address the controversies that have emerged around predictive policing concerning

---

[73] Mackenzie, *Machine Learners*, 149.

bias and discrimination. Algorithmic decisions through calculations of be-tweenness and the partitioning of abstract spaces produce lines as separations. The abstract feature space becomes a space of decision through calculations of geometrical distances and their partitioning. In predictive policing, these par-titions appear first and foremost as interventionist tools. Based on his analysis of PredPol, sociologist Bilel Benbouzid has argued that the problem was 'to do something rather than nothing, following the machine's recommendations'.[74]

In 2017, former Chicago-police member and founder of CivicScape Brett Goldstein left the company to work with the Department of Defense as Di-rector the Defense Digital Service.[75] PredPol had built on Pentagon funding for its co-founder Brantingham to develop a counterinsurgency model fore-casting casualties in Iraq.[76] These intersections between military and police speak to an expansive government of difference across internal and external boundaries. Yet, we have shown that the discriminatory results of algorithmic decision are not only the result of self-fulfilling data prophecies or long-standing institutional racism. Sociologist Dorothy Roberts has argued that 'data collection, automation, and predictive analytics facilitate the carceral mission to deal with social inequality by punishing the communities marginal-ized by it'.[77] These insights need to be supplemented by the political rationality of partitioning that works in infra-sensible and supra-sensible ways upon calculations of betweenness in feature spaces.

We have proposed to understand algorithmic decisions within mundane human–nonhuman workflows, rather than as a mutually exclusive relation between humans and machines. As Anders's analysis of human acts in the in-dustrial society has highlighted, technologies combine the supra-sensible with the infra-sensible. The partitioning of feature spaces is not just supra-sensible because of its high dimensionality but it also takes multiple infra-sensible forms, where it becomes unclear how and where decisions emerge from small steps in the human–machine workflows. By appearing to work in banal and highly segmented ways, algorithmic decision-making creates the impression of simultaneously doing less and more than we might anticipate that it could do. It does less in the sense that, as Anders has noted about machines, 'their appearance does not betray anything about their function'.[78] In following the

[74] Benbouzid, 'Values and Consequences in Predictive Machine Evaluation', 131.
[75] Miller, 'Brett Goldstein Leaves Ekistic'.
[76] Stop LAPD Spying Coalition, 'Predictive Policing'.
[77] Roberts, 'Book Review', 1709.
[78] Anders, The Obsolescence of Man, 20.

algorithmic human-machine workflow, every step seems to be a mundane one. Yet, algorithmic decision-making always does more, as it proliferates differences through the rationality of partitioning. As we will see in Chapters 3–5, these rationalities of transcending binaries and partitioning are materialized in the targeting of potentially dangerous others, the power of platforms, and the politics of economic value.

PART II
MATERIALIZATIONS

3

Others

On 31 March 2017, two journalists, Ahmad Zaidan and Bilal Abdul Kareem, filed a lawsuit against the Trump administration for having been wrongly put on the US 'Kill List' and targeted by drone strikes. The plaintiffs argued that they were targeted as a 'result of arbitrary and capricious agency action' by the US government and asked to be allowed to challenge their inclusion on the Kill List.[1] Ahmad Zaidan was already a known figure to the media, as the Snowden disclosures had shown that he had been singled out algorithmically as a 'person of interest' for the National Security Agency (NSA).

The NSA's infamously named SKYNET application became the object of public controversy for identifying innocent people as anomalies and potential targets for drone attacks. Documents made public by Snowden and the Intercept showed that NSA analysts were interested in finding 'similar behaviour' based on an analysis of the Global System for Mobile Communications (GSM) metadata collected from the surveillance of mobile phone networks in Pakistan.[2] Deemed to work 'like a typical modern Big Data business application,'[3] SKYNET collected information on persons of interest. It used travel and mobile phone usage patterns such as 'excessive SIM and Handset swapping' and relied on cloud behaviour analytics employing 'complex combinations of geospatial, geotemporal, pattern-of-life, and travel analytics ... to identify patterns of suspect activity'.[4] SKYNET also built on behaviour patterns generated from previous targets' metadata to then derive both similar and unusual behaviour. According to the Snowden disclosures, Zaidan had been identified as a courier for Al Qaeda and was potentially selected as a US target. Through the algorithmic use of his GSM metadata, Zaidan becomes a suspect terrorist, being cast simultaneously as a member of the Muslim Brotherhood and an Al Qaeda courier.

---

[1] *Zaidan et al. v Trump et al.*, 'Memorandum Opinion'.
[2] NSA, 'SKYNET: Courier Detection'; Currier, Greenwald, and Fishman, 'U.S Government Designated Prominent Al Jazeera Journalist as "Member of Al Qaeda"'.
[3] Grothoff and Porup, 'The NSA's SKYNET Program'.
[4] NSA, 'SKYNET'.

Algorithmic Reason. Claudia Aradau and Tobias Blanke, Oxford University Press.
© Claudia Aradau and Tobias Blanke (2022). DOI: 10.1093/oso/9780192859624.003.0004

In the case before the US courts, the UK NGO Reprieve, supporting both Zaidan and Kareem, argued that they were at risk of drone attacks given their inclusion on the Kill List and challenged their designation as potential terrorists. Reprieve explained that the journalists were effectively 'serving time on a death row that stretches from America out across the globe—one without bars or gates or guards, and none of the trappings of a recognizable justice system, either'.[5] Zaidan's case is based on the Snowden documents showing his inclusion in the SKYNET programme, while Kareem brings evidence of five near misses by drones to account for his targeting.

In their opposition motion, the US government argued that Zaidan's designation as 'potential terrorist' does not necessarily mean that he would have been included on the Kill List:

Indeed, even assuming the truth of Plaintiff's allegation that the alleged SKYNET program identifies 'potential terrorists' based on 'electronic patterns of their communications writings, social media postings, and travel,' id. at 33, it remains wholly unsupported that 'potential terrorists'—as Plaintiff alleges, he has been judged—are nominated and approved for lethal action.... In fact, it is well established that the Government undertakes other non-lethal measures against known or suspected terrorists, including through economic sanctions or other watchlisting measures, such as aviation screening and No Fly List determinations.[6]

The US government also dismisses Kareem's frequentist inference that five near misses mean that he is a target of lethal action by deeming it a 'bald speculation'.[7] The connection between the selection of individuals through metadata collection and machine-learning algorithms and their targeting by drones is severed by inserting uncertainty about the actions of the US government. The relation between the production of others in the masses of data and the targeting of real people is rendered unknowable and thus unaccountable in courts, subject to an initial imputation of conjecture and speculation, and the subsequent invocation of state secrecy.

This chapter traces the diffuse contours of the production of algorithmic others and their targeting as potentially dangerous. Even as the 'other' as a target emerges through algorithmic operations, we know little about the situated practices that ultimately produce gendered or racialized bodies as killable

---

[5] Reprieve, 'Two Journalists Ask the US Government'.
[6] *Zaidan et al. v Trump et al.*, 'Memorandum of Points and Authorities in Support of Defendants' Motion to Dismiss'.
[7] *Zaidan et al. v Trump et al.*, 'Motion to Dismiss'.

or neutralizable.[8] The figure of the enemy is often imagined as an extension or amplification of enemies 'offline' to an 'online' realm. The metaphor of the 'data double' or digital twins extends the line between online and offline embodiment.[9] Yet, as we have seen in Chapters 1 and 2, algorithmic reason entails distinctive rationalities of governing through decomposing the large and the small as well as partitioning data spaces. Algorithmic operations can multiply the enactment of difference, often seemingly without recourse to the dominant ethnic, religious, or racial categorizations that have produced dangerous and risky others historically. How is the algorithmic enactment of dangerous others reinforcing or redrawing the lines between friend and enemy, normal and abnormal, identity and difference?

To trace how lines of differentiation between self and potentially dangerous others are materialized algorithmically, the chapter focuses on the extended public scene where computer science discussions on anomaly detection and intelligence practices play out in the detection of Zaidan. We argue that dangerous or risky others are constituted through algorithmic operations like anomaly detection. Firstly, we attend to how the figure of the enemy has been analysed in critical scholarship and how the enemy appears to be waning from both military and political discourse. If not the enemy, then who is the dangerous 'other' today? Secondly, we explore the enactment of otherness algorithmically through the hunt for anomalies or small irregularities, discrepancies, and dissimilarities. Anomaly detection has become one of the key practices of intelligence agencies, which supplements behaviour analytics by attending not to the general or collective patterns that emerge in the mass of data, but to what escapes these patterns, what 'stands out' in some way.

An anomaly, we argue, is neither the dangerous enemy nor the abnormal criminal. An anomaly is a discrepancy, an often banal dissimilarity whose emergence relies on almost insignificant details—the time or length of a phone call, an overnight stay, or rare use of a mobile device. Yet, although apparently devoid of explicitly racializing categories, anomaly detection does not erase the racial and colonial practices of producing and governing difference. Instead,

---

[8] For discussions that address the production of difference in drone warfare, see Wilcox, 'Embodying Algorithmic War'; Pugliese, 'Death by Metadata'; Chamayou, *A Theory of the Drone*.

[9] Formulated by Richard Ericson and Kevin Haggerty, the 'data double' is probably one of the most used metaphors that renders practices of governing the self with and through data (Haggerty and Ericson, 'The Surveillant Assemblage'). Yet, as we have seen in Chapters 1 and 2, there is no direct connection between the individual and a 'data double'. Olga Goriunova has also criticized the representational implications of the 'data double' or 'digital traces' and argues that we need to understand the 'operation of distance' between the digital subject and the living person (Goriunova, 'The Digital Subject').

and thirdly, we see modes of reactivation and reconfiguration of racial formations. In the final section, we draw on Achille Mbembe's conceptualization of nanoracism to render the political consequences of this algorithmic conjunction between the very small and the very large in the figure of the 'other'.

The enemy multiple

Who is the enemy? This question has been central to philosophical and political thought. The figure of *hostis humanis generis* ('enemy of all humanity') has not only served to justify the use of violence, but it has informed contemporary engagements with the production of the figure of the enemy in the 'war on terror'. Distinctions between friend and foe—or what Schmitt has expressed as the political separation of *hostis* and *inimicus*[10]—have often been analysed in terms of historical continuity and discontinuity. For cultural studies scholars, the figure of the enemy resurfaces in similar terms, as '[t]he enemy of all humankind is cast as one archetypical pirate figure; the international terrorist thus become recognizable as a quasi-pirate'.[11] Yet, the figure of the enemy emerges not just through cultural practices, but through relations of power, military, and political rationalities, and technological devices, all of which vary historically.

Critical scholars have explored these multiform figures, while attending to continuities of race and gender that underpin relations of power and professional worlds of practice. Historian Reinhart Koselleck has shown that modernity brought a 'radicalization of concepts of the enemy' through the language of the inhuman and subhuman. According to him, this language of representing the enemy would have been unconceivable before.[12] More recently, political philosopher Achille Mbembe has analysed the exacerbation of the figure of the enemy to the extent that he comes to diagnose the present as a 'society of enmity'.[13] His diagnosis of the present resonates with international relations theorist Vivienne Jabri's analysis of the 'domestication of heterogeneity', which draws on the 'trope of "humanity"' to legitimize discourses and practices of governing formerly colonized others.[14]

For philosopher Byul-Chung Han, the digital entails a complete transformation of the relations between self and other to the extent that he comes to

[10] Schmitt, *The Concept of the Political* 28.
[11] Schillings, *Enemies of All Humankind*, 9. Schillings' assessment refers to Daniel Heller-Roazen's analysis in *The Enemy of All*.
[12] Koselleck, *Sediments of Time*, 201.
[13] Mbembe, 'The Society of Enmity'.
[14] Jabri, *The Postcolonial Subject*, 116–17.

speak about the 'expulsion of the other' in digital times. Han argues that 'the negativity of the Other now gives way to the positivity of the Same'.[15] Without negativity, there are no others and there are no enemies. If the language of the enemy appears transitory in digital practices, does it mean that practices of othering are also transitory, subsumed to the continuous positivity of the self? However, Han's provocative argument does not account for practices of algorithmic othering. Even if the language of enemies is increasingly eschewed by professionals of the digital, othering is mutable and multiform. Distributions of humanity, subhumanity, and infrahumanity continue to be produced algorithmically.

Rather than privileging digital transformations, international relations scholars have attended to the transformation of the enemy in the 'war on terror'. They have explored how and why the enemy is produced as more fluid, elusive, and abstract. In analysing how the category of the 'the universal adversary' was invented in US Homeland Security, Mark Neocleous draws attention to the motley adjectives of invisible, faceless, elusive, or abstract mobilized to describe it, thereby leaving the category of the enemy 'open to endless modification'.[16] Christian Olsson similarly argues that contemporary wars evince an avoidance and even absence of officially declared enemies.[17] A plethora of substitutes or euphemisms are deployed to avoid the explicit reference to an enemy in the wars in Iraq and Afghanistan. Olsson's insights are particularly relevant for us, as he focuses on military and political discourses, which have historically been most authoritative in articulating figures of the enemy. In an analysis of the legal languages of 'civilian' and 'combatant', Christiane Wilke points out that the plethora of categories that have come to replace the combatant—unlawful combatant, illegal enemy aliens, insurgents, irregular force, militants, or warlords—'enable the modification and withdrawal of legal protections that are attached to the standard categories of the laws of war'.[18]

While much of the work in the humanities and social sciences has privileged representations of the enemy in legal texts, political discourses, and mass culture, science and technology studies (STS) scholarship has attended to technological enactments of enemy figures.[19] For instance, Peter Galison has

---

[15] Han, *The Expulsion of the Other* 109.
[16] Neocleous, *The Universal Adversary*, 4.
[17] Olsson, '"The Enemy" as Practical Object of Political-Military Controversy'.
[18] Wilke, 'Seeing and Unmaking Civilians in Afghanistan', 1045.
[19] For discussions of the social construction of the enemy and its constitutive effects for politics and the self, see Neumann, 'Self and Other in International Relations'; Huysmans, *The Politics of Insecurity*. For the transformation of enemy figures, see Laurence and Pandolfi, 'The Enemy Live'; Bigo, 'The Möbius Ribbon of Internal and External Security(ies)'.

shown that cybernetics developed its own vision of the enemy when it was summoned to stage an encounter with the enemy during World War II. Galison presents us with several visions of the enemy: the racialized representation of the German and Japanese enemy in public discourse, the quasi-racialized figure of the anonymous enemy of air power, and the non-racially marked emerging cybernetic enemy in Norbert Wiener's work.[20] The cybernetic enemy was a third emergent figure of the enemy as the 'machinelike opponent', where the boundary between the human and nonhuman became blurred. In Galison's analysis, racialization is gradually loosened and largely disappears, once we move from the opposition human–subhuman in public discourse to that of individual human–anonymous mass in air wars and then human–machine in cybernetics. Given Galison's attention to cybernetics, there is less discussion of how different figures of the enemy relate to each other, and how race might be implicated in technological enactments, even if not explicitly invoked or immediately visible in a machinelike human.

Figures of enmity emerge in variegated worlds of technoscience as well as in the world of the professionals of politics and security. We propose the notion of 'enemy multiple' to account for the coexistence, contestation, and coordination of enactments of enemies across social and political worlds of practice.[21] The enemy multiple does not simply refer to a more fluid or evanescent figure of the enemy. It renders the decomposition and recomposition of figures of the enemy and the redrawing of racializing lines between self and other with algorithmic reason. Angela Davis reminds us that 'it is extremely important to acknowledge the mutability of race and the alterability of the structures of racism'.[22] We trace how the enemy multiple emerges through the methodological orientation to scenes of controversy and enactment, which helps attend to how transformations of otherness and mutations of racism intersect, are juxtaposed, align, or clash.

The schema of friend–enemy, self–other appears as 'vastly complicated by close analysis of contemporary sites and events of violent confrontation, both "at home" and "abroad."'[23] The complex and fragile architecture of security has always been enacted in fraught ways, dispersed (epistemic) practices,

---

[20] Galison, 'The Ontology of the Enemy', 230.
[21] Our coinage of the 'enemy multiple' follows Annemarie Mol's phrase of the 'body multiple' to capture the diverse enactments of the enemy in different sites of practice. Mol raises an additional question about how 'different objects that go under a single name avoid clashes and explosive confrontations' (Mol, *The Body Multiple*, 18).
[22] Davis and Mendieta, *Abolition Democracy*, 52.
[23] Suchman, Follis, and Weber, 'Tracking and Targeting', 9.

techniques, and devices.[24] For instance, international relations scholar Didier Bigo has shown that different categories of security professionals enact otherness by deploying heterogeneous security techniques.[25] Diverse figures of the other emerge depending on professional expertise, techniques, and devices, as well as contestations among professionals. However, we also need to attend to how both professional routines and practices of security are subject to change, in relation to other worlds of practices, internal transformations, and technological challenges. Enemy figures are modulated through modes of expert knowledge, practice, and socio-technical devices.

A textbook introduction to Homeland Security for emergency management professionals reiterates the view that contemporary terrorism is diametrically opposed to the identifiable and known enemy of traditional conflicts.[26] Potential terrorists cannot be easily located and identified. They are often not distinguishable from normal citizens, as they have foregone all insignia of distinction (uniforms, contained battlefield, or intent to attack). What distinguishes potential terrorists can only be captured at the level of minuscule detail. It is through data collection and algorithmic operations that minute details can come to indicate dangerous otherness. As Antoine Bousquet has argued, the martial gaze has been relocated from 'its native biological substrate to myriad technical apparatuses'.[27] Although the scholarship on drone targeting, for example, has often focused on the visibility of the enemy and the potentially dangerous other, drones need to be understood as a 'vast sociomaterial assemblage, spanning three continents, which brings together networks of people, technology, and control centres'.[28]

How is the dangerous other detected in the masses of data and made legible? We argue that intelligence and security professionals have made use of the figure of the 'anomaly', drawing on its centrality in machine learning. The anomaly as the figure of the dangerous other is not equivalent to the enemy. It is also not indicative of a combatant, militant, warlord, or criminal. Therefore, the transformation that we see today is not from 'political adversaries to be opposed' to 'criminals to be apprehended or eliminated'.[29] Once produced as an anomaly, Zaidan can be folded onto the figure of a potentially dangerous Al

---

[24] Balzacq et al., 'Security Practices'; Bueger, 'Making Things Known'; Davidshofer, Jeandesboz, and Ragazzi, 'Technology and Security Practices'; Huysmans, *Security Unbound*; Bigo, 'Freedom and Speed in Enlarged Borderzones'; Amicelle, Aradau, and Jeandesboz, 'Questioning Security Devices'.

[25] Bigo, 'The (In)Securitization Practices of the Three Universes of EU Border Control'.

[26] McEntire, *Introduction to Homeland Security*, 136.

[27] Bousquet, *The Eye of War*, 11.

[28] Qaurooni and Ekbia, 'The "Enhanced" Warrior', 66.

[29] Chamayou, *A Theory of the Drone*, 65.

Qaeda courier and member of the Muslim Brotherhood. The other as anomaly unmakes the binaries of friend–enemy, normal–abnormal, identity–difference by producing relational uncertainty. In the section 'Knowing the other like an algorithm', we show how anomaly detection renders the other detectable and knowable algorithmically at the intersection of security practices and machine learning.

Knowing the other like an algorithm

[T]o distinguish between friends and enemies is one thing; to identify the enemy with certainty is quite another.

—Achille Mbembe, 'The Society of Enmity', 26

Documents disclosed by Snowden show that for the NSA, anomaly detection names the promise of big data to capture the 'unknown unknowns' and departs from digital techniques that concentrate on analysing known suspects or profiling risky individuals.[30] NSA job descriptions for data scientists list anomaly detection among the essential skills required: 'data mining tools and/or machine learning tools to search for data identification, characteristics, trends, or anomalies without having apriori knowledge of the data or its meaning'.[31] Similarly, the UK government argues in the Investigatory Powers Bill that access to bulk data allows the intelligence agencies to search for 'traces of activity by individuals who may not yet be known to the agencies … or to identify potential threats and patterns of activity that might indicate national security concern'.[32] The role of anomaly detection to target the not yet known was afterwards confirmed in a review of the Investigatory Powers Bill.[33]

In the wake of an attack at the Soldier Readiness Centre at Fort Hood in Texas in 2009, the US Defense Advanced Research Projects Agency (DARPA) issued a call for funding of projects addressing Anomaly Detection at Multiple Scales. In its call, DARPA identifies a problem of targeting anomalies in vast amounts of data by taking the relatively 'small' case of the Fort Hood military base:

---

[30] GCHQ, 'HIMR Data Mining Research'. HIMR stands for the Heilbronn Institute for Mathematical Research at the University of Bristol, UK.

[31] NSA, 'Data Scientist. Job Description'.

[32] UK Home Department, 'Draft Investigatory Powers Bill', 20.

[33] Anderson, 'Report of the Bulk Powers Review'.

For example, there are about 65,000 personnel at Fort Hood.... Under a few simple assumptions, we can show that the data collected for one year would result in a graph containing roughly 4,680,000,000 links between 14,950,000 nodes. There are currently no established techniques for detecting anomalies in data sets of this size at acceptable false positive rates.[34]

DARPA's initiative made anomaly detection into a key research project for machine learning and big data. It envisaged anomaly detection to 'translate to significant, and often critical, actionable information in a wide variety of application domains'.[35] Following on from DARPA and similar investments around the world, computer scientists have declared it 'a vital task, with numerous high-impact applications in areas such as security, finance, health care, and law enforcement'.[36] Anomaly detection has also become a key part of machine-learning books focusing on security applications as a technology that is crucial for the education of future professionals.[37]

One of the documents disclosed by Snowden, which maps the current cloud capabilities developed by the NSA and GCHQ and continuing gaps in their services, contains a matrix that includes four variations of known–unknown target and known–unknown query (Figure 3.1). This matrix starts from the case of known knowns where both the target and the query about the target are known—e.g. has X been in regular contact with Y? The remainder of the matrix gradually adds further unknowns, obscuring either query or target or both until the most challenging case is reached: 'unknown target, unknown query'. This fourth case in the matrix resonates with Donald Rumsfeld's 'unknown unknowns' of the war on terror, but now it is firmly associated with anomaly detection. Something is going on somewhere, but it is not known by who, where, and how. The document points out that GCHQ's and NSA's techniques aim to find exactly these anomalies, which are the holy grail of their new digital capacities.[38]

For security professionals and data scientists, one of the greatest promises of machine learning is that it appears to 'offer the possibility of finding suspicious activity by detecting anomalies or outliers'.[39] A report by the Heilbronn Institute for Mathematical Research, disclosed by Snowden and the Intercept a few

---

[34] DARPA, 'Anomaly Detection at Multiple Scales', 3.
[35] Ibid.,
[36] Akoglu, Tong, and Koutra, 'Graph-Based Anomaly Detection', 626.
[37] Chio and Freeman, *Machine Learning and Security*. At the time of writing, David Freeman's LinkedIn profile identifies him as an 'anti-abuse research scientist/engineer at Facebook', while Clarence Chio is a consultant advising on security data science.
[38] GCHQ, 'GCHQ Analytic Cloud Challenges'.
[39] GCHQ, 'HIMR Data Mining Research' 15.

Understand usage of capabilities
Use Case Class Mapping

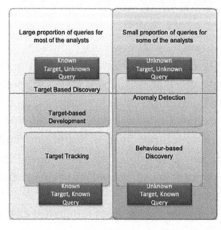

- Developed jointly between GCHQ and NSA to understand
  - the benefits of our current capabilities
  - where respective strengths and weaknesses exist
- Provides a clear set of drivers for architectural evolution
  - Missing capabilities
  - Suboptimal use of capabilities
  - Opportunities for collaboration and reuse

Fig. 3.1 GCHQ capabilities

Source: Snowden Archive. GCHQ, 'GCHQ Analytic Cloud Challenges'.

years later, acknowledges that '[o]utliers (e.g. low-volume telephone numbers, small connected components) are often exactly what SIGINT is interested in'.[40] In an earlier document detailing the capabilities of XKeyScore, an NSA programme used to analyse Internet data, the question '[h]ow do I find a cell of terrorists that has no connection to known strong-selectors?' is answered by '[l]ook for *anomalous* events'. Anomalous events are then illustrated by a series of examples: 'Someone whose language is out of place for the region they are in; Someone who is using encryption; Someone searching the web for suspicious stuff'.[41] The language of security professionals seamlessly moves from anomaly and outlier to suspicion, and that which becomes of interest, 'out of place', or otherwise unusual.

Security professionals are not the only ones praising the potential of anomaly detection. An overview of computer science research on anomaly detection notes that 'knowing what stands out in the data is often at least, or even more important and interesting than learning about the general

---

[40] Ibid., 39.

[41] NSA, 'XKeyScore'. Anomaly detection through machine learning has come to supplement or even replace the work of 'sensing' what is 'out of place' that citizens were enjoined to do in the global counterterrorism efforts. For a discussion of sensing the unexpected, potentially catastrophic event in the context of what has come to be known as the 'war on terror', see Aradau and van Munster, *Politics of Catastrophe*, Chapter 6.

structure'.[42] Anomaly detection is the result of developing algorithmic techniques to look for 'non-conformant' behaviour, for that which is different from computational regularities.[43] Despite receiving growing attention in the computer science research literature, anomaly remains a rather elusive concept. We find a plethora of vocabularies of 'abnormalities, discordants, deviants, or anomalies'.[44] Anomalies and outliers are sometimes metaphorically defined as that which stands out in vast masses of data and are often used interchangeably.[45] In another literature survey of anomaly detection in computing, anomalies are simply the 'odd ones in the mist of data'.[46] Ultimately, anomaly remains ambiguous, as it refers to 'an observation (or subset of observations) which appears to be inconsistent with the remainder of that set of data'.[47] Thus, anomalies emerge in relation to regular, rather than statistically 'normal' data. The authors of a book on *Machine Learning and Security* caution the reader against confusing 'regular data' that a machine-learning application can process with 'normal or standard data'.[48]

Computer science sees a special role for machine learning in anomaly detection, with new application areas in terrorism, cybersecurity, online fraud, and critical infrastructure protection.[49] Unlike statistics, which is considered to be 'mathematically more precise', outlier or anomaly detection with machine learning makes it possible to use 'large amounts of data and with far fewer assumptions—the data can be of any type, structured or unstructured, and may be extremely large'.[50] While statistics often considers anomalies as noise or 'abnormal data' that risks 'distorting the results of the analysis', machine learning refocuses the analysis and makes anomalies the special target using a wide range of data.[51] Similarly to the predictive suspicious practices for policing in Chapter 2, machine learning can be deployed to partition a dataset into anomalous and other items. The right machine-learning algorithms can distinguish anomalies from other noise in the data across fine distinctions in the analysis of extreme values, which are 'collectively referred to as the distribution

---

[42] Akoglu, Tong, and Koutra, 'Graph-Based Anomaly Detection', 627.
[43] Chandola, Banerjee, and Kumar, 'Anomaly Detection', 1. In the computing literature, the turning point for research on anomalies is located around the early 2000s, as argued by Goldstein and Uchida, 'Unsupervised Anomaly Detection'.
[44] Aggarwal, *Outlier Analysis*, 1.
[45] Chandola, Banerjee, and Kumar, 'Anomaly Detection'.
[46] Agyemang, Barker, and Alhajj, 'A Comprehensive Survey of Numeric and Symbolic Outlier Mining Techniques', 535.
[47] Barnett and Lewis, *Outliers in Statistical Data*, 7.
[48] Chio and Freeman, *Machine Learning and Security*, 80.
[49] Eberle and Holder, 'Anomaly Detection in Data Represented as Graphs'; Akhgar et al., Application of Big Data for National Security; Akoglu, Tong, and Koutra, 'Graph-Based Anomaly Detection'.
[50] Aggarwal, *Outlier Analysis*, xiii.
[51] Daroczi, *Mastering Data Analysis with R*, 291.

tail.[52] Targeting data irregularities with machine-learning algorithms and partitioning into anomalous and non-anomalous data have become vital to the anticipatory efforts of security agencies.

In the case of Ahmad Zaidan, a set of PowerPoint slides about SKYNET, entitled 'Courier Detection via Machine Learning', shows that network or graph analysis is part of the machine-learning techniques employed for anomaly detection. In this section, we concentrate on graph analysis, because it has its own special history in security applications. As IBM researcher Charu Aggarwal has explained, in graph analyses, anomalies can take a multitude of forms. They can be nodes, edges, or small graphs with peculiar linkage relations, whose anomalous status proliferates, depending on the method of calculation. In a network, '[t]here are virtually an unlimited number of ways that outliers could be defined.'[53] In algorithmic decompositions of data, anomalies emerge as potentially infinite. It is this productivity of large-scale data and small-scale anomalies that is of particular interest to both computer scientists and security analysts. From the massive volume of data, anomaly detection promises to delve into the very small detail of discrepancy or dissimilarity. It is the movement between the large and the small that produces the plasticity of the other-as-anomaly.

As we have seen in Chapter 1, algorithmic reason entails the decomposition and recomposition of binary oppositions: the small and the large, population and individual, saying and doing. If we look closely at the bottom-right network visualization in Figure 3.2, the target emerges as an anomaly through the delinking of a small subgraph that stands out from the overall social network derived from GSM metadata. Network-based targeting is described in the slides as algorithmically 'looking for different people using phones in similar ways without using any call chaining techniques from known [suspects].'[54] The network of phone behaviour and travel patterns is then fed together with other data into machine-learning algorithms to partition out Zaidan as a 'Member of Al-Qaeda', 'Member of Muslim Brotherhood', who—without any hint of contradiction—also 'Works for Al Jazeera' according to the slides.

The production of anomalies through network analysis and machine learning marks an important shift from the earlier uses of network analysis in security and intelligence practices. For security professionals, social networks and other graph analysis techniques have long played a critical role in discovering the networks of 'known extremists' and identifying their previously unknown

---

[52] Aggarwal, *Outlier Analysis*, 43.
[53] Ibid., 344.
[54] NSA, 'SKYNET: Courier Detection'.

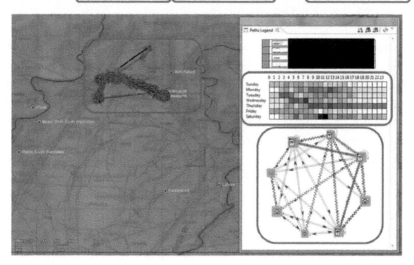

Fig. 3.2 SKYNET

Source: Snowden Archive. NSA, 'SKYNET: Courier Detection'.

contacts, which the Snowden slides dismiss as 'call chaining techniques from known [suspects]'.[55] The technique was one of linking or connecting, proceeding from the known to unknown and thereby producing 'known unknowns'. Social network analysis has been used to render risks amenable to intervention by enacting and expanding connectivity.[56] For GCHQ in the UK, such networks have been traditionally a vital component of intelligence work. As they outline,

> [c]ontact chaining is the single most common method used for target discovery. Starting from a seed selector ..., by looking at the people whom the seed communicates with, and the people they in turn communicate with ..., the analyst begins a painstaking process of assembling information about a terrorist cell or network.[57]

---

[55] Home Office, 'Operational Case for Bulk Powers', 37.

[56] See the discussion of social network analysis as a risk technology in de Goede, 'Fighting the Network'.

[57] GCHQ, 'HIMR Data Mining Research', 12. A 2011 NSA memo revealed by Snowden shows that the NSA's contact chaining using metadata can be extended from any selector, independent of location and nationality. Previous guidance limited contact chaining to foreign selectors (NSA, 'New Contact-Chaining Procedures').

Although contact chaining is described as a 'painstaking process', it is popular because it can be highly productive, as it enables the tracing of connections both retroactively and proactively.

Algorithmic operations have supplemented traditional contact chaining with anomaly detection by utilizing networks. Rather than proceeding from the known to the unknown through a process of tracing connections and infusing them with meaning, anomaly detection is much more flexible in exploiting graph structures. It might target anomalies in the whole of the network through node and linkage outliers as in Figure 3.2. It might also look for subgraph outliers or 'a set of strongly connected components in the graph where the nodes of a component have high affinity or attraction'.[58] A subgraph outlier could be seen as 'a part of the graph which exhibits unusual behavior with respect to the normal patterns in the full graph'.[59] 'Closed loops' are such subgraph outliers and deserve specific attention in target discovery, as they might refer to 'cliques or near cliques with few connections to the remainder of the graph'.[60] They can refer to connections, phoning each other frequently but rarely communicating with other group members and therefore raising suspicion.

Like other algorithmic operations, graph-based anomaly detection prefers what we have called 'truth-doing' rather than 'truth-telling' data. Both computer scientists and security professionals often refer in their papers to activities such as phone calls or linking Web pages as the best ways to define nodes and links in an anomaly detection network. In the previously cited Snowden document, it was GSM metadata that defined the targeted social graph. For graph anomaly detection, the suspicious content of a part of the graph is always related to its structure. In a typical example offered by a computer scientist, 'an unofficial US Government web site is unlikely to link to a web page containing certain kinds of questionable content'.[61] While this connection appears commonsense, it does not consider that certain governments could decide to refer to questionable content or even destroy links and Web content, as the US Trump administration had done.

If contact chaining started with assumptions of a known enemy or suspect, anomaly detection traces divergences anywhere in the network. Suspicion can be related to anything that can be expressed as graph structures. Within graph-based anomaly detection, it is not the content of a node, but the kind

[58] Bhattacharyya and Kalita, *Network Anomaly Detection*, 81.
[59] Aggarwal, *Outlier Analysis*, 353.
[60] GCHQ, 'HIMR Data Mining Research', 46.
[61] Aggarwal, *Outlier Analysis*, 355.

of connection that is the target of interest. Connections are determined by neighbouring nodes that are 'hops' away according to the graph's topology. Computers learn what should be topologically normal hops and unsuspicious connections by partitioning out any kind of network discrepancies. Should the topological attributes of nodes, subgraphs, etc. differ significantly from others, this is an indication of anomalies, which can be anything that is or seems different. Anomalies might be disconnected or integrated as 'closed loops'. The geometry of the graph becomes the plastic substance of self–other relations.

The plasticity of the graph means that, firstly, identity and behaviour are neither aligned nor contradictory. Tensions harboured in a statement of the type 'X would not do Y' are not subject to dispute or further justification. Zaidan was singled out by SKYNET as part of an anomalous pattern in a network topology based on 'who travels together, have shared contacts, stay overnight with friends, visit other countries, or move permanently'.[62] As we have seen and as it was widely publicized in the media, Zaidan was in fact the Al Jazeera Islamabad Bureau Chief in Pakistan.[63] This ascription of identity does not contradict the topology of anomaly. Zaidan is both a journalist and a suspected member of the Muslim Brotherhood and Al Qaeda. Anomaly detection effectively dispenses with the processing of contradictions, and Zaidan can be 'both ... and', even when this might appear contradictory. As computer scientists highlight, anomalies remain ambiguous, as not all of them have to be threatening and can have 'innocent explanations'.[64] Anomaly detection materializes the rationality of transcending epistemic and social binaries, as we discussed in Part I of this book.

Anomaly detection is made possible by the multiplicity of connections and the ambiguities of being at a distance from another data point in continually changing graph topologies. Anomaly detection is a particular materialization of the algorithmic rationality of attending to small differences in order to partition an abstract feature space. Even when mobilized to target potentially dangerous others, anomalies seem to eschew the language of race or hierarchies of humanity, subhumanity, and inhumanity, which have been historically associated with practices of othering. This does not mean that anomaly detection is devoid of racializing effects, as some lives become exposed to the possibility of killing and premature death. However, anomaly detection entails mutations

---

[62] Grothoff and Porup, 'The NSA's SKYNET Program'.
[63] Ibid.,
[64] Craddock, Watson, and Saunders, 'Generic Pattern of Life and Behaviour Analysis'.

in how racism takes hold in masses of data, as anomalies are distinct from both norms of humanity and population normalities.

Algorithmic nanoracism

Historian of medicine Georges Canguilhem has shed light on the unusual position of the concept of anomaly in relation to normality, abnormality, and pathology.[65] Canguilhem is one of the few scholars to have noted the epistemic difference of anomaly as a term that cannot be collapsed into the abnormal or the pathological. He draws attention to an etymological error that has effaced the distinction between anomaly and abnormality in ordinary language. Unlike the normal and the abnormal, anomaly is not derived either from the Greek *nomos* or from the Latin *norma*. According to Canguilhem, '"anomaly" is, etymologically, *an-omalos*, that which is uneven, rough, irregular, in the sense given these words when speaking of a terrain'.[66] Rather than a normatively inscribed deviation from the normal, anomaly refers to what is simply an irregular existence. Like a terrain, anomaly is an asperity, leading Canguilhem to argue that anomaly, unlike normative abnormality, is simply descriptive. Even though anomalies are also suffused with normative assumptions, Canguilhem's retrieval of the specificity of anomaly in the history of medicine helps us situate it as a supplementary term, irreducible to abnormality or pathology. In medicine, an anomaly is not necessarily a sign of disease or abnormal development. Moreover, an anomaly is not marked negatively as it can also mean an improvement of the normal. In an additional comparison, Canguilhem sees anomaly as 'an irregularity like the negligible irregularities found in objects cast in the same mold'.[67]

Canguilhem's distinction between anomaly and abnormality resonates with the two objectives of anomaly detection developed historically by statistics and machine learning.[68] The first statistical approach tends to identify anomalies as errors or noise that must be eliminated for a statistical regularity to hold. As O'Neil has observed, 'statisticians count on large numbers to balance out exceptions and anomalies'.[69] Irregularities in the object that Canguilhem talks about would be eliminated in such a statistical approach, unless they reached a point where they became too large. The second approach makes anomalies

---

[65] Canguilhem, *The Normal and the Pathological*.
[66] Ibid., 131.
[67] Ibid., 136. See Aradau and Blanke, 'Governing Others'.
[68] Agyemang, Barker, and Alhajj, 'A Comprehensive Survey of Numeric and Symbolic Outlier Mining Techniques'.
[69] O'Neil, *Weapons of Math Destruction*, 10.

the object of analysis through minor differences, which machine learning has perfected. Here, anomalies do not need to be 'very much different from other instances in the sample'.[70] A 'minor deviation from the normal pattern' is sufficient to designate an anomaly.[71] Appearing as a minor deviation, anomaly detection is inflected by the knowledge of security professionals, who assume that someone trying to hide suspicious behaviour would make it look as 'real' as possible. In research supported by the US Air Force Research Laboratory, experts in anomaly detection advise that 'if some set of data is represented as a graph, any nefarious activities should be identifiable by small modifications, insertions or deletions to the normative patterns within the graph'.[72] We are back to the small detail or 'almost nothing' that could be barely noticeable and that lives on the threshold of the normal.

As this chapter has shown, the detection of small discrepancies or anomalies in the structure of data leads to the production of a different figure of otherness. Although vocabularies of anomaly detection have not received much analytical attention in the critical literature on big data or algorithmic governmentality, anomalies have become increasingly problematized in other social and scientific fields. For instance, sociologist Nikolas Rose has suggested that, in the field of neuroscience, there has been a mutation from the binary of normality and abnormality to variation as the norm and anomaly without abnormality.[73] For security professionals, anomaly detection names the promise of big data and algorithms to partition discrepancies from the general patterns and tendencies in data and addresses the limitations of statistical knowledge and risk governmentality.[74]

Rather than statistical abnormalities or deviations from the norm, anomalies are supplementary terms that disturb binaries of normal–abnormal, friend–enemy, self–other. As we have argued, an anomaly is identifiable neither with an individual nor with a statistically formed category. Anomalies do not rely on categorizations of high-risk or low-risk groups and do not work with stabilized social norms. We are far from the radically evil other or the 'crude image of pathological individuals and groups, involving the trope of the "barbarian" with whom political engagement is unthinkable'.[75] We are also far from the statistical production of abnormal others who are to be governed

---

[70] Alpaydin, *Introduction to Machine Learning*, 199.

[71] Eberle and Holder, 'Anomaly Detection in Data Represented as Graphs', 664.

[72] Ibid.,

[73] Rose, 'The Neurochemical Self'.

[74] For analyses of these anticipatory techniques and limitations of statistical knowledge, see Amoore, *The Politics of Possibility*; Aradau and van Munster, *Politics of Catastrophe*; Bigo, Isin, and Ruppert, 'Data Politics'.

[75] Holmqvist, *Policing Wars*, 30.

according to social norms and narratives or whose conduct is to be shaped through interventions upon their living milieu. As an almost infinitesimal discrepancy and relational form, an anomaly is 'both … and' or 'neither … nor'.

The potentially dangerous other is recomposed through minute acts of noncognition, which are therefore difficult to hide. The banal combination of small fragments of travelling, calling, staying, moving data seems to eschew the recognizable categories of gender, race, or class. Yet, both Kareem and Zaidan entered the litigious scene of the court because their lives were summoned within wider racialized practices of transnational war. The 'racial-imperial spacetime of drone warfare'[76] is also decomposed algorithmically, overlaid through partitioning, network formations, and multiple data points. Racism is recomposed algorithmically while being simultaneously decomposed from the wider imaginaries of war, which rely on the separation of humans and machines and thus obscure the distributions of human-machine work.

Let us return to the US government's motion of opposition in the journalists' case with which we started this chapter. The complaint against the Trump administration points out that 'Zaidan does not pose any threat, let alone an immediate threat, to the United States, its citizens, residents or persons, or its national security. Zaidan has no association with Al-Qaeda or the Taliban'.[77] The plaintiffs argue that he was falsely identified as an enemy and erroneously included on the Kill List. The US government counterargues that Zaidan 'merely engages in conjecture' without any 'facts' that can show that he was included in the Kill List and targeted for lethal action.[78] A similar counterargument is made about the second journalist, Abdul Kareem, who had been targeted by drone strikes on five occasions in Syria. The government also dismissed the inference made by Kareem that he was on the Kill List as 'wholly implausible' given that 'Syria is an active war zone with numerous warring factions vying for influence and terrain'.[79] Therefore, no inference based on repeated targeting and near misses can dispel the uncertainty of strikes within a war zone.

In her Memorandum Opinion, the US District Judge Rosemary Collyer dismissed all claims made for Zaidan. However, she agreed that—based on the rights of due process—the US citizen Kareem has made a plausible claim that he was on a Kill List. The allegations using the Snowden revelations by the Syrian and Pakistani citizen Zaidan remained 'conjectural', as the judge

---

[76] Atanasoski and Vora, *Surrogate Humanity*, 148.
[77] *Zaidan et al. v Trump et al.*, 'Complaint', 7.
[78] *Zaidan et al. v Trump et al.*, 'Motion to Dismiss', 6.
[79] Ibid., 13.

argued that 'he has failed to allege adequately a link between SKYNET and the Kill List'.[80] Zaidan made his case of being wrongly targeted based on the NSA's data-driven inferences in documents disclosed by Snowden. Kareem employed frequentist inferences to support his case—having been targeted five times, at different locations, and having narrowly escaped death. For Zaidan, the judge explains that '[w]hile it is possible that there is a correlation between a list like SKYNET and the Kill List, the Court finds no allegations in the Complaint that raise that possibility above mere speculation'.[81] While the judge accepts Kareem's frequentist and experiential argument as plausible, she rejects Zaidan's argument as conjectural.

Even as both journalists have most likely been targeted by employing similar data collection and algorithmic operations, their targeting can only be the object of litigation when it becomes perceptible and knowable within everyday experience. Algorithmic operations of partitioning data spaces and tracking anomalies through networks and machine learning remain infra-sensible and do not raise to the surface of perception. They are also supra-sensible as rationalities of partitioning are part of wide-ranging human-machine workflows, to which security professionals add further ambiguity under the guise of secrecy. The connection between the SKYNET programme and the Kill List remains speculative, as it is materialized in dispersed and diffuse practices, even more so than in Kareem's argument.

The workflows of anomaly detection are entangled with unknown intelligence decisions, the translation of the SKYNET programme into military operational decisions, and questions of secrecy and accountability. Algorithmic infra-sensible operations are inflected by the list as 'a preemptive security device', which targets individuals for what they might do in the future.[82] Such opacities are reinforced at the intersection of computational and security practices. Given that the US government has a panoply of actions targeting suspect terrorists, Zaidan might or might not have been 'approved for lethal action'. The formation of a counter-list of lethal and non-lethal measures reinforces the speculative nature of security practices, even as it appears to 'arrange disparate items into a coherent semantic field'.[83] Furthermore, Kareem's case is stopped short by the US government's invocation of state secrecy. Indeed, the US government's invocation of the state secrets privilege is

---

[80] *Zaidan et al. v Trump et al.*, 'Memorandum Opinion', 11. On 24 September 2019, Rosemary Collyer also dismissed the second case, *Bilal Abdul Kareem v Gina Haspel*, given the US government's invocation of the state secrets privilege. *Kareem v Haspel*, 'Memorandum Opinion'.

[81] *Zaidan et al. v Trump et al.*, 'Memorandum Opinion', 12.

[82] Sullivan, *The Law of the List*, 23.

[83] De Goede and Sullivan, 'The Politics of Security Lists', 82.

accepted as reasonable, given that its disclosure might endanger national security. In Kareem's case, the judge accepts the government's argument that 'disclosure of whether an individual is being targeted for lethal action would permit the individual to alter his behaviour to evade attack or capture and could risk intelligence sources and methods if an individual learns he is under surveillance'.[84] She repeats almost word by word the arguments made by the then US Acting Secretary of Defense, Patrick M. Shanahan.[85] This commonsense inference does not account for the continuous recomposition of data to detect anomalies, and it does not consider the conditions of possibility of human action. A suspect terrorist is deemed to hold vast—if not unlimited—capacities of knowledge and action.

Later, the US Court of Appeal for the District of Columbia Circuit reversed Collyer's judgement of plausibility by entangling Kareem's experience of near miss targeting into the ambiguities of a diffuse and opaque war. Because Idlib City and Aleppo were the sites where the strikes occurred, the judge argues that it is not clear that the US was responsible. There were 'numerous actors involved in the Syrian conflict in the specific areas identified in Kareem's complaint', from state actors including Russia, Iran, Turkey, and the US, to pro-Assad government forces and many different factions. Even Kareem's allegation that one of the strikes was launched by a Hellfire missile, which is 'employed by numerous U.S. allies' is not sufficient given the circulation of drones and impossibility of seeing with certainty what type of drone it was.[86] Moreover, even assuming that a Hellfire missile was launched by the US, the appeal judge holds that there is no plausible inference that can be made about Kareem having been targeted by US drone strikes.

These cases highlight the distinctiveness of anomaly detection through a scene of controversy at the intersection of algorithmic operations, security, and legal practices. As metadata, algorithms, drones, and intelligence methods are summoned upon the legal scene, their materializations eschew both accountability and responsibility. The anomaly shapes distinctions between hierarchies of lives that count and lives that do not, while remaining both infra-sensible and supra-sensible, both beneath and beyond the threshold of legal and public perceptibility. In his book *Politiques de l'inimitié* (Politics of Enmity), Mbembe reflects on a new form of racism—nanoracism—which has come to supplement what he calls the 'hydraulic racism' of the state apparatus. The institutional macroracism of the state is supplemented by microracisms.

---

[84] *Kareem v Haspel*, 'Memorandum Opinion', 6.
[85] Shanahan, 'Public Declaration', 7.
[86] Haspel, 'Appeal from the United States District Court', 12–15.

Nanoracism, argues Mbembe, is 'that narcotic brand of prejudice based on skin colour and expressing itself in seemingly anodyne everyday gestures, often apropos of nothing'.[87] What is characteristic of nanoracism is not only its infiltration into the everyday, but a racism that takes hold of minuscule details, that seizes the small and recomposes it into macroracism. While Mbembe's coinage of nanoracism has so far received little attention, it is particularly helpful to render the racializing effects of algorithmic othering through anomaly detection. Nanoracism helps us understand the transformation of minute or banal details, a 'small modification' into a potentially dangerous other. As Mbembe reminds us, racializing entails 'procedures of differentiation, classification, and hierarchization aimed at exclusion, expulsion, and even eradication'.[88]

Anomaly detection intensifies nanoracism at the intersection with anticipatory security and extensive war apparatuses. As a result, both journalists are disallowed from claiming full human status, as their lives hover on the threshold between life and death as potential targets of killing. Multiple devaluations of their lives are produced through the 'strategic ignorance' of security professionals and the state secrets privilege, through law's ambiguity about plausible inference and conjecture, and finally by the infra-sensible plasticity of anomaly detection.[89] Both Zaidan and Kareem continue to be subjected to state-sanctioned distribution of 'premature death'.[90]

In the absence of categories of group or individual vulnerability that can lead to public claims, anomalies cannot enter channels of causality and accountability for premature death. The plaintiffs argue that Zaidan's connections with known militants, travel patterns, and interests resulted in 'his social media account understandably and innocently containing words and phrases associated with terrorism'.[91] Yet, the category of 'journalist' and the practice of journalism as justifications for the data intelligence agencies have collected cannot undermine practices of anomaly detection. Moreover, decomposition and delinking are also made possible by the ambiguities, opacities, and uncertainties of governmental action and the apparatuses of war. The US

[87] Mbembe, *Politiques de l'inimitié*. Chapter 2 has been translated as Mbembe, 'The Society of Enmity'. The full English translation was published under the title *Necropolitics* in 2020.
[88] Mbembe, *Critique of Black Reason*, 24.
[89] Sociologist Linsey McGoey has defined strategic ignorance as 'any actions which mobilize, manufacture or exploit unknowns in a wider environment to avoid liability for earlier actions, (McGoey, *The Unknowers*, 3).
[90] We refer here to Ruth Wilson Gilmore's definition of racism as 'the state-sanctioned and/or extralegal production and exploitation of group-differentiated vulnerabilities to premature death' (Gilmore, 'Abolition Geography', 301).
[91] *Zaidan et al. v Trump et al.*, 'Complaint', 8.

government relies on ambiguities in their lists and the transitions between different lists, so that a connection between the documents disclosed by Snowden and their practices of targeting becomes untenable. As the distinction between lives to be protected and dispensable lives is intensified by exposing some to the possibility of being killed, these distinctions are made possible by the algorithmic reason of partitioning out anomalies.

In tethering anomaly detection to the practices of targeting and warfare, its constitutive ambiguity is mobilized in the erasure of responsibility rather than the contestation of the designation of 'anomaly'. As a detected anomaly, Zaidan hovers on the threshold between life and death. Neither social norms nor statistical normalization can account for his selection as a potential target and attribution of danger to his banal acts. Anomaly detection promises to capture the 'unknown unknowns', thereby addressing limitations of statistical and probabilistic knowledge with its emphasis on frequencies and the assumption that certain behaviours are repeated. In materializing partitioning through the composition and recomposition of small differences, anomaly detection enacts new hierarchies and (de)valuations of life. The two journalists' lives become 'ungrievable' so that potential loss neither registers as a loss, nor can it be contested so that their lives come to matter equally.[92] Can this materialization of othering practices and the nanoracism of insignificant but potentially deadly irregularities become the objects of friction or resistance? Before answering this question in Part III of this book, we need to trace two further materializations of algorithmic reason in the power of platforms and the economies of value.

---

[92] Butler, *The Force of Nonviolence*.

4

Platforms

'A lack of connectivity constrains the capacity of refugee communities to organize and empower themselves, cutting off the path to self-reliance. But it
also constrains … transformative innovation in humanitarian assistance at
a time when such a transformation has never been more necessary'.[1] Thus,
the United Nations Refugee Agency (UNHCR) diagnosed key problems that
refugees encounter today. This diagnosis has led the UNHCR to develop a
set of initiatives for digital connectivity and new platforms, from the use
of digital cash assistance to promoting digital identity and financial inclusion for refugees. As digital technologies promise to enable nongovernmental
organizations (NGOs) and other humanitarian actors to connect, provide information, reach out to target communities, or deploy resources in zones of
humanitarian emergency, small and large NGOs are developing initiatives in
collaborating with small and large tech platforms.

Digital Humanitarians, Patrick Meier's manifesto-book published in the
wake of the 2010 earthquake in Haiti, makes the case for the transformative
effects that digital technologies have had for humanitarian action, from social media to machine learning and AI. According to Meier, humanitarian
actors can no longer ignore these digital technologies and the datafication
surrounding them: 'new digital sources of information from social media to
high-resolution satellite imagery, and new platforms powered by advanced
computing are catapulting digital humanitarians forward and defining the future of disaster response'.[2] Since then, a long list of digital technologies has
continued to unfold. Crisis mapping, use of GIS technologies to locate refugees
trying to cross the Mediterranean, estimating numbers of displaced people
through satellite imaginaries, mobile applications, social media, and even un-
manned aerial vehicles are reconfiguring the practices of humanitarian actors
globally. Digital humanitarians now regularly collect tweets to map sites of

---

[1] UNHCR, 'Connecting Refugees'.
[2] Meier, *Digital Humanitarians*, 19.

Algorithmic Reason. Claudia Aradau and Tobias Blanke, Oxford University Press.
© Claudia Aradau and Tobias Blanke (2022). DOI: 10.1093/oso/9780192859624.003.0005

crisis, use satellite technologies to estimate refugee numbers, employ biometrics to identify refugees, deploy digital cash tools, and develop apps to support refugee mobility and integration.

Meier and other digital humanitarians replicate the techno-utopian promises of the digital revolution and a future of 'platformization', which this chapter investigates. They seem captivated by the imaginary of digital platforms as a 'new business model that uses technology to connect people, organizations, and resources in an interactive ecosystem in which amazing amounts of value can be created and exchanged'.[3] Even when digital humanitarians acknowledge the challenges that digital technologies can pose—like 'big false data', misinformation, or the unstructured 'meadows' of data—the answer is found in yet more technology like AI to verify social media content during disasters.[4] Digital platforms seek to connect humanitarian organizations with displaced populations and refugees at low cost. They appear to combine rationalities of efficiency with the promise of speed, precision, and global reach. The authors of a typical book envisaged for business leaders, *Platform Revolution*, celebrate the main effects of platforms as 'little short of miraculous', as these condense time and space, while connecting people around the globe.[5]

Critical geographer Ryan Burns has drawn attention to the entanglements between 'philantro-capitalism' and digital humanitarianism, as humanitarian actors rely on 'Tech for good' interventions to develop and deploy digital technologies.[6] Many big tech companies have created 'Tech for good' or 'AI for good' initiatives, funding digital projects for humanitarian action. International relations scholar Katja Lindskov Jacobsen has questioned the humanitarian practices of experimenting with technology, particularly technologies that extract digital traces from migrants' bodies in the forms of biometric data. As she explains, these practices replicate forms of experimentation in the 'colonial periphery' and produce renewed harms or displaced populations.[7] Digital technologies reproduce power asymmetries in ways that 'reinvigorate and rework colonial relationships of dependency'.[8]

By using digital technologies developed elsewhere and for different purposes, humanitarianism becomes entangled in discourses and practices of

---

[3] Parker, Van Alstyne, and Choudary, *Platform Revolution*, 3.
[4] Meier replaces the metaphor of 'needle in a haystack' with that of the needle in 'vast meadows of unstructured information, meadows that stretch from horizon to horizon as far the eye can see' (Meier, *Digital Humanitarians*, 96).
[5] Parker, Van Alstyne, and Choudary, *Platform Revolution*, 5.
[6] Burns, 'New Frontiers of Philanthro-Capitalism'.
[7] Jacobsen, *The Politics of Humanitarian Technology*.
[8] Madianou, 'Technocolonialism', 2.

productivity and surveillance: from market efficiency to security threats and from 'Tech for good' to technological empowering. Meier recently cofounded WeRobotics and the FlyingLabs network to advocate for the use of drones in humanitarian action.[9] As discussed in the Introduction to this book, the NGO Save the Children suggested using predictive analytics for estimating the length and type of crisis to tailor their responses to displacement. Other NGOs like Privacy International have sounded the alarm that the humanitarian adoption of digital technologies risks supporting state surveillance.[10] As the UNHCR issued biometric IDs to Rohingya refugees in Bangladesh, they subsequently caused public consternation by sharing this biometric data with Bangladesh, which in turn offered the data to Myanmar to identify people for repatriation.[11]

This chapter investigates how algorithmic reason materializes through the infrastructure of digital platforms and the emergent platform power that reconfigures social and political relations, including humanitarian ones. We show that it is important to avoid overstating the digital revolution and to rethink platforms as emergent and mundane infrastructures, rather than unprecedented and exceptional. Platforms raise political questions in that they 'press us into relations with others', while enacting asymmetries of power.[12] Humanitarianism is situated at the 'periphery' of big tech platforms which have attracted most attention: Google, Facebook, Twitter, Apple, and Amazon. Despite this peripheral position, it is a particularly significant scene for the analysis of platform power, as humanitarianism situates it within spatial and political asymmetries globally. Therefore, we also analyse how humanitarian action has been reconfigured through the materialization of algorithmic reason in digital platforms.

To understand the effects of platform power for humanitarianism, we do not start from assumptions that it is simply extending neoliberal rationalities of efficiency and speed, colonial rationalities of dependency, or state rationalities of population surveillance. We propose to focus on the modes of power and humanitarian government made possible through digital platforms. On the one hand, we argue that digital platforms materialize algorithmic reason. On the other, they transform humanitarian work through platformization. We show that digital platforms are material compositions of the small and the large, while platform power works through decomposing and recomposing algorithmically constituted relations. In the final section, we unpack this mode

[9] https://werobotics.org/.
[10] Hosein and Nyst, 'Aiding Surveillance'.
[11] Human Rights Watch, 'UN Shared Rohingya Data'.
[12] Honig, *Public Things*, 21.

of power in the humanitarian drive to develop apps for refugees as apparently banal devices of communication and information.

Platformization: large and small forms

How have digital platforms become so powerful? How are these different from traditional infrastructures of modernity? The fast and global platformization of all digital spaces has given rise to a wide range of theories explaining why these new infrastructures have become so powerful. Infrastructures promise stability and continuity. They have come to order relations between state and citizens, require long-term planning and vast collective efforts.[13] Infrastructures of modernity are often invisible until they fail. This perceived invisibility might hide how they are entwined with the asymmetries and inequities of social and political life globally. As the editors of a volume on *The Promise of Infrastructure* point out, 'infrastructures are critical locations through which sociality, governance and politics, accumulation and dispossession, and institutions and aspirations are formed, reformed and performed'.[14] As infrastructures stabilize and render asymmetries of power invisible, critical work has focused not only on bringing visibility to infrastructural exclusions and dispossessions, but also on tracing controversies and frictions afforded by socio-technical infrastructures. In these approaches, infrastructures are 'hybrids that join and rely on elements too often separated under the (bogus) headings of "technical" and "social"'.[15]

Like other infrastructures, platforms are hybrids of different technical and social elements that become visible in controversies about their power. Compared to the stability of other infrastructures, platforms are often associated with a sense of deep disruption. The authors of *Platform Revolution* welcome this disruption and its challenge to our understanding of modern infrastructures which otherwise ensure 'the sense of stability of life in the developed world, the feeling that things work, and will go on working, without the need for thought or action on the part of users beyond paying the monthly bills'.[16] Unlike the supposed stability and durability of infrastructures, platforms appear as permanently changing, as they are not evenly distributed but characterized by a dynamic opposition of a central core and its peripheries.

---

[13] Edwards et al., 'An Agenda for Infrastructure Studies'.
[14] Apel, Anand, and Gupta, 'Introduction', 3.
[15] Edwards et al., 'Knowledge Infrastructures', 12.
[16] Edwards, 'Infrastructure and Modernity', 188.

Jean-Christophe Plantin and Alison Powell aptly summarize the distinction between infrastructures and platforms: 'Infrastructure studies combine historical and sociological approaches to focus on who and what is excluded from infrastructure; platforms studies scholarship ... focuses on what is decentralized and recentralized through platforms'.[17] The power of infrastructures is read through relations of inclusion–exclusion, while that of platforms is manifest through decentralization–centralization.

The dynamic of centralization and decentralization plays out through the politics and economics of platform enclosure and openness. Platforms have a tendency towards 'enclosure as a key means of competing against their rivals'.[18] They need to be '"open enough" to generate a whole ecosystem of applications ..., but possess as their end goal to simultaneously position themselves at the centre of such an ecosystem, to eventually become the entity that regulates data circulation'.[19] Platforms have to be open to other applications and provide a sense of continuity as a central single access point. Platforms 'rose up out of the exquisite chaos of the web'[20] to provide continuity from a centre. They evince a centralized logic of control and at the same time its distribution among heterogeneous actors. In 2014, Facebook changed its motto to 'move fast with stable infrastructure', departing from the Silicon Valley mantra to 'move fast and break things'. It was still aiming at breaking things but with assured continuity.[21]

Providing stability while adding disruption, offering a stable core and expansion into peripheries, platforms have been hailed as a new 'open, participative infrastructure for these interactions [between external producers and consumers]'.[22] With their dynamics of a central stable core connected to ever more new peripheries, platforms are seen in this optimistic view as simply the latest advance in the digital world's biggest utopian promise of the 'death of distance'.[23] By entering platforms, actors seem to be able to access, reproduce, and distribute anything anywhere and anytime. According to platform utopians, they are 'online environments that take advantage of the economics of the free, perfect, and instant. To be more precise, a platform can be defined

---

[17] Plantin and Powell, 'Open Maps, Closed Knowledge', 6.
[18] Srnicek, *Platform Capitalism*, 113.
[19] Plantin and Power, 'Open Maps, Closed Knowledge', 9.
[20] Gillespie, 'Governance of and by Platforms', 254.
[21] Statt, 'Zuckerberg'.
[22] Parker, Van Alstyne, and Choudary, *Platform Revolution*, 5.
[23] Cairncross, 'The Death of Distance'. This myth that place and distance would no longer matter for digital technologies endures despite its long-standing criticism and well-known failures. For a discussion of how this myth shapes the deployment of digital technologies, see Srinivasan and Oreglia, 'The Myths and Moral Economies', 218.

as a digital environment characterized by near-zero marginal cost—of access, reproduction, and distribution.'[24] We will see why this promise inspires not just tech companies, but also humanitarian actors.

To shrink distance and scale access, reproduction, and distribution, platforms have to go large and collect so-called 'complementors'. Their economic logic is one of connecting to peripheries on a large scale. While the language of core/periphery is reminiscent of imperial and colonial vocabularies, peripheries are understood here first and foremost as complementary business actors, from start-ups to developers. In this business logic, platforms 'act as a foundation upon which an array of firms … can develop complementary products, technologies or services.'[25] Platforms promise control over the production of 'complementary products'.[26] For instance, Apple innovated several such complementor platforms and developed mobile apps. A product like the iPhone has become such a success as it leveraged the power of platforms to develop new 'complementors that selectively benefit [its] particular product'.[27] Complementors' apps expand the possibilities and use of the iPhone platform and in turn need it to run. Following the logic of a central core and peripheries, the means to organize and manage platforms are not distributed to the complementors but centralized by the platform. They are in the hands of those with the resources to maintain the centre of the platform, thus inscribing strong assymetries of power and knowledge. Having to work 'with a proprietary platform over which the great majority of the players have no control' has become the fate of most actors in the digital realm.[28] Critical authors thus lament the nature of platforms as effective monopolists that need to be broken up and become state controlled.[29]

By connecting peripheries and collecting complementors, platforms have been made to control the chaos of the Web that stems from its socio-technical design of evenly distrusted peers. With digital platforms, the Web is not open anymore. The Web's original 'exquisite chaos' shrinks into an ordered but asymmetric digital space focused on 'specific control arrangements' that are a signature of platforms.[30] Through platforms, the Web is seen differently—not as an open peer space but as 'programmable' and thus controllable from

---

[24] McAfee and Brynjolfsson, *Machine, Platform, Crowd*, 137.
[25] Gawer, *Platforms, Markets and Innovation*, 57.
[26] McIntyre and Subramaniam, 'Strategy in Network Industries'.
[27] Ibid., 1512.
[28] Newfield, 'Corporate Open Source', 10.
[29] Srnicek, *Platform Capitalism*.
[30] De Reuver, Sørensen, and Basole, 'The Digital Platform', 127.

a central space, which is the platform. The development of platforms started with the idea of a 'programmable Web'. The programmable Web was as much a technical innovation as a socio-economic movement that predated and kick-started platformization.[31] It condensed this relation in its credo that '[i]f you can program it, then it's a platform. If you can't, then it's not.'[32] Through the principles of the programmable Web, platforms could achieve both control and decentralization.

Platformization, a term introduced by media theorist Anne Helmond, entails the 'extension of platforms into the rest of the Web and their drive to make external web data "platform ready"' and programmable.[33] Helmond offers several examples of platform extension such as the creation of the Facebook Like button widget, which logs external like events within Facebook. YouTube has similar tools to distribute its content to other sites. In order to extend, Facebook and YouTube rely on one of the core drivers of the programmable Web, the so-called APIs (Application Programming Interfaces). APIs are small software services that function as intermediaries for technical systems to be able to talk to each other. For platforms, they are bridges into their outside, which allow them to pull in data. Through API services, Facebook aspires to embed itself in as many other websites as possible and make its users available to advertisers. To this end, it connects all the 'likes', 'plays', and other data from inside and outside the Facebook platform to a large social graph of relations connected through its APIs. Facebook's platformization activities target the ever-growing expansion of this social graph. APIs are the drivers for the widely shared concern that Facebook penetrates all corners of the Web and 'embed[s] itself in our daily existence'.[34] APIs stand for the relationality of platform power or the ability to 'mandate organisational alignment'.[35]

Facebook's Like button and YouTube's widgets are by now classical examples of platform expansion, but APIs are also increasingly shaping digital humanitarianism. For instance, the Brazilian private bank Itaú uses the Facebook/WhatsApp business API 'to distribute over two million digital books to Brazilians in parts of the country where literature is not easily accessible'.[36] The books are sent as PDF attachments in WhatsApp messages, because the platform is widely used within Brazil for everyday communication, especially in

---

[31] The movement is organized around the website https://www.programmableweb.com/.
[32] See Musser, 'What Is a Platform?'.
[33] Helmond, 'The Platformization of the Web'.
[34] Plantin et al., 'Infrastructure Studies Meet Platform Studies', 304.
[35] Helmond, Nieborg, and van der Vlist, 'Facebook's Evolution', 141.
[36] Facebook, 'Itaú'.

parts of the country that are otherwise difficult to reach. Once the integration of WhatsApp into the Facebook marketing world is complete, the platform will have drawn book readers in diverse Brazilian communities into its social graph. Through APIs, platforms create connections between everything on the Web and act as single access points—in Facebook's case for social connections, in Google's case for information, while Amazon started with books and now does almost everything. This allows platforms to appear as a central point of control and an enabler of heterogeneity at the same time.[37] Then, WhatsApp can be used to control the distribution of books in a heterogeneous Brazilian environment.

APIs are small changes that enable the effective integration of outsides into a larger platform. They were, however, only the first step of platformization. In the 2000s, a new business model called 'platform-as-a-service' (PaaS) was created, which was tasked not only with the internalization of external websites, but also with the externalization of platform internals. Through PaaS, platforms offer internal services, allowing everybody access to their largeness by promising, for example, (limitless) storage options or advanced computational processing services such as facial recognition and natural language processing. Having concentrated on connecting peripheries through APIs, PaaS provided platforms with the means to strengthen their core and remain at the centre. PaaS (together with its siblings software-as-a-service (SaaS) and infrastructure-as-a-service (IaaS)) became the basis for commercial cloud platforms such as the Google Cloud Platform and Amazon Web Services. Where the APIs shape the outside of the platforms, PaaS and Clouds form its inside. Therefore, we need to understand platforms as blurring inside–outside boundaries through the dual move of taking the inside out and bringing the outside in.

If the programmable Web and APIs were enablers of platformization, the principles of PaaS have transformed the power of platforms. Google's PaaS, for example, has made it indispensable for mobile and web applications. In 2008, Google launched its App Engine, which kickstarted a whole new industry of providing advanced computational resources to everyone.[38] Microsoft has used its Azure platform to reinvent itself and end its dependency on Windows-based desktop applications. As a PaaS provider, Microsoft won at first the $10 billion Joint Enterprise Defence Infrastructure (JEDI) contract,

---

[37] Blanke, *Digital Asset Ecosystems*.
[38] Hinchcliffe, 'Comparing Amazon's and Google's Platform-as-a-Service Offerings'.

the largest contract ever to provide cloud services for the US Department of Defense.[39] In 2021, the contract with Microsoft was cancelled with the expectation of creating a new programme open to several cloud platforms. The most successful PaaS example, however, is Amazon, whose Web Services division has been its greatest driver of growth,[40] making it the largest Internet company at the time of writing.

Although late arrivals to the digital world, humanitarian organizations have become active users (and creators) of PaaS and clouds. Google Crisis Response became famous for demonstrating the use of Google services during the 2010 Haiti earthquake, also inspiring Meier and his seminal book. It has since customized the Google platform to provide crisis tracking and identification services such as Google Person Finder, which helps identify missing persons, or the Google Maps Engine for real-time disaster information to the public.[41] Google Maps has become a vital PaaS solution for many humanitarian applications. GeoCloud, which was set up as an integrated digital humanitarian solution, used Google as its 'geospatial data backbone'.[42]

To kickstart such work, Google and several other tech companies like Amazon have funding programmes to provide cloud 'credits' and 'consultancies' for humanitarian and crisis response purposes.[43] In a typical example for such a collaboration, the Humanitarian OpenStreetMap Team used 'portable Amazon Web Services (AWS) servers' to identify target areas for surveillance and mapping drones.[44] Based on the success of the commercial platforms, humanitarian organizations have begun to replicate PaaS businesses. DroneAI is a project by the European Space Agency for humanitarian and emergency situations. They developed a PaaS 'covering all the requirements in term of application hosting, deployment, security and scaling',[45] which exploits neural networks to analyse drone data for on-time disaster assessment. Meier also cofounded the Digital Humanitarian Network, which

---

[39] BBC, 'Microsoft Pips Amazon for $10bn AI "Jedi" Contract'. The contract was widely expected to be awarded to Amazon, after a controversy that saw Oracle challenge an earlier award in an administrative court. Services, 'Amazon Web Services, Inc.'s Response'. Google had decided to withdraw from the bid, following the internal controversy concerning its participation in Project Maven, which we discuss in Chapter 6. In 2021, the Pentagon cancelled the entire $10 billion contract given continued legal challenges (Conger and Sanger, 'Pentagon Cancels a Disputed $10 Billion Technology Contract').

[40] Amazon.com, 'News Release'.

[41] Google, 'Helping People'.

[42] PRNewswire, 'NJVC Platform as a Service'.

[43] Fuller and Dean, 'The Google AI Impact Challenge'; AWS, 'AWS Disaster Response'.

[44] Fitzsimmons, 'Fast, Powerful, and Practical'.

[45] European Space Agency, 'DroneAI—DroneAI Solution for Humanitarian and Emergency Situations'.

provides extensive 'platform-as-a-service support to a variety of sites ranging from ReliefWeb to the Humanitarian Data Exchange to the Financial Tracking Service.'[46]

Driven by its potential as a PaaS, Amazon does not limit its platform services to machines, but it seamlessly integrates humans. It has pioneered a new commercial cloud-based crowdsourcing platform called Amazon Mechanical Turk (AMT), which allows it to link to human microwork or microtasking for work that computers cannot do. It connects to human workers in the same way it connects to machines in order to, for instance, provide image annotations to train machine-learning algorithms. According to tech writer Jaron Lanier, this process of outsourcing tasks and creating so-called microwork now takes place 'in a framework that allows you to think of the people as software components.'[47] This reframing of humans as a service has political consequences, as 'by hiding workers behind web forms and APIs, AMT helps employers see themselves as builders of innovative technologies, rather than employers unconcerned with working conditions.'[48]

These dynamics are further amplified for migrants and refugees, as in the case of a Syrian refugee in a Kurdish refugee camp trying to make a living as a microworker but being limited by access conditions.[49] People in Iraq were stopped from registering on platforms and had difficulties receiving payment for their microwork. A report by the International Labour Organization (ILO) on refugees' digital labour has highlighted some of the problems of microwork for refugees: '[Refugees] may lack documentation to verify their identity or find their IP addresses and profiles blocked from platforms, due to international sanctions against financial transactions with certain nationalities. Prominent digital payment mechanisms, such as PayPal, do not operate in some refugee host countries.'[50] While platforms project their inside elements to the outside, these projects are not equally distributed, but there are various zones of asymmetric platform operations, which are obscured by the imagination and practices of 'servicification'.

It is therefore not surprising that the incorporation of microwork as an element of platforms has led to public complaints and controversies. Amazon Mechanical Turk's reputation was hit hard by workers' complaints almost from the beginning. A widely cited 2016 survey of platform-based microwork by the

---

[46] Digital Humanitarian Network, 'Digital Humanitarian Network'.
[47] Lanier, *Who Owns the Future?*, 177.
[48] Irani and Silberman, 'Turkopticon', 613.
[49] Gonzalez, 'The Microworkers Making Your Digital Life Possible'.
[50] ILO, 'Digital Refugee Livelihoods', 19.

Pew Research Center found that 24% of all workers had to use these platforms to make a living.[51] Another earlier report by the International Labour Organization about platform microwork, which was based on interviews with 3,500 workers living in seventy-five countries around the world and working on five major globally operating microtask platforms, found that average earnings were $3.31/hour.[52] Stories persist of tasks on Amazon Mechanical Turk that pay $1/hour but last up to two-three hours. The *New York Times* reported that the Cambridge Analytica scandal from Chapter 1 also began on the Mechanical Turk site, where users were invited for $1 or $2 to install a Facebook app and complete a survey in order to collect their profile information.[53]

This brief history of platformization shows how digital platforms have reshaped economic transactions, social interactions, work, and even humanitarian action. As the analysis of digital platforms has focused on the big international companies, digital humanitarianism has been largely neglected in these discussions. How have humanitarian practices been reshaped through platformization? As we have seen, platforms have become essential infrastructures of digital life, even though they 'were not infrastructural at launch, [and] rather gained infrastructural properties over time by accumulating external dependencies through computational and organisational platform integrations.'[54]

While there are different types of platforms, their emergence can be traced to the programmable Web and then centralized PaaS/clouds as new engines of platform growth. In the section 'Platform power: Decomposing and recomposing', we show how the power of platforms can be understood through the ways in which they have transcended the inside–outside boundaries by offering their own components to be decentrally embedded across the Web. This has always been part of their architectures but it has significantly increased in recent years, leading to a new microphysics of platform power. This new microphysics allows Google to collect more and better data from all its Google Map users and to make its services indispensable for disaster management, while Amazon knows which kinds of machine-learning algorithms are deployed to process drone images for humanitarian work. These practices of offering platform components appear mundane and innocuous even if their effects are debilitating and produce relations of dependency.

---

[51] Smith, 'Gig Work'.

[52] Berg et al., 'Digital Labour Platforms and the Future of Work: Towards Decent Work in the Online World', 49. This includes paid and unpaid hours.

[53] Herrman, 'Cambridge Analytica and the Coming Data Bust'.

[54] Helmond, Nieborg, and van der Vlist, 'Facebook's Evolution', 141.

Platform power: decomposing and recomposing

Not too long ago, only technical experts working on PaaS or programmable Web applications knew of platforms, defined then as 'the extensible code-base of a software-based system that provides core functionality shared by the modules that interoperate with it and the interfaces through which they inter-operate'.[55] Platforms in this sense served specific developer needs of modular-ization and reuse. The benefits of such an extensible codebase, which provides modules for code to be assembled into larger applications, are based on shar-ing existing solutions across organizations and—if needed—with the outside world. Since those early days when platforms were discussed mainly within technical communities, they have become the subject of many controversies, both public and academic.

Most of the critical research on platforms has highlighted their monopoly or oligopoly character and their concentration of power. Media theorists José van Dijck, Thomas Poell, and Martijn de Waalon describe how platform monop-olies are driven by processes of datafication and commodification.[56] Alphabet (Google's parent company) can be taken as indicative of how platforms operate and concentrate value and power:

> Alphabet's ability to integrate its own hardware, software, analytics, distribu-tion, and marketing services allows them to collect, store, and process more data, which in turn provides enormous competitive advantages when enter-ing new markets, using them against competitors who lack historical data.[57]

Tarleton Gillespie similarly puts the movement of control at the centre of plat-form interests.[58] For him, platforms permanently work on making themselves economically valuable by moderating and curating the content they organize, while at the same time publicly claiming that they do not influence what their users do and are 'just' platforms to surface their activities. Across disciplines, researchers concur that platforms are not neutral and actively shape social-ity, as they 'extend analyses of concrete configurations of power and identify control points, structural dynamics and crucial resources'.[59]

As the theorist of *Platform Capitalism* Nick Srnicek has argued, the logic of concentration of power and monopoly is built into platforms as 'the more

---

[55] Tiwana, Konsynski, and Bush, 'Platform Evolution', 675.
[56] Van Dijck, Poell, and De Waal, *The Platform Society*.
[57] Van Dijck, Nieborg, and Poell, 'Reframing Platform Power'.
[58] Gillespie, 'The Politics of "Platforms"'.
[59] Rieder and Sire, 'Conflicts of Interest and Incentives to Bias', 208.

numerous the users who interact on a platform, the more valuable the entire platform becomes for each one of them.[60] Through such network effects, achieved by means of increased numbers of participants, global platforms have emerged as a 'new business model, capable of extracting and controlling immense amounts of data, and with this shift we have seen the rise of large monopolistic firms.'[61] According to this view, all platforms tend to become monopolies, as they integrate third parties, replace the computational capacities of all Internet actors with their own, and accumulate large amounts of data. However, platforms also do not fit the traditional understanding of monopolies, as they work through the small and distributed forms such as 'complementors' and APIs. This makes it difficult to track platform power, as one needs to trace microrelations. Their expansion is as much asymmetric as it is centralized. We can say that platforms have reinvented a microphysics of power. Following Foucault's methodological advice, we need to 'decipher in it a network of relations, constantly in tension, in activity, rather than a privilege that one might possess.'[62]

Attention to this microphysics should not ignore that power is 'the overall effect of strategic positions.'[63] Google and Facebook, but also their Chinese counterparts Alibaba or Tencent have taken up strategic positions in all digital ecosystems. They are reminiscent of the large-scale railway monopolists of the nineteenth century or the US Steel Corporation controlling the essential building material of the Industrial Age. The big Internet companies provide the services to make all things digital and extract data and information as the essential building materials of the Digital Age. Thus, they display the extractive and colonial characteristics of companies such as the East India Company. However, the microphysics of platform power also entails practices of breaking up, decomposing, and recomposing existing digital components rather than simply extracting and expanding, as past monopolies had often done. These practices were already present in the history of platforms and realized as APIs and PaaS but have further accelerated.

While most political and economic commentators on digital platforms are concerned with the power to centralize and even become monopolistic, we argue that platform power emerges through the dual move of decomposing into small components and recomposing these across the Web. Amazon became a platform by breaking up its book-selling application into smaller and smaller

---

[60] Srnicek, *Platform Capitalism*, 95.
[61] Ibid., 6.
[62] Foucault, *Discipline and Punish*, 32.
[63] Ibid.,

parts that can be recombined to add value in new environments, offered first to the outside world as a PaaS and through APIs. The Amazon platform embraced heterogeneity once Amazon found out that it could sell its cloud computing platform independently from its book-selling activities. This made it the biggest Internet company in the world. Value is hidden in the many parts of the platform, and the concealed history of a platform is that of broken-down and decomposed applications.[64]

The latest step in platformization emerges through a shift from a 'monolith' application to the holder of a well-defined set of functionalities that can be reused, which are called 'services' in the computing world. Such services are modular and can be composed and recomposed indefinitely. There is not a single Facebook (or Google) anymore since they are not single Web applications and stacks to bring together Harvard students (or Stanford searchers). There are assemblages of services that together make up digital platforms. The biggest platforms provide their users with almost global reach through their instant assemblage of underlying services that appear to the various users as one. As the services of the platform have become integrated into online applications, the Internet user is permanently connected to platforms—often without realizing it. Through their computing services, platforms provide a 'rhizomatic' form of integration.[65]

The mobile ecosystem offers a clear picture of the new platform microphysics.[66] Based on an analysis of almost 7,000 Android apps for their permissions and embedded services, one of us conducted research together with social AI scholar Jennifer Pybus on the technical integration of services within apps. We investigated the repeated co-occurrences of services within the same apps. The largest platforms dominate the mobile ecosystem because they provide key services for everybody else. They offer monetization services that others depend on to make money from apps. As we use our mobile phones, we are permanently connected to some parts of the Google and Facebook platforms as decomposed into services. For Facebook, dominance through mobile services has become its central concern because, as of the third-quarter of 2019, 90% of its advertising revenue came from the mobile ecosystem.[67] The section 'Platform humanitarianism' will analyse in more detail what this mobile expansion means for humanitarian action and organization.

[64] Tiwana, Konsynski, and Bush, 'Platform Evolution', 678.
[65] Srnicek, *Platform Capitalism*, 103.
[66] Blanke and Pybus, 'The Material Conditions of Platforms'.
[67] Tankovska, 'Facebook'.

We need to understand platformization as a permanent process of decomposing and recomposing services, where users are never really logged out. By decomposing their platforms into service collections, the Facebooks and Googles could expand their reach deep and not just wide. A large platform is thus characterized by permanent shifts in its components, while maintaining control over its core. Like Facebook, Airbnb has decomposed its original 'monolith' application into what its engineers call 'microservices'. Microservices are the latest innovation in the decomposing and recomposing shifts that have come to define the recent platformization push.[68] The author of a textbook on microservices simply defines them as 'small, autonomous services that work well together'.[69] They escape a clear definition and are perhaps best rendered as combinations of services that offer particular elements of a platform to outsiders, which focus on one task such as authenticating a user through a platform. Like APIs, they are directly embedded in outside applications while always relating back to a central core like PaaS and clouds. Microservices optimize the decomposing of platforms so that components can be used independently by outsiders.

In the humanitarian sector, microservices are now part of ongoing experimentation in order to create applications that are attractive to a wider community of developers. Prometeo is such a humanitarian experimentation with microservices for fighting wildfires. It uses microservices from the IBM platform to monitor the health of firefighters during a fire, for which it won the 2019 IBM Call for Code Global Challenge.[70] The application OpenEEW works on earthquake detection and employs microservices to allow outside developers to connect and develop their own localized earthquake emergency systems.[71] Microservices are thus designed to fit into any humanitarian application and to communicate and cooperate with all other parts of the platform permanently. In the section 'Platform humanitarianism', we will see how microservice structures have been already integrated within humanitarian mobile apps.

Microservices are the latest innovation to enable the breaking-down or decomposition of platforms in order for them to become essential building blocks elsewhere. They are the techno-material manifestation of platformization as the creation of decentralized heterogeneous elements and centralized, monopolized control by means of a single business aim. Microservices

[68] Currie, 'Airbnb's 10 Takeaways from Moving to Microservices'.
[69] Newman, *Building Microservices*, 2.
[70] Klipp, 'Prometeo Wins'.
[71] OpenEEW, 'IoT-Based Earthquake Early Warning System'.

combine the business dimension with the technical one at the large scale of permanent change and modularity. Whereas application domains like digital humanitarians are beginning to follow microservices, the Airbnb platform already deploys 3,500 microservices per week, with a total of 75,000 production deploys per year. Airbnb now has what it calls 'democratic deploys', which means that 'all developers are expected [to] own their own [microservice] features from implementation to production.'[72]

Although microservices seem like a new concept, they continue many of the existing mundane platform practices we have already encountered. APIs and PaaS come into their own within the concept of microservices. Microservices are the building blocks by which a PaaS is exposed to the outside world while maintaining control at the core. APIs allow them to connect with each other and collaborate.[73] This flexibility has aided the grand emergence of microservices across platforms. Airbnb, Amazon, eBay, etc. have all become microservice-based architectures, and Netflix is scaling to billions of requests for content every day. As Netflix explains on the company's technology blog, their 'API is the front door to the Netflix ecosystem of microservices.... So, at its core, the Netflix API is an orchestration service that exposes coarse grained APIs by composing fine-grained functionality provided by the microservices.'[74]

The scale and speed of platforms built around microservices make full human control impossible. At any moment in time, Airbnb's algorithms enable and make decisions about which microservices are deployed and constitute the Airbnb platform. The platform becomes a socio-technical self-composing system run by machines for machines, which also organizes the required input from human developers and microworkers. Platforms are so dispersed and heterogeneous that only machine learning can bring them together again. Machines learn to complete the tasks necessary to keep platform insides and outsides together. They have become part of the workflows of digital production as permanent interpretation engines of our likes and dislikes or which disaster to react to next.

Thus, digital platforms have evolved into infrastructures that allow for the permanent recomposition of their component services and devices that they themselves permanently compose and decompose. The big platforms have already perfected this movement and smaller ones like humanitarian platforms have begun to follow. Operating through microservices, platform power

[72] Currie, 'Airbnb's 10 Takeaways from Moving to Microservices'.
[73] Newman, *Building Microservices*.
[74] Netflix, 'Netflix API Re-Architecture'.

is both more insidious and more dispersed than the power of monopolies. Platform monopolies are much harder to identify than Big Oil or US Steel were. Of course, we can still see the Facebook application shaping social relations or Google's worldwide network of 'campuses' that provide services and community places to start-ups globally. However, digital platforms have become so much more than these visibilities. Platform power is as deep as it is wide. Through the compositions of the small and large forms of services, platformization shapes practices that at first sight appear removed from the social media and advertising platforms attracting much public attention. In the section 'Platform humanitarianism', we unpack the effects of platformization through the production of mobile apps for digital humanitarianism.

Platform humanitarianism

In the projects we have mentioned so far in this chapter, digital humanitarians have focused on the joint use of social media, crowdsourcing, and mapping to respond to suffering and emergencies around the world. Humanitarian actors have tended to present technology development as affordances for more efficient, speedier, and targeted action to save lives. A report by the UN Office for the Coordination of Humanitarian Affairs (OCHA) repeats this discourse of a 'paradigm shift from reaction to anticipation by enabling earlier, faster and potentially more effective humanitarian action'.[75] The OCHA report lists a range of digital technologies from AI to mobile apps, and from chatbots to drones as emerging technologies that will transform humanitarian work.[76] Critical scholars have analysed the effects of technology in humanitarianism as increasing risks, producing control, and depoliticizing calls for justice by focusing on addressing victimhood and suffering.[77] Jacobsen has drawn attention to the invisible and unexpected consequences emerging out of technologies such as biometrics, remote sensing, and drones.[78] As we saw in the introduction to this chapter, other scholars have analysed the entanglements of humanitarianism and digital technology through the prism of philantro-capitalism and techno-colonialism.[79] This section will pay further attention to how humanitarian technologies and associated data collection

---

[75] OCHA, 'From Digital Promise to Frontline Practice', 2.
[76] Ibid.,
[77] Didier Fassin's work has been seminal in these debates: Fassin, *Humanitarian Reason*.
[78] Jacobsen, *The Politics of Humanitarian Technology*. See also Sandvik, Jacobsen, and McDonald, 'Do No Harm'.
[79] Burns, 'New Frontiers of Philanthro-Capitalism'; Madianou, 'Technocolonialism'.

become part of digital platforms and how platforms have become the core of digital humanitarianism and everything else digital.

Apps are particularly interesting for understanding how platform power shapes more and more areas of social and political life. They are generally accessible from only one or more of the major platforms—like the Apple App-store or Google Playstore—and have quickly become the subject of public suspicion of platform control. They have been shown to 'spy' on Internet users and track their behaviour for the big Internet companies. Computer scientists have investigated the scale of the penetration of apps by the big Internet companies and other parties interested in tracking users' behaviour.[80] In exploring almost one million apps from the Google PlayStore, they found that most of these apps contain some kind of tracking through services by outside providers, with News and Games apps being the worst offenders. The biggest Internet companies also provide the largest and most widely used tracker services. Many of the trackers work transnationally and many are based outside European jurisdictions. Other investigations into API systems and microservices for mobiles have found similar results globally. Liu et al., for instance, have analysed how analytics services track users' in-app behaviour and leak data to outside actors, mainly in the Chinese mobile ecosystem.[81] This creates a strong capacity for the analytics companies to profile users.

These contributions reveal how much digital platforms track everything and how they achieve this by offering their platforms as services. Critical research on platform monopolies has traced the digital materiality of third-party actors and the accumulation of data for the purpose of value extraction.[82] In attending to the materiality of platforms, this critique brings an important perspective to platform power. Investigating mobile ad networks, Meng et al. call data leakage to the big Internet providers the 'prize of free'.[83] This has developed to such an extent that we cannot speak of 'data leakage' anymore, as data circulations have become an unexceptional, mundane practice of how platforms work.[84] Thus, the problem of 'humanitarian metadata' generated by humanitarian actors through the increasing use of digital technologies, digital interactions, and digital transactions with tech companies cannot be addressed through the lens of privacy and data protection alone.[85]

---

[80] Binns et al., 'Third Party Tracking in the Mobile Ecosystem'.
[81] Liu et al., 'Privacy Risk Analysis'.
[82] Blanke and Pybus, 'The Material Conditions of Platforms'.
[83] Meng et al., 'The Price of Free'.
[84] Aradau, Blanke, and Greenway, 'Acts of Digital Parasitism'.
[85] International Committee of the Red Cross (ICRC) and Privacy International, 'The Humanitarian Metadata Problem'.

In the humanitarian mobile ecosystem, platforms are foundational services without which the whole ecosystem would not be possible. There is no app anymore without platform services, and data transactions are part of the workings of platforms.

Humanitarian apps for refugees have proliferated in the wake of the so-called 'refugee crisis' of 2015 in Europe.[86] Many apps were developed within 'Tech for good' initiatives, while other established commercial apps such as WhatsApp, Viber, and Facebook Messenger were used for communication and other verification purposes. Although humanitarian actors have started to reflect on the data protection challenges stemming from digital technologies, the development and use of apps demonstrate that it has become impossible to avoid platforms today. Humanitarian actors often do not have in-house knowledge to develop digital technologies and work with private actors either through contract work or 'Tech for good' initiatives, which resonate with Burns's diagnosis of philanthro-capitalism from this chapter's introduction. At the same time, the critique of data extraction needs to be supplemented by an account of the power of breaking up and recomposing elements on the platforms, and how compositions of small and large forms enable new modes of control.

Humanitarian apps for refugees have generally been developed with the aim to provide services for refugees and help communication between them and humanitarian actors.[87] Beyond the call for connectivity, we have investigated humanitarian apps to understand the socio-technical constitution of platform power. To this end, we chose eighteen apps developed for refugees by humanitarian actors.[88] In collaboration with a developer, we analysed the apps' manifest files, which should list the permissions for each app, some service components, and further hardware and software requirements.[89] But we could also go further than this, as we concentrated on a smaller subgroup of apps with the clearly defined purpose of supporting refugees. For each identified app, we created a script, which decompiled the app into its readable source code looking for embedded APIs, microservices, and other links to the outside world.

Figure 4.1 summarizes the embedded service connections we have discovered in refugee apps. The services are represented as nodes, while the links

---

[86] We draw in this section on our work on apps for refugees, as described in Aradau, Blanke, and Greenway, 'Acts of Digital Parasitism'.

[87] UNHCR, 'Connecting Refugees', 8.

[88] At the time of finishing the book, even the website collecting apps for refugees has stopped working: http://appsforrefugees.com/. We will reflect on this systematic obsolescence of apps and other digital technologies developed for humanitarian action later.

[89] In Aradau, Blanke, and Greenway, 'Acts of Digital Parasitism', we discussed the methods we developed through hacking as 'acts of digital parasitism' to analyse apps and their APIs.

Fig. 4.1 Network visualization of APIs

Source: Aradau, Blanke, and Greenway, 'Acts of Digital Parasitism'.

mean that they co-occur within the same apps. The thicker the link the more frequent is the co-occurrence. The size and shade of the nodes in the network correspond to the number of links.

Overall, at this microlevel of code, the big platforms clearly dominate. Google and Facebook are at the centre of the network and define the digital humanitarian ecosystem as we know them to define the whole mobile ecosystem. They provide the essential service building blocks even for humanitarian apps that do not aim to monetize their users. They have succeeded in becoming the technological foundations of the (mobile) Internet itself. Users are immediately connected to them once they open an app.

While Google and Facebook clearly dominate the exchanges that underpin the production of refugee apps, there are many other interesting connections from and into digital humanitarianism on the microlevel of code. There are, for instance, service links that are used in the day-to-day development of apps and are an indicator that our investigation concentrated on the deeper technical building blocks of apps. Apache.org relates to open-source tools provided by Apache Software Foundation projects and often used in software production. Services such as fasterxml and okhttp3 respond to specific common challenges in app development. Daichi Furiya is a Google developer expert for Android who wrote himself into the code (wasabeef.jp) and has become a connection towards other Japanese sites.

The visualization of the networks of APIs also revealed connections and nodes we had not expected. We still do not know why booking.com features in the network of apps and APIs. We were also surprised to see Airbnb, which turned out to be important in countries where some Google services like Google Maps are blocked. Airbnb had a service to circumvent this, automatically selecting the best available map provider for a particular country. Airbnb created an open-source software—AirMapView—which could 'choose by default the best map provider available for the device'.[90] The presence of Airbnb in the network of humanitarian apps demonstrates its successful transition from a monolith to a provider of detailed microservices that are deeply embedded everywhere. As a result of this labour, Airbnb does not need to take part in social good hackathons or provide 'Tech for good' funding for humanitarian actors to become an essential part of digital humanitarianism.

Services and the most recent development of microservices are the culmination of the microphysics of platform power. They are highly effective but come at an increased cost for both platform centres and their peripheries. The decomposing and recomposing of platforms into tens of thousands of (micro)services means that platform centres must rely on intensive algorithmic and human labour. Airbnb had to hire 900 expensive engineers to split up its monolith into microservices.[91] After release, microservices require constant updating. If microservices are updated, the apps that embed them must often be reworked at the platform peripheries. The continuous modularity of platform elements, however, makes the updating of any app an arduous task, which further reproduces the humanitarian actors' dependency upon tech companies.

Platform centres and other embedded services might alter or even disappear completely, which then forces changes throughout the mobile ecosystem. As refugee apps rely on platform services and on organizations that generally lack extensive resources, they quickly contain obsolete and depreciated elements. Many of the eighteen apps we investigated stopped working fully soon after their creation because they lost too much functionality. In Figure 4.1, koushik-dutta.com and oblador.com are two examples of services that are obsolete at the time of writing, thus debilitating humanitarian action. Even worse, apps

---

[90] Petzel, AirMapView.
[91] Cebula, 'Airbnb, from Monolith to Microservices'.

sometimes use platforms only to create the appearance of connected functionality. In 2016, Apple pulled the 'I sea' app, which claimed to provide satellite images in real time and thus help find refugees at sea, but effectively only showed old Google Maps data.[92]

As platforms continually turn the inside out and the outside in, their components are permanently changing. This affects digital technologies for humanitarian organizations. Apps need regular updating and maintenance as platform requirements change. Humanitarian actors often lack in-house digital expertise, have built technological innovation with time-limited 'Tech for good' initiatives, or lack sustained capacities for technical development, maintenance, and repair. Therefore, they are often unable to tackle the depreciation, messiness, and obsolescence of platforms, their APIs and software, and reproduce the debilitation of refugee lives.[93]

The combination of small and large forms, the decomposition of the large into recomposable microservices means that platforms are always transforming in ways that are not visible. Small forms of app creation, APIs, and code both disperse and recombine the material power of platforms. The microphysics of platform power emerges not so much or not only through the ability to conquer new digital territories and integrate new populations of digital consumers. Rather, it emerges through the invisible recompositions of code and services, which entangle more and more actors within platforms. The power of platforms is that of decomposing its elements and dispersing them on the Web, of blurring their own boundaries through the dual move of what we have called bringing the outside in and taking the inside out.

Platform power is not the direct continuation of techno-colonialism and capitalist logics of monopolization (or oligopolization), even as platforms contain elements of both. As this chapter has argued, the material power of platforms emerges through socio-technical relations. Techno-colonialism does not fully capture digital platforms that do not follow the paths of colonialism and do not move from the Global North to the Global South—or are not experimentations in the Global South by Global North actors. The Ushahidi mapping software, for example, was initially created to crowdsource information about post-election violence in Kenya in 2008. Since then, Ushahidi has become a global platform with 'an entire ecosystem of software and tools

[92] Plaugic, 'App Pulled from App Store'.
[93] However, large transnational NGOs can increasingly build digital capacity, as is the case, for instance, with Amnesty International or the Red Cross.

built to facilitate the work done by human rights advocates, journalists, election monitors and those responding to disaster and crisis'.[94] The diagnosis of centralization and monopolization does not account for how platforms break up and disperse their components across the Web. Digital platforms materialize algorithmic reason in that they transcend binaries of small and large forms by splintering large forms and recomposing small forms. Platform power as indefinite decomposition and recomposition does not only conquer new areas of the practice, expand to different spaces, and reconfigure tech users. It also creates new forms of dependency and debilitation for many actors such as humanitarian organizations and refugees themselves.

[94] Doran, 'How the Ushahidi Platform Works'.

5
Value

In 2021, the digital rights organization Access Now wrote a letter to the Spotify CEO raising questions about a Spotify patent on speech recognition.[1] The Access Now letter was followed by another letter written by a group of almost 200 'concerned musicians' and human rights organizations.[2] Both letters challenged the claims in the speech recognition patent that Spotify could detect 'emotional state, gender, age or accent' to improve its music recommendations. Both letters highlighted privacy concerns, data security, potential discrimination against trans and non-binary groups, and the possibility of manipulation. Access Now pointed out that Spotify already had 'troves of data on the people that use its service, down to the specific neighbourhoods where they live'.[3] Further intrusive surveillance could not be justified. The letter by the concerned musicians also drew attention to the effects of AI and big data on the music industry. They argued that '[u]sing artificial intelligence and surveillance to recommend music will only serve to exacerbate disparities in the music industry'.[4] The musicians based their argument on the strong normative position that '[m]usic should be made for human connection, not to please a profit-maximizing algorithm'. In their response letter, Spotify reiterated their commitment to ethics, privacy, and responsible innovation and argued that the technology in the respective patent had not been implemented at the company.[5] While Spotify claimed that they did not have plans to implement this technology, the question remained why Spotify was patenting it if there were no plans to use it. In this chapter, we suggest that one answer to this question lies in the production of economic value.

Value has indeed emerged as one of the key dimensions of big data and its algorithmic operations. Expressing a widely held opinion, the *Economist* muses that '[t]he world's most valuable resource is no longer oil, but data'.[6]

---

[1] Access Now, 'Dear Spotify'.
[2] Access Now, 'Spotify, Don't Spy'.
[3] Access Now, 'Dear Spotify'.
[4] Access Now, 'Spotify, Don't Spy'.
[5] Spotify, 'Letter to Access Now'.
[6] *The Economist*, 'The World's Most Valuable Resource'.

Algorithmic Reason. Claudia Aradau and Tobias Blanke, Oxford University Press.
© Claudia Aradau and Tobias Blanke (2022). DOI: 10.1093/oso/9780192859624.003.0006

According to Andrew Ng, this data needs algorithmic operations and AI capacities to become valuable, which makes AI 'the new electricity',[7] transforming the production and circulation of data. A business report on 'The Data Value Chain' explains that 'the true value of input or source data' can be discovered only through 'mining and interrogating large datasets'.[8] The IBM's outline on extracting business value from big data focuses on the need for 'fast and actionable insights' from data.[9] Sociologist Martha Poon summarizes this allure of data as 'raw fuel', which 'grows a powerful new form of operational infrastructures that companies can use to manage markets: algorithms imbued with techniques from artificial intelligence that learn, recursively, on the job'.[10] Scholars and practitioners agree that big data and advances in AI have transformed value production in digital capitalism.

This chapter proposes to shed light on the political implications of multiple productions of value from data. The controversy around Spotify's patents highlights different understandings of value that circulate among various actors. The concerned musicians' letter emphasizes value as profit and the disruptive effects that algorithmic operations have on music as a human experience. Access Now concentrates on the extraction of data for surveillance purposes, while Spotify replies by emphasizing the value of 'giving a million creative artists the opportunity to live off their art and billions of fans the opportunity to enjoy and be inspired by it'.[11] At the same time, Spotify acknowledges that they operate in a 'highly-competitive market' where their success depends on implementing competitive business values.

What are the connections between these different articulations of value in the three letters, as they resonate with public debates about AI and big tech companies? What is of value in the world of big data and AI has become a deeply political question, as it has been split between value extraction by big tech companies and the values of their users. Questions of how value is produced, by whom and for whom have not only concerned academics but public debates more broadly. 'Uberization' has become a media shorthand for value extraction through precarious gig labour in digital economies. Other controversies have focused on the business model of Facebook and other social media companies, which is based on amassing data about their users through

---

[7] Ng, 'The State of Artificial Intelligence'.
[8] GSMA, 'The Data Value Chain', 3.
[9] IBM, 'Hybrid Data Management'.
[10] Poon, 'Corporate Capitalism', 1100.
[11] Spotify, 'Letter to Access Now'.

digital surveillance. Finally, the Amazon model has been widely discussed for its capacity to move beyond the traditional model of the market and extract value from the 'free labour' of users.

Between precarization, extraction, surveillance, and monopolization, how are we to understand the production of value in digital economies? In this chapter, we focus on the production of economic value and its political consequences and therefore speak of processes of valorization. As we have seen, governing rationalities foster relations between people and things, and hierarchies of subjectivity. Processes of valorization add another dimension to the government of self and other, of individuals and populations. We argue that algorithmic reason is newly materialized within a specific form of economic value, which relies on combining small datasets to produce new situations of commodity consumption.

To develop this argument, we expand the public scene around Spotify's patent with other patent applications and granted patents to the big tech companies, so that we can trace how valorization is imagined in the daily business of digital companies. Patents also trace problems and limitations, which they aim to address through innovation. The Spotify patent from the beginning of this introduction and the controversies attached to it exemplify how we can productively use patents. Independent of whether a specific patent has been implemented, patents offer a site of inquiry into value. Indeed, they should not be understood to be direct translations of how a company produces, as too little is known about the status of the patented products within the company.[12] Nevertheless, they help us recognize which actors are involved, their interests in valorization, and how the problem of value is formulated and addressed. Patents are particularly useful for shedding light on value when juxtaposed to other company documents and legal or news items about their practices of valorization. Our reading of the patents investigates how value is not only materialized through the extraction of personal data and global exploitation of labour, or just through surveillance or network effects.

The chapter starts with an analysis of value as developed by scholars who focus on the continuities between digital and industrial capitalism. In a second section, we turn to authors who have diagnosed a new stage in the development of capitalism and new forms of digital value. Here, we concentrate on the controversies that surrounded Shoshana Zuboff's idea of behavioural surplus value in surveillance capitalism and Nick Srnicek's network value through platform domination. We have selected these authors from a vast range of

---

[12] Bucher, 'The Right-Time Web'.

literature on digital economy as their work has been mobilized in public debates about digital value. In a final section, we show how analyses of value in digital capitalism need to be supplemented by a new form of value accumulation from small data contexts. Patents help us explain how companies attempt to overcome human subjectivity limitations that hinder valorization by focusing on ever smaller details of human experience. The various forms of value production underpin different practices and imaginaries of politics, to which we return in the chapter's conclusion.

Exploitation and extraction in digital capitalism

There is a long tradition of a political critique of value that is not data-centric, as outlined in the introduction to this chapter, but labour-centric. This critique would not start from data as raw material, privacy, surveillance, etc. but from human labour. In much of the nineteenth-century analysis of industrial capital, for instance, the exploitation of labour is seen as the sole source of value. The value that big data and AI analytics create does not efface the question of labour but is challenged by new forms of labour that at least at first sight do not fit strong labour-centric interpretations, where labour is employed by capital to produce value. The extraction of 'free labour' given in 'free time' can be found everywhere in the new digital economy and has made companies such as Amazon more than an online bookshop, paving the way for it to become one of the largest enterprises in the world. With 'free labour', books are valued not just through price, but through the production of online opinions and rankings. Allocating 1, 3, or 5 stars to a book could propel it to the top or bottom of rankings in a seemingly unlimited market of competing products. The value of a book thus depends on more or less 'free labour', the labour that 'unpaid' users produce for the site.

Such new forms of 'free labour' are often closely intertwined with regular practices of paid or underpaid labour. The media has recently highlighted the extent of 'fake reviews' on Amazon;[13] these reviews are not produced through the 'free labour' of users but are bought on markets of so-called clickwork. Clickworkers are far from the public image of Silicon Valley engineers and developers. They are precarious workers in centres around the world, from the Philippines and Indonesia to Madagascar, Ivory Coast, and Venezuela.[14] While these clickworkers as well as their better-known gig work cousins, Uber

---

[13] BBC, 'Amazon "Flooded by Fake Five-Star Reviews"—Which? Report'.
[14] Casilli, 'Automating Credulity'. See also Chapter 8 in this book on the international politics of digital content moderation.

drivers, remind us of established practices of exploitation through piece rate work, the unpaid contribution of labour challenges traditional labour-centric critiques of industrial capitalism.

For both sides of the early capitalism labour-centric view on value, Karl Marx and Adam Smith, the contribution of 'free labour' to value production is hard to comprehend. Smith famously stated that labour is 'toil and trouble' and as such valuable.[15] Marx generally agrees on the hardships of laboured value production. His analysis is also historical and includes detailed descriptions of the hardships in a worker's life at home and at the factory. For Marx, only labour ruled by capital produces surplus value, which assumes that labourers have sold their labour force in exchange for the means of living, which does not really happen with the new digital 'free labour'. Marxist scholars thus struggle with free labour as a source of value. This is the case of Dan Schiller's earlier *Digital Capitalism* and, more recently, Christian Fuchs' work on digital value.[16] A labour-centric critique finds it difficult to integrate the idea of human 'free labour' that seems to open up value creation around big data.[17]

Alongside Marxist attempts to explain the digital value chain, cognitive capitalism approaches have gained a lot of interest to cover the new type of digital production.[18] They argue that cognitive capitalism has replaced industrial capitalism and that the big platforms we discussed in Chapter 4 could be seen as rentiers, whose platform monopolies allow them to extract value from surpluses produced elsewhere. Fumagalli and colleagues explain that 'data are created as use values, produced and socialized by users/consumers in the performance of daily cooperation and relation activities'.[19] Fuchs argues strongly against cognitive capitalism. For him, Facebook users and other 'free labourers' should be considered as value producers just like anybody else.[20] Free labour should be seen to follow the idea of transport labour in Marx.[21] But free labourers on social media sites do not sell their labour force as workers, in contrast to other online crowds such as clickworkers or microworkers, where labour and capital relations seem to be much easier to define.[22] Those writing

---

[15] Smith quoted in Dupré and Gagnier, 'A Brief History of Work', 553.

[16] Schiller, *Digital Capitalism*; Fuchs and Sevignani, 'What Is Digital Labour?'.

[17] This dilemma has also found felicitous expression in Trevor Scholtz's *Digital Labor: The Internet as Playground and Factory*. Scholtz, Digital Labor.

[18] For a definition see Moulier-Boutang, *Cognitive Capitalism*.

[19] Fumagalli et al., 'Digital Labour in the Platform Economy', 1757.

[20] 'Facebook invests money into production and constantly lets users produce data commodities in order to sell ever more advertisements and accumulate ever more capital' (Fuchs, 'The Digital Labour Theory of Value', 34).

[21] See Fuchs, 'The Digital Labour Theory of Value', 30.

[22] 'Turkers' has become the colloquial name for freelance workers selling their labour on the Amazon Mechanical Turk platform.

book reviews on Amazon also do not rent out their assets for capitalization. Attempts to define social media 'prosumers' as 'productive workers' seem to mainly serve the interest that they can be organized in labour movements to overcome social media capital according to Marxist political ideas of a struggle between labour and capital.

The capitalization of unpaid time and a range of other new values would have been unknown to Marx, as he concentrates on industrial production with well-defined factory floors. Yet, feminist scholars have already drawn attention to the invisibilization of reproductive and other forms of feminized and racialized labour in Marx that happens outside factory floors. In the 1970s, feminist Marxists argued that reproductive labour was indispensable to capitalism. According to one of its key voices, Silvia Federici, feminist theorists discovered that 'unpaid labour is not extracted by the capitalist class only from the waged workday, but that it is also extracted from the workday of millions of unwaged house-workers as well as many other unpaid and un-free labourers.'[23] Black feminists highlighted the invisibilization of black women's labour within transatlantic chattel slavery, 'in which women labored but also bore children who were legally defined as property and were circulated as commodities.'[24] Today, feminist scholars attend to the 'heterogeneity of living labor' and differentials of exploitation in order to shed light on what Verónica Gago has called the 'very elasticity of the accumulation process.'[25] Not only is valorization not limited to labour officially guided by capital, but it is also made possible through the constitution of gendered and racialized hierarchies of labour. These hierarchies cut across geopolitical borders, as we will also see in Chapter 8 on the International.

This perspective that attends to the heterogeneity of capitalism and valorization has inspired political theorists Mezzadra and Neilson to expand the idea of exploitation in capitalism and focus on 'extraction' to understand how capital extricates value from its 'outsides', whether understood in spatial terms or as non-capitalist 'outsides' of social activity. According to them, extraction names 'the forms and practices of valorization and exploitation that materialize when the operations of capital encounter patterns of human cooperation and sociality external to them.'[26] Mezzadra and Neilson do not argue that extraction is the exclusive logic of capitalism, but that extractive operations intersect

[23] Federici, 'Social Reproduction Theory', 55.
[24] Vora, 'Labor', 206.
[25] Gago, *Feminist International*, 148.
[26] Mezzadra and Neilson, *The Politics of Operations*, 44.

with other capitalist operations and logics of valorization.[27] Capitalist operations depend on conditions that they cannot (re)produce and which therefore constitute their outside. This means that the analysis is focused on the expansionist boundaries of capitalism and the relation with its 'outsides'. Digital extractive logics operate on a multiplicity of differences, which capitalism both constitutes and mobilizes.

Valorization depends on the constitution of differences and the multiplication of 'outsides'. 'Free labour' is no exception here. Originally envisioned as contributions made possible through organizing the users' 'free time' in highly industrialized societies, it quickly started to entail the exploitation of 'outsides' of capitalism. Although the use of 'free labour' at scale can be seen as a historically unique moment of the digital economy, it is important to keep in mind that direct exploitation of more or less paid labour does not disappear but accelerates through the global extension of platform power, as we have seen in Chapter 4. We have already mentioned precarious clickworkers, who might not exist without the development of 'free labour'. While we give 'free labour' to Amazon in the varied forms of reviews, scores, and traces of our activities on the site and beyond, the exploitation and extraction implicated in the work of Amazon services, from Amazon logistics to products sold on its platforms, have received increasing attention.[28]

Much of the critical literature on labour in platform economies has concentrated on the exploitation of labour on crowd-working sites such as Amazon Mechanical Turk from Chapter 4, and emphasized the microtasking, repetitive, and low-paid nature of crowd work. Amazon Mechanical Turk appears as a 'model of digital Taylorism, which offers compartmentalized tasks for any user connected to the Internet around the world'.[29] More recently, Tech Republic wondered whether clickwork 'data labelling' had become the 'blue-collar job of the AI era'.[30] Cheap data-labelling labour drives the AI revolution in China. As AI needs to learn from humans and their understanding of data, it is a competitive advantage of China to have large amounts of human labour resources that can feed AI cheaply: 'If China is the Saudi Arabia of data, as one expert says, these businesses are the refineries, turning raw data into the fuel

---

[27] As such, the operations differ from Nick Couldry and Ulises Mejias's analysis of data colonialism, which poses appropriation and extraction as the homogenizing logic of a new mode of capitalism (Couldry and Mejias, *The Costs of Connection*). Similarly, Kate Crawford argues that 'practices of data accumulation over many years have contributed to a powerful extractive logic, a logic that is now a core feature of how the AI field works' (Crawford, *The Atlas of AI*, 121).

[28] Crawford, *The Atlas of AI*, Chapter 2.

[29] Boullier, *Sociologie du numérique*, 211 (translation ours).

[30] Reese, 'Data Labeling'.

that can power China's A.I. ambitions.'[31] According to Mark Graham and Mohammad Amir Anwar, AI has led to a 'planetary labour market' of exploitation and extraction.[32]

How economic value is produced remains a central political question and even more so if all our time produces value. As we have seen, for many Marxist scholars, the political question remains that of worker organization and intensifying the struggle between labour and capital. Feminist and postcolonial scholars have expanded these questions to the differentials of labour that subtend both digital and non-digital extraction. They have renewed questions about capitalism's 'outsides' and the conflict over capitalist expansion through extractive logics. In the section 'New capitalism? Surveillance and networks', we discuss two understandings of value in digital capitalism, which build upon these new forms of exploitation and extraction, and which speak to wider controversies about what is new in digital capitalism and related political struggles.

New capitalism? Surveillance and networks

In her book *The Age of Surveillance Capitalism*, shortlisted for the *Financial Times* 2019 Business Book of the Year, Shoshana Zuboff has coined 'behavioral surplus' to render the new value that emerges through the companies' attempt to control and ultimately predict our behaviour based on how we spend our time online, where life is rendered as data.[33] Generating value from all our time has been made possible by new forms of digital surveillance, leading to surveillance capitalism, which 'claims human experience as free raw material for translation into behavioural data.'[34] The extracted 'behavioural surplus' is transformed into prediction products traded on 'behavioral futures markets'.[35]

Zuboff is not the first scholar to point out the new centre stage of behavioural data for valorization through extensive surveillance by digital platforms, but she offers a comprehensive theorization of 'surveillance capitalism', where she goes beyond existing theories of the 'quantified self' with a deeper and more detailed understanding of value and digital surveillance.[36] Our social and cultural world is transformed through the unprecedented growth in the data

---

[31] Yuan, 'How Cheap Labor Drives China's A.I. Ambitions'.
[32] Graham and Anwar, 'The Global Gig Economy'.
[33] Zuboff, *The Age of Surveillance Capitalism*.
[34] Ibid., 14.
[35] Ibid., 93-6.
[36] There is a vast literature on surveillance and quantified/datafied selves. Seminal contributions to these debates are Andrejevic and Gates, 'Big Data Surveillance'; Lupton, *The Quantified Self*; and Lyon, *Surveillance after Snowden*.

generated about ourselves at all times. In this process, we are made into big data through the billions of pieces of content shared daily on Facebook, the millions of daily tweets, etc.[37] According to Zuboff, the self is not just quantified in becoming behavioural data but radically transformed. Surveillance capitalism is ultimately about behavioural change. Zuboff identifies Google's Hal Varian as the new Adam Smith. For Varian, queries into Google's search engine describe how users feel and act right now: what they are interested in, which disease they are worried about, or which house they want to buy.[38]

Throughout her book, Zuboff remains preoccupied with Google as the 'master' of secondary data exploitation, which is data removed from its primary use, such as entering a search query, and employed to predict secondary future behaviour. Google's patents seem to support Zuboff's version of surveillance capitalism. It has numerous patents to exploit secondary data such as, for instance, a system to predict which Web content users might be interested in after they have searched for and visited several websites. The patent defines 'navigation events', which 'may be predicted by various indicators, including but not limited to a user's navigation history, aggregate navigation history, text entry within a data entry field, or a mouse cursor position.'[39]

Google was not the only company to generate surplus from its users' online behaviour in the 2000s. However, compared to Yahoo!'s clickstream analysis, its data was better 'raw' material. Anonymous search queries became a gold mine for marketers. All they had to do was to link a product to an information need in the query by means of Google's many ad services. Google is a master of what we called in Chapter 1 'truth-doing'. Since Google paved the way for exploiting behavioural futures, others have followed. Facebook owns numerous patents to predict user behaviour and extend its social graph. For example, the company has registered a US patent that focuses on analysing textual information to track and enable links between users and predict character traits. 'Based on the linguistic data and the character', the patent proposes, 'the social networking system predicts one or more personality characteristics of the user' so that 'inferred personality characteristics are stored in a user profile'.[40]

Yet, there is more to Google's behavioural data valorization than just the primary user interactions during online searching. In a critical reading of surveillance capitalism, Internet critic Evgeny Morozov has shown that Zuboff leaves aside other practices of digital value production that are crucial to

---

[37] For an overview of up-to-date Internet usage data, compare Statistica, 'Business Data Platform'.
[38] Choi and Varian, 'Predicting the Present with Google Trends'.
[39] Hamon, Burkard, and Jain, 'Predicting User Navigation Events', 2.
[40] Nowak and Eckles, 'Determining User Personality', 1.

Google's success.[41] Without the underlying content that the Google search engine ranks, it could not exploit behavioural surplus. This view is confirmed by Google's patents (and especially earlier ones), whose primary concern is often to exploit online content created by others. It has, for instance, patented a 'user-interaction analyzer' that checks for specific interests in particular parts of digital media on the Web, comparing 'normal' and 'specific' interests: 'Normal user behavior with respect to the media is determined and stored.... Whether ... user behavior of a particular media segment deviates from normal relative to the determined normal user behavior is determined.'[42]

What Zuboff calls 'instrumentarian power' is the ability to shape extracted behaviour to instrumentalize it for new ends. The concern with instrumentarian power of capital is not new. In industrial capitalism, all of nature was instrumentalized, which famously led the Frankfurt School of critical theory to make instrumentalization a focus of their critique of contemporary society. According to Max Horkheimer, instrumental reason is only concentrated on the means to an aim without reflecting on the aim itself.[43] This led to an absolute drive to dominate nature in capitalism. The targeting of behavioural value and how we spend our time is a manifestation of this drive by concentrating on a particular part of nature—human nature—and the creation of new subjects. Our actions are abstracted to become a set of behavioural data items, which are readily modifiable for the purpose of creating new capital.[44]

Zuboff remains focused on the instrumentarian power of one form of valorization from behavioural data. Not only does she ignore the time needed to create online content by others for Google and the free (and not so free) labour that goes into it, but she also misses out on a crucial other component of Google's success. Google's economic success also came from exploiting 'network effects' to support the monetization of advertising.[45] Google AdSense, still the main source of Google's income, places ads on websites based on their content and thus matches advertisers to larger and smaller sites. As far as we can see, AdSense is only mentioned once in Zuboff's book in the

---

[41] Morozov, 'Capitalism's New Clothes'.
[42] Sherrets, Liu, and Lider, 'User Behavior Indicator', 3.
[43] Horkheimer, *Critique of Instrumental Reason*.
[44] Zuboff, *The Age of Surveillance Capitalism*, 99.
[45] Zuboff seems dismissive of the idea of 'network effects', which are only discussed twice in her book. The first time she cites 'network effects' as an excuse by surveillance capitalists for their wealth (Zuboff, *Surveillance Capitalism*, 106). The second time 'network effects' are discussed, Zuboff dismisses the claim that they could explain 'Facebook's dominance', which is 'initially derived from the demand characteristics of adolescents and emerging adults, reflecting the peer orientation of their age and stage. Indeed, Facebook's early advantage in this work arose in no small measure from the simple fact that its founders and original designers were themselves adolescents and emerging adults.' (Ibid., 446).

context of 'content-targeted advertising'.[46] However, AdSense is about more than just extracting value from the content of websites; it also draws them into Google's world. The more sites are reached, the more advertisers will follow. This succinctly captures network value as the other defining practice of digital capitalism that has led to many controversies.

In his analysis of the digital economy, sociologist Tim Jordan points to the importance of network value for digital economic practices, 'potentially reaching a point where the network has so much value, because it has so many connections, that it becomes dominant'.[47] Many patents across the large digital corporations concentrate on exploiting network values. Facebook suggests an approach to roll out products that are 'network-aware' in order to socially cluster users.[48] The social media company has many patents that make claims towards network-aware products such as technology to complete user profiles if users do not fill in all the details when they register. The system uses the networked friend relations on Facebook to deduce missing profile parts. 'The inferred user profile attributes may include age, gender, education, affiliations, location, and the like.'[49]

Across the patents, we find a strong belief in the benefits of network effects and their values. Network values are generated by relations users develop and are acquired after a product is inserted in circulatory processes online. The more connections are established online, the higher the network value, because the network grows. Patents like the Facebook one about completing missing user profile data based on networked friend relations follow the optimism of economists, who believe that new digital networks enable scale and flow. Mayer-Schönberger and Ramge argue that digital networks are the condition of developing 'data-rich markets' that will overcome traditional information shortages in capitalism, as 'massive amounts of data can flow quickly, easily and cheaply between transaction partners.'[50] These data flows are not to be interrupted by data limitations such as incomplete Facebook profiles and can extend across social clusters thanks to network effects.

In the early days of the Internet Age, network effects had been thought to lead to what was called a 'commons-based peer production'[51] and the collective creation of value. The early free software movement, such as Wikipedia, has been often cited as an example of a modern form of 'barn-raising—a collective

[46] Ibid., 83.
[47] Jordan, *The Digital Economy*, 169.
[48] Marlow et al., 'Network-Aware Product Rollout'.
[49] Zhou and Moreels, 'Inferring User Profile', 1.
[50] Mayer-Schönberger and Ramge, *Reinventing Capitalism*, 63.
[51] Benkler and Nissenbaum, 'Commons-Based Peer Production and Virtue'.

effort of individuals contributing towards a common goal in a more-or-less in-formal and loosely structured way'.[52] Today, network effects are less linked to common goals (and collectivity), but generally associated with controversies about the dominance of social media platforms such as YouTube and Face-book, where networks are utilized to expand the user base. Non-users are only interesting in so far as they are potential users/consumers empowered by net-works. Network effects are important not only to social media companies, but they permeate the whole digital economy. Netflix owns several US patents that focus on using network effects to help keep existing users and make new ones by offering new content. For example, they have developed a 'take-rate' signal system, which consists of 'information derived from recording user interac-tions with a system relating to viewing, playing, renting or otherwise taking a content item.'[53]

In the controversy about digital capitalism, valorization through network effects is considered to be the main reason for creating enclosures or 'walled gardens' of the same software and hardware environment that lead to monop-olies. Srnicek summarizes such concerns with monopolies driven by network valorizations: 'In the end, the tendency of major platforms to grow to immense size thanks to network effects, combined with the tendency to converge to-wards a similar form, as market pressures dictate, leads them to use enclosure as a key means of competing against their rivals.'[54] Apple, which Zuboff seems to sometimes consider to be some kind of traditional valorization alternative to Google's surveillance capitalism, was an early master of enclosure with the invention of dedicated hardware and app stores. With every new product, the dependency of Apple's customers on its other products grows, as we have seen in Chapter 4.

Apple has shown how to excel at a strategy long linked to network valoriza-tion and feared by many, because it generates winner-takes-it-all effects. The theory behind network effects is credited to a 1996 article in the *Harvard Busi-ness Review*.[55] Based on 'positive feedbacks' in a chain of user evaluations, a commodity can become a success and ultimately achieve market dominance. This dominance can be achieved through 'early leads', while 'influencing cus-tomer expectations plays a crucial role in "winning" in a network market'.[56] 'Winning the market', however, does not have to rely on better products.

[52] Ibid., 395.
[53] Singh and Gomez-Uribe, 'Recommending Media Items', 2.
[54] Srnicek, *Platform Capitalism*, 113.
[55] Arthur, 'Increasing Returns and the New World of Business'.
[56] Sundararajan, 'Network Effects'.

Whereas Apple seems to still care about the quality of its products (or at least their design) to achieve positive user feedback, this is not required for network valorization. Facebook started off in a tiny market when it was launched as a website to connect Harvard students. Its product played a secondary role. Facebook did not care about the quality of the posts of its users and still seems to not care much today.

Public controversies about the seemingly unstoppable monopolization and expanding size of very large platforms persist—while often ignoring the specifics of digital platforms, which we have analysed in Chapter 4 as algorithmic composition and recomposition of inside/outside, core/periphery. Given such enduring concerns about platform monopolies and expansion, it is not surprising that many of the critics of new forms of capitalism have recourse to regulation or state control to limit the effects of network valorizations and behavioural surplus. Srnicek moves from the private to the public by arguing for platforms to become public utilities supported by state resources—and by implication, we could add, by state regulation.[57] Increased political regulation and protection of privacy is also the answer for those concerned by surveillance capitalism. Zuboff asks for legal regulation given her diagnosis that the surveillance capitalists 'vigorously lobby to kill online privacy protection, limit regulations, weaken or block privacy enhancing legislation, and thwart every attempt to circumscribe their practices because such laws are existential threats to the frictionless flow of behavioral surplus'.[58]

The literature that has analysed a new mode or stage of capitalism—independent of the attributes attached to it—has tended to focus on the processes of value production, expansion, and exploitation through networks and surveillance. Both the enthusiasts of network effects and behavioural surplus and their strongest critics generally agree on how effective and seemingly limitless the expansion of the network and behavioural surveillance are. Less attention is paid to how what we called 'truth-doing' in Chapter 1 underpins new mechanisms of valorization and their limits. Valorizing the small entails the permanent reconfiguration of differences between and within subjects to generate new consumption situations. While the Spotify patent with which we started this chapter focused on gendered differences, we argue that new forms of value generally emerge through the proliferation of smaller and smaller differences. Companies like Spotify do this by focusing not so much on ever more content and connections, but by casting already existing products as 'new' through valorizing small actions and predicting ever more different subjectivations. In the section 'Algorithmic valorization through difference', we enter the abode of Spotify's patents again to explore these practices of valorization.

Algorithmic valorization through difference

Spotify is an online music streaming service turned global platform employing network effects and surveillance machines. Its business model is based on transforming music consumption from a time-limited experience of mix tapes and records into endless streams. The proliferation of data and digitization have made music another digital content experience like Facebook posts or Google-indexed webpages. With digital music, Spotify seems to have a seemingly endless music offer, which it can stream online. It generates the impression of an infinite music offer by linking songs no longer to just one particular album or to a special artist but by making them appear in a variety of guises and categories of activities such as 'music for concentration' or 'Discover Weekly'.

For music listeners, Spotify's apparently unlimited and complex offer can be disorientating. In one patent application, Spotify acknowledges that the 'nearly limitless access to media content introduces new challenges for users', as 'it may be difficult to find or select the right media content that complements a particular moment, activity, environment, or purpose'.[59] Despite its motto of 'No.More.Limits', Spotify used different modes of restricting access to music content—from limited downloads for free versus paying users to monthly and geographical download restrictions.[60] Concerned with getting small differences in 'moments' and 'environments' right, the platform modulates music consumption through various compositions produced algorithmically based on traces offered by users. As Mounia Lalmas, Director of Research at Spotify explains, '[w]hen users interact with the recommendations served to them, they leave behind fine-grained traces of interaction patterns, which can be leveraged to predict how satisfying their experience was'.[61] To algorithmically find the right context, Spotify concentrates on 'fine-grained traces of interaction' in another example of how algorithmic reason is constituted through rationalities of truth-doing.

---

[59] Jehan et al., 'Identifying Media Content', 2.
[60] Welch, 'Spotify Raises Limit for Offline Downloads'.
[61] Lalmas, 'Engagement, Metrics and Personalisation', 2.

Since the 1990s, critical theorists have coined the phrase 'attention economy' to capture the claim that 'human attention is productive of value'.[62] In a 1997 *Wired* article, Michael Goldhaber defined for the first time a 'radical theory of value', which specified that the '[t]he currency of the New Economy won't be money, but attention.'[63] Since then, attention has featured in the titles of numerous books: from *The Attention Economy* and *The Attention Complex* to *The Ecology of Attention*.[64] Two decades later, big data and AI have added the limitless attention of algorithms to the original 'attention economy'. Hayles has highlighted the supposed benefits of machine-learning technologies as they have 'the huge advantage of never sleeping, never being distracted by the other tasks'.[65] Algorithms always pay attention, while human attention is limited and can only be harnessed with difficulty. The rendition of attention as human–machine capacity turns it into a key component of value creation and orients the analysis towards the algorithmic reproduction of an attentive subjectivity through granular digital traces.

However, attention is too generic a term here, as it points to a common human process of selecting subjective objects of interest. Spotify and other platforms care about the continued consumption of their products and the creation of marketable user data. From the perspective of consumption, the attention economy folds onto analyses of surveillance, as attention is deemed to be productive of consumerist subjectivity, which also justifies the extraction of 'behavioural surplus'. In a critique of earlier industrial capitalism, critical theorist Günther Anders', whom we have already encountered in Chapter 2, coined the phrase 'consumerist continuum'.[66] While specified for industrial capitalism and its material 'disjunction between what we produce and what we can use',[67] 'consumerist continuum' fits digital valorizations even better, as this disjunction is exacerbated through the seemingly infinite production and reproduction of digital products. Valorization implies that there is the danger of not using enough, of not needing enough products, which can only be overcome by the consumption of other/new commodities so that individual lives can become the 'consumerist continuum'. In the patents of Spotify, this plays out as the intensive search for new datafication possibilities that will help with the algorithmic capture of subjectivities that keep consumption going.

[62] Beller, 'Paying Attention'.
[63] Goldhaber, 'Attention Shoppers!'.
[64] Davenport and Beck, *The Attention Economy*; Rogers, *The Attention Complex*; Citton, *The Ecology of Attention*.
[65] Hayles, *How We Think*, 71.
[66] Anders', *The Obsolescence of Man*, 52.
[67] Ibid., 8.

As we discussed in the section 'New capitalism? Surveillance and networks', Morozov criticized the theory of surveillance capitalism for ignoring how digital content from billions of websites and sources around the world is extracted in addition to the users' personal data. There are so many websites that are permanently produced that it is sometimes easy to forget that Google does not just valorize behavioural data, but it extracts content from the online digital content productions of many. Spotify's dependence on digital content is difficult to miss and it keeps reappearing in its patents. The company valorizes a combination of limited commercial content from music artists with the 'free labour' contributions of its users. A limited offer of songs and their potentially infinite combinations in user playlists make up its products. Analysing Spotify's patents highlights these different forms of valorization, while drawing attention to a new form of valorization made possible by algorithmic reason. Spotify's music artefacts need to be produced, circulated, and consumed in a continuum.

Spotify has often been criticized for extracting its content from artists and producing precarity. According to a famous calculation, in 2010 an artist on Spotify needed over four million plays to earn a minimum US monthly wage of $1,160.[68] Spotify has also been denounced for its extensive technologies of algorithmic surveillance, as we have seen in the introduction. Yet, there has been less attention to how Spotify uses the music content and playlists for valorization through algorithmic decomposition and recomposition of data. If surveillance capitalism assumes that bodies and minds are transformed into data to be traded on platforms as behavioural futures, Spotify has a limited amount of music it can sell and must focus on generating new experiences to keep the 'consumerist continuum' expanding. The Spotify patents tell the story of searching for small data recompositions, which can be transformed into new commodifications from existing music collections.

'Old' music artefacts appear as 'new' through minuscule datafied alterations. While this also takes place at the very large platforms, it is easier to spot and explain for a company working within the limited realm of music. Spotify keeps the 'consumerist continuum' running with a finite amount of music by recommending new combinations of music to listen to. Its recommendation engines work by combining music sound data, textual information like descriptions and titles, and interaction data from its users playing tracks.[69] Like other platforms, Spotify combines deep and detailed surveillance of its users with

---

[68] Information Is Beautiful, 'How Much Do Music Artists Earn Online?'.
[69] Johnson, 'From Idea to Execution'.

network effects to promote the 'smallest, strangest music'.[70] Matthew Ogle, who led the development of one of Spotify's core recommendation engines, explained their motivation with the digital economy model of connecting the dots to expand the network of users and developing a long tail of music offers:

> We now have more technology than ever before to ensure that if you're the smallest, strangest musician in the world, doing something that only 20 people in the world will dig, we can now find those 20 people and connect the dots between the artist and listeners.[71]

User profiles are created, and music consumption is built around finding people through data that 'are just like you—musically at least'.[72]

In the Spotify world, producing value takes the shape of a search for new data and different infrastructures to intensify predictions about how to keep users consuming music. Spotify needs to always generate new situations of digital music consumption when it does not produce new commodities. A typical patent activates a number of devices that a user carries with them 'to identify patterns of user interaction that account for both context and listening behavior, where, for example, a same behavior could indicate different meanings in different contexts'.[73] Small changes in lived situations can make for new music experiences so that 'old' music is rendered as 'new'. By identifying user interaction patterns, machine-learning algorithms learn to classify preferences within a user situation. The algorithm queries whether music is skipped or whether shuffle mode is activated in order to cluster the sessions into an endless 'consumerist continuum'.

Permanent modulations of lived situations from small data have become very important for Spotify. Another one of its patents shows how small data makes it possible to match music experience to real-world sports activities.[74] The patent provides the example of a fictional Playlist 23 about rock music, which is linked to the 'afternoon run', while 'jogging' might go better with Country Playlist 15. In the patent, running is identified as 'repetitive motion activity' and as such datafiable using sensors from smartphones. It can be transformed algorithmically into 'cadence-based' playlists using correlations with different music tempo ranges. An afternoon run, for example, would require music with a 140–5 tempo. Figure 5.1 illustrates the idea that cadence

---

[70] Pasick, 'Spotify's Discover Weekly Playlists'.
[71] Ibid.,
[72] Ibid.,
[73] Gibson et al., 'Methods and Systems for Session Clustering'.
[74] Ibid.,

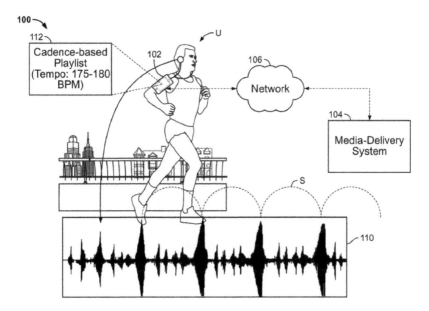

Fig. 5.1 Spotify patent
Source: US Patent Office. Garmark et al., 'Cadence-Based Playlists'.

measurements of running or the 'frequency of ... repetitive motions' can be
another means of enriching music listening to keep the runner consuming. For
Spotify, cadence is a simple way to algorithmically decompose data in order
to recompose music products and experiences as 'new'.

As growth towards a larger user base becomes more difficult for Spotify in a saturated music market with a finite amount of digital content, the
cadence–tempo connections demonstrate how valorization is ensured through
the recomposition of new smaller data details to produce novel music contexts. When the 'attention economy' idea first developed in the 1990s and
2000s to describe the subjectivity challenges to the digital 'consumerist continuum', it was mainly concerned with changing user experiences through
new interfaces. Mobile, permanently connected cadence measurement devices that could correlate to playlists using tempo assumptions did not exist
then. The principal means of accelerating consumption were user A/B experiments to measure the modification of an (external) effect on consumer
behaviour. If an interface button's colour would be changed from blue to red,
will that make it more likely that a user clicks on it? Now variations are prop-
agated all the time by algorithms and progressed through the whole system of
situation-aware infrastructures reusing data of all kinds. The Spotify patents

are employing 'repetitive motion data', 'user interaction data' like skipping, 'speech recognition data', and many more.

Algorithms produce new situations of consumption by decomposing and recomposing small data fragments to predict how more content is accessed after existing content is already consumed. In another patent, Spotify connects parking suggestions with media provision, thus producing a new experience of music commodities and consumption while parking cars.[75] The use of car environmental metadata is particularly revealing for Spotify's search for new situations to keep consumption going. Environmental metadata is seen as productive for making consuming subjects, because it reveals 'a physical environment (e.g., bus, train, outdoors, school, coffee shop), as well as a social environment (e.g., alone, small group, large party)'.[76] Considering this wealth of data possibilities, it is not surprising that Spotify could distance itself from the patent that attracted the attention of digital rights activists, as we discussed at the beginning of the chapter. The Access Now letter emphasized emotion and gender as problematic categories both scientifically and in terms of discrimination. The patent, however, lists a multitude of other data that could be used: age, accent, physical environment, or number of people.

With big data and AI, large data assets are shaped from small data signals and human–machine labour enables the generation of new situations of consumption. For Spotify, a global, very large, and expensive machine-learning infrastructure employing a range of devices is now largely concentrated on predicting how to link data to users' music consumption.[77] The prediction looks to modulate subjectivities. A typical Spotify patent sets out to predict 'taste profiles': 'In response to a query [the algorithm] retrieves terms and weights associated with an artist, song title, or other preferences of a user and use the terms and weights to predict demographic data or other taste preferences'.[78] This decomposition and recomposition of data and small changes in context can also be used to 'output value and confidence level ... for a target demographic metric' such as 'age', 'gender', or 'relationship status'.[79] In predicting taste profiles and demographic metrics, subjectivities are algorithmically recomposed to make new connections between musical artefacts and contexts of situated consumption.

---

[75] Swanson and Oskarsson, 'Parking Suggestions'.
[76] Hulaud, 'Identification of Taste Attributes', 7.
[77] Garmark et al., 'Cadence-Based Playlists'.
[78] Whitman, 'Demographic and Media Preference Prediction', 10.
[79] Ibid.,

As music theorist Eric Drott has shown, surveillance is part of Spotify's business model, which focuses on two types of markets: a market for the circulation of music and a market for the circulation of data. He argues that this intersection is made possible by rendering music as 'something that pervades our everyday lives, and for that reason can function as an ideal tracking device, providing unique insights into who we are, how we feel, what we do, and how these fluctuate from one moment to the next'.[80] Yet, valorization through the algorithmic decomposition and recomposition of data to produce new commodities and situations of consumption has many limitations. Drott observes that user profiles never reflect the 'real' individual moment independent of how much data is collected and analysed.[81] The *New York Times* also detects that Spotify recommendations can 'feel cold', as its personalization fails us.[82]

Algorithmic predictions of situations to consume fail more often than proponents and critics of the new valorization practices from the section 'New capitalism? Surveillance and networks' are ready to admit, as human attention to objects is not easily datafied. Facebook, for instance, has a well-documented history of failed attempts to datafy users' consumption, as well as exaggerated claims of capturing it. The digital marketing and content industries started investing heavily in digital videos in what was called the 'pivot to video' because of Facebook's viewing statistics.[83] The investment in video did not pay off, as Facebook exaggerated the video consumption it generated. In a class action lawsuit, advertisers accused Facebook of inflating its metrics for how long users viewed videos.[84] For Facebook, the algorithmic view metrics included all attention for longer than three seconds. In comparison, YouTube defines a view as a consumption situation of 30 seconds and more.[85] How the consumption of digital products is computed is a political and economic fabrication. As Anders cautions, there are limits to our abilities of consumption even as datafication transforms all parts of our lives into a 'consumerist continuum'.

According to Zuboff, surveillance capitalism started at Google in the early 2000s. Google turned to advertising to finance its desire to monetize the world's online information using its detailed knowledge about us from the search queries we enter. Hal Varian, Google's chief economist saw the potential

---

[80] Drott, 'Music as a Technology of Surveillance', 239.
[81] Ibid., 246.
[82] Klosowski, 'Personalization Has Failed Us'.
[83] Kozlowska, 'The Pivot to Video'.
[84] Kates, '"Far from an Honest Mistake"'. A notice of settlement in November 2019 shows a settlement proposal of $40 million. LLE ONE, 'Plaintiffs' Motion'.
[85] Kozlowska, 'The Pivot to Video'.

of treating people as 'raw' material by using advanced analytics to extract behavioural data. Zuboff, however, ignores the problems behind the ideas of 'raw
data' and humans as data. As she bases her analysis on Google's relative success
in monetizing search, she seems to assume that the extraction of behavioural
data is largely successful and can therefore create a new large-scale capital.
As we have argued in previous chapters, producing knowledge about humans
with data is neither easy nor straightforward. As data is collected, stored,
cleaned, and algorithmically processed, it evinces an often-messy process that
is necessarily incomplete.

To return to the Spotify patent on identifying media content, it draws a distinction between direct qualities which can be measured—for instance, the
tempo or pitch of a song—versus indirect qualities that not might be easily
measurable. 'Typically', they argue, 'whether a media content item will induce
a particular emotional response cannot be measured directly from data representing the media content (e.g., audio signal, video signal, etc.). Additionally,
indirect qualities may lack a unit of measurement.'[86] Algorithmic valorization
has not eliminated frictions, tensions, and conflict. At this threshold between
valorizations with algorithmic reason and 'multiple outsides', we need to attend to what Mezzadra and Neilson have called 'a drama of frictions and
tensions in which the efficacy of the operation appears far more fragile and elusive than might otherwise be assumed.'[87] As we will discuss in Chapter 8, these
frictions and tensions of valorization become a matter of political struggle over
how borders are drawn in international politics.

The analysis of valorization is therefore a deeply political question, which
adds a different dimension to the relation between governing rationality and
subjectivity. In the labour theory of value, the politics of value is read through
the labour force, the workers who produce the massive quantities of data that
are then appropriated and commodified by the big tech companies. Politics
emerges in the labour–capital conflict. These theorists of value are focused on
the possibilities of organizing the working class to resist capital and big tech
companies. For the theorists of surveillance or platform capitalism, the political questions are primarily about the relation between the state and companies
that extract data from users. Capital accumulation relies on the data surplus
that is sold on predictive markets or monopolized on platforms. Therefore,
the focus has been largely on the regulation of these companies, through varied means: from transparency and privacy rights to breaking up monopolies

---

[86] Jehan et al., 'Identifying Media Content'.
[87] Mezzadra and Neilson, *The Politics of Operations*, 67.

and remaking platforms as state-funded public utilities. A different politics emerges when heterogeneous modes of valorization are held together, including algorithmic valorization through decompositions and recompositions of small data fragments that enhance digital commodities. As we have argued in this chapter, any difference that is computable is a productive difference for companies like Spotify. These differences can coincide with hierarchies of race, ethnicity, or gender but they can also be differences between the pace of walking, the habit of shuffling music and so on. The proliferation of difference in machine learning has enabled new forms of valorization and new political effects.

In 2006, *Time* magazine produced one of the iconic images of the emerging new social media age when it announced that 'You' are the 'Time Person of the Year' because 'You control the Information Age' and 'You control the world'.[88] The cover was an image of a YouTube player that reflected as a mirror the reader of the magazine ('You'). While the cover was controversial at the time, it reflected an earlier optimism that the Web and especially social media would lead to new age of global democratization and empowerment of the self. Since then, this optimism has been replaced by controversies about surveillance capitalism and the powerlessness of datafied subjects compared to the monopolies resulting from network effects. The algorithmic valorization that traverses Spotify's patents focuses on exploiting small differences and new datafications from cadence, etc. in order to formulate new algorithms that redefine valorization practices. Given the limits of production and extraction of digital content, algorithmic valorization recasts old digital artefacts—in this case musical artefacts—as new, not just by recombining them but also by generating ever new situations of consumption. If value is produced through an intense focus on all parts of digital traces and how they can be used to reconfigure experiences and situations of consumption, subjectivity is also one of the territories of resistance and potential ungovernability. The third section of the book turns to three interventions to make algorithms governable and the frictions, refusals, and resistances these interventions generate.

[88] Grossman, 'Time's Person of the Year'.

PART III
INTERVENTIONS

6

Ethics

'What if algorithms could abide by ethical principles?', asked a report on scientific foresight for the European Parliament.[1] Rather than remaining a speculative question, ethics has become embedded in social and political responses to algorithms, big data, and artificial intelligence (AI) and their deployments in more and more spheres of social life. From the ethics of big data to ethics of algorithms and AI, technological developments have become deeply associated with ethics.[2] The Organization for Economic Cooperation and Development has extended principles for an AI that is 'right' to its 42 member states.[3] Acknowledging that AI 'is bound to alter the fabric of society', the European Commission's High-Level Expert Group on Artificial Intelligence (AI HLEG) developed an ethical framework for trustworthy AI after receiving more than 500 public submissions.[4] The European Union (EU) has since promoted a what they call the 'third way' for trustworthy AI in Europe—avoiding state surveillance in China and corporate surveillance in the United States. This ethical 'third way' has found its most recent expression in the attempt to supplement the General Data Protection Regulation (GDPR) with a broad proposal for a regulation on AI, which was hailed as the first ever legal framework of AI.[5]

Making algorithms and AI governable follows the assumptions that they are necessary and already embedded in institutions, processes, and our lives more generally. The EU's AI HLEG group speaks for many proponents of AI technology, as it defines trustworthy AI as our 'north star, since human beings will only be able to confidently and fully reap the benefits of AI if they can trust in technology'.[6] In order to follow this north star, the new AI regulation proposed for EU member states takes a risk-based and sector-specific approach to

---

[1] European Parliament, 'What If Algorithms Could Abide by Ethical Principles?'.
[2] European Economic and Social Committee, 'The Ethics of Big Data'; European Commission's High-Level Expert Group on Artificial Intelligence, 'Ethics Guidelines for Trustworthy AI'.
[3] OECD, 'Recommendation of the Council on Artificial Intelligence'.
[4] European Commission's High-Level Expert Group on Artificial Intelligence, 'Draft Ethics Guidelines for Trustworthy AI'.
[5] European Commission, 'Proposal for a Regulation on AI'.
[6] European Commission's High-Level Expert Group on Artificial Intelligence, 'Draft Ethics Guidelines for Trustworthy AI'.

Algorithmic Reason. Claudia Aradau and Tobias Blanke, Oxford University Press.
© Claudia Aradau and Tobias Blanke (2022). DOI: 10.1093/oso/9780192859624.003.0007

AI and is generally concerned that 'high-risk' applications are 'safe' and 'fair'. It remains unspecific on what qualifies as high risk and how hierarchies of risky AI are to be established. More generally, the AI regulation concentrates on AI system providers who need to undertake 'assessments' and comply with 'regulatory requirements'. It has been criticized for largely ignoring multiple subjects affected by AI systems, a tendency that continues those of earlier debates around ethics and AI, which also mainly focused on 'experts', 'providers', and 'developers'. For instance, the Institute of Electrical and Electronics Engineers (IEEE), which describes itself as the world's largest technical professional organization, published its second version of ethically aligned design in 2019, targeting the behaviour of engineers.[7] One of the largest and most influential AI conferences, NeurIPS, has installed an ethical review system for its submissions.[8] The tech industry followed along by designing and publishing its own ethics guidelines, with most Silicon Valley companies professing adhesion to some form of ethical guidance or ethical responsibility.[9] Elon Musk has donated $10 million to keep AI beneficial,[10] while Google's DeepMind launched a separate unit on ethics and AI.[11] The list of AI ethics targeting engineers, experts, and providers keeps growing. How are we to understand this rush to make algorithms and AI ethical through expert knowledge, and this almost viral spread of ethics from the European Parliament and European Commission to IEEE and Google's DeepMind?

Alongside governmental institutions, many media organizations, think tanks, universities, and civil society groups have been engaged in the search for ethical principles in response to the challenges that algorithms and AI raise for our lives individually and collectively. The turn to ethics to manage algorithms is not that surprising, given the long history of mobilizing ethics in response to difficult social, political, and economic questions. Scholars in the humanities and social sciences have devoted a lot of attention to the limits of ethics formulated as 'as an achieved body of principles, norms and rules already codified in texts and traditions'.[12] The recent formulations of an ethics for algorithms rely on 'abstract ethical principles' based on fundamental rights commitments, which are envisaged to apply to almost any possible situation of AI tech. What matters here are less the different ethical commitments that

[7] IEEE, 'Ethically Aligned Design'.
[8] NeurIPS, 'Reviewer Guidelines'.
[9] See for instance IBM, 'Everyday Ethics for Artificial Intelligence'; Deutsche Welle, 'Facebook Funds AI Ethics Center in Munich'; Microsoft, 'Microsoft AI Principles'.
[10] Tegmark, 'Elon Musk Donates $10M'.
[11] Deep Mind, 'Ethics & Society'.
[12] Walker, *Inside/Outside*, 50.

inform these documents and the exact principles that are selected by various authorities, but the appeal to and desire for ethics as a political technology for governing algorithms.

Ethics has played an important role in expert and public discussions of the societal impact of algorithms and as an intervention that aims to shape algorithmically mediated relations. In this chapter, we analyse ethics as a political technique deployed to tame power relations and make corrective interventions on algorithmic reason. As a technology of government, ethics has a limiting or constraining role on the failures or excesses of social action. We do not propose an alternative type of ethics to displace or supplement ethics as code. We approach ethics as political practice to understand how it emerges relationally. We discuss its limitations by inquiring into its speedy adoption by AI researchers, engineers, and big tech companies alike.

We make a two-pronged argument about the ethics of algorithms. For us, the move to ethics pre-emptively eliminates dissensus and draws lines of separation between humans and things. Firstly, the ethics of algorithms effaces dissensus by focusing on certain categories of subjects, who are interpellated to become ethical subjects. As we have already indicated, these subjects are the technologists and engineers who will develop and implement ethical principles, and who will need to consider the concerns of 'users' to be designed into the technology. The racialized and gendered bodies most affected by algorithmic operations are generally not imagined as participants in the dissensus over what an ethics of algorithms is. Algorithms are, secondly, assumed to be mouldable at will, as tools to be subsumed to the ethical decisions of engineers, coders, and computer scientists. We address these differential exclusions through altered modes of ethico-political interventions opening scenes of friction that turn algorithms into public things.

To unpack this proposal, we start by showing how recent invocations of ethics for big data, algorithms, and AI are geared towards consensus. While there are many different ethics guidelines between the various actors involved, including academic authors, ethics as a technique of government is deployed to pre-empt dissensus and render invisible racialized and gendered bodies that challenge the algorithmic distribution of the sensible or the perceptible.[13] In a second section, we reformulate the relation between ethics and politics through what Bonnie Honig has called 'public things', which make political action in concert possible.[14] Thirdly, we explore two ethico-political scenes

[13] Rancière, *Disagreement*, 57–9.
[14] Honig, *Public Things*.

that make algorithms public things by producing and multiplying frictions. One scene has emerged around the petition signed by 4,000 Google employees against Google's involvement in the weaponization of AI; the second scene is that of collaborative hacking of technology to explore its frictions.

Ethics of consensus

As we have started to outline, many organizations have embarked on projects that develop ethical guidelines and principles to be implemented in the use of big data, algorithms, and AI. Ethics has emerged as a public vocabulary and practice of engaging and taming the effects of digital technology. Despite the multiplicity of ethical frameworks and guidelines produced by various actors, these are underpinned by shared assumptions and norms. Some of these norms concern international law and fundamental rights, as in the case of data protection and privacy. Other guidelines focus on principles of conduct, such as 'Do no harm!', fairness, respect for human rights, and transparency.[15] The European Commission's AI HLEG argues that AI ethics needs to be 'based on decades of consensual application of fundamental rights.'[16]

The organizations calling for or implementing AI ethics remain largely silent over what 'fundamental rights' might look like, as rights are hardly ever subject to 'consensual application'. Rather, rights are claimed by different subjects in variable situations and often against considerable resistance. Moreover, there is no abstract human who is a subject of rights as envisaged by the ethics reports and guidelines. Human rights discourses enact a version of the 'human', which excludes multitudes of others deemed 'lesser humans'. Against this dominant version of the human, rights also emerge in situated contestations over who counts as human and what challenges implicit hierarchies of humanity. A fighter pilot needing to make a strike decision based on digital data processed and visualized algorithmically, their human target (often a racialized and gendered 'other'), the developer of an algorithm, and the companies providing the software are all subjects within specific situations where different modes of conflict and coordination are possible and where multiple kinds of justifications are called upon.

The ethical principles of algorithmic beneficence ('Do good!'), non-maleficence ('Do no harm!'), autonomy ('Preserve human agency!'), and

---

[15] For example, e.g. Winfield and Jirotka, 'Ethical Governance'.
[16] European Commission's High-Level Expert Group on Artificial Intelligence, 'Draft Ethics Guidelines for Trustworthy AI'.

openness ('Operate transparently!') endorsed by EU politicians and others are so general that they would entail not just different, but often contradictory practices. What does 'Do no harm!' mean for a drone pilot or for Pentagon's deployment of AI technologies? Or for the border police extracting biometric data from people on the move? What does 'Do good!' entail for a data broker or credit scoring company? Or finally, what does 'Operate transparently!' say about the NSA or other security agencies, when we have seen how they invoke secrecy even when their citizens' lives are at stake? Ethics is imagined as a corrective political technique, as indicated by the addition of the attribute 'ethical' to governance, research, medicine, and so on. Even when non-Western modes of ethics are called upon to displace the monopoly of Western ethics, ethics is still assumed to enable the correction and taming of power from Western centres.[17]

What is at stake here is the aim of consensually taming power, its failures, and excesses. For many, however, this corrective imaginary has been either incomplete or misguided. The AI Now 2018 Report has been one of the first critical public interventions in this landscape of ethicizing AI, big data, and algorithms. Under the heading 'Why ethics is not enough', its authors explain that '[w]hile we have seen a rush to adopt such codes, in many instances offered as a means to address the growing controversy surrounding the design and implementation of AI systems, we have not seen strong oversight and accountability to backstop these ethical commitments'.[18]

A similar concern about the lack of 'independent, informed and transparent review' has been voiced by the Electronic Frontier Foundation (EFF) in response to Google's AI Ethics principles, which were developed in the wake of the controversy concerning Google's involvement in the US military's Project Maven.[19] However, the EFF sees Google's seven principles for ethical AI as a step in the right direction to be replicated by other tech companies. Unlike the EFF, the AI Now Institute points out that such ethical guides and codes of conduct developed by the industry 'implicitly ask that the public simply take corporations at their word'.[20] A stronger criticism has been expressed by proponents of legal regulation. For them, ethics lacks the force of law. Relying on ethics instead of regulation is not just an insufficient strategy, but a misguided one. According to legal scholar Mireille Hildebrandt, 'law provides

[17] The IEEE contributors to *Ethically Aligned Design for AI* proposed to include non-Western ethical principles in future drafts, such as principles from the Chinese and the Vedic traditions (Mattingly-Jordan, 'Becoming a Leader in Global Ethics').
[18] Whittaker et al., 'AI Now Report 2018', 29.
[19] Eckersley, 'How Good Are Google's New AI Ethics Principles?'.
[20] Whittaker et al., 'AI Now Report 2018', 30.

closure whereas ethics remains in the realm of reflection as it does not have *force of law*.[21] In these readings, ethics itself is limited and cannot therefore provide a fully corrective or limiting intervention. Ethical guidebooks lack the force of legal codebooks.

Next to these established criticisms, it is important to also ask what the proliferation of ethics does, what form of control it enables, and within which limits this happens. Ethics is effectively deployed as a technique of governing algorithms, which relies on codes, coordinates issues of implementation, and shapes subjectivities as well as possibilities of action. To borrow Foucault's terms, ethics is a political technique for the 'conduct of conduct' of individuals and groups. Governing through ethics is deemed to 'build and maintain public trust and to ensure that such systems are developed for the public benefit'.[22] To function, ethics should not be asking for the impossible, the philosopher of technology Luciano Floridi tells us.[23] Ethics needs to straddle the gap between what should be done and what can be done. As the IEEE initiatives on ethics point out, ethics is about the alignment between implementation and principles and the generation of standards to coordinate conduct.[24] Ultimately, ethics is subordinated to rationalities of feasibility and consensus-building between multiple and distributed actors.

International relations scholar Maja Zehfuss is particularly instructive for an analysis of the effects of governing through ethics. While not discussing algorithms directly but focusing on ethically justified war, Zehfuss sheds light on the effects of ethical invocations that present war 'as making the world a better place for others',[25] which resonates with by now infamous self-descriptions of Silicon Valley tech companies such as Google's 'Don't be evil' or Facebook's 'Build Social Value'. Instead of making war more benign and less violent, 'this commitment to and invocation of ethics has served to legitimize war and even enhance its violence',[26] because it makes violence 'justified through its aims and made intelligible'.[27] Zehfuss's argument about how ethics enables a particular form of war, which is neither more benign nor less violent, offers a different prism to understand the turn to algorithmic and AI ethics. What algorithms are and do will be shaped by vocabularies and practices of ethics. Paraphrasing

---

[21] Hildebrandt, *Law for Computer Scientists and Other Folk* 283 (emphasis in text).
[22] Winfield and Jirotka, 'Ethical Governance', 1.
[23] Floridi, 'Soft Ethics', 5.
[24] IEEE, 'Ethically Aligned Design', 1.
[25] Zehfuss, *War and the Politics of Ethics*, 2.
[26] Ibid., 9.
[27] Ibid., 186. A similar argument is made by Grégoire Chamayou, who draws attention to the emergence of necroethics as a 'doctrine of *killing* well' (Chamayou, *A Theory of the Drone*, 146).

Zehfuss's claim that war is made through ethics, we can say that algorithms and AI are now made through the political technique of ethics.

This diagnosis of ethics as an enabler of governance and violence leads Zehfuss to the question of politics and an understanding of ethics as limit or constraint. For her, it is this 'cordon[ing] off against the real world, against politics' that is the limit of ethical engagements.[28] A different conceptualization of ethics would not solve the problems of ethical war. According to Zehfuss, political decisions would surpass any existing rule and ethical quest for clarity, as they are inseparable from uncertainty, ambiguity, and the possibility of negative consequences. This understanding of politics rather than ethics is tethered to decisions and decision-makers. Uncertainty and ambiguity endure on the side of the decision-maker, the one who gauges the reality of the world, rather than the individuals and collectives who experience the consequences of decisions. Decisions remain hierarchical and exclusionary, as those who become the target of technologies of killing cannot reconfigure decisions and only appear as a silent concern to the decision-maker. As we saw in Chapter 2, not only are decisions much more dispersed and mediated through work and infrastructures, but the subjects most affected by algorithmic operations have generally no say in these decisions.

Ethics as a political technique of governing algorithms similarly turns those potentially most affected by these decisions into what philosopher Jacques Rancière has called the 'part of those who have no part'.[29] The part of no part is formed by those made invisible by the dominant arrangement of people and things. This invisibilization allows for the reproduction of and policing of consensus. For Rancière, dissensus politicizes this invisibility through collective action and makes visible 'whoever has no part—the poor of ancient times, the third estate, the modern proletariat'.[30] Whereas AI ethics guidelines render the 'part of no part' invisible or absent in the consensual rendition of the world, dissensus can redistribute what is visible and sensible. Take for instance, Google's ethical promise that '[w]e will seek to avoid unjust impacts on people, particularly those related to sensitive characteristics such as race, ethnicity, gender'.[31] The category of 'people' remains a general one like in many other AI ethics guidelines, which can be divided in processable sociological categories without any residuals or absences. Ethical algorithms 'promise to render all agonistic political difficulty as tractable and resolvable', as Amoore

---

[28] Zehfuss, *War and the Politics of Ethics* 195.
[29] Rancière, *Disagreement*, 15.
[30] Ibid., 9.
[31] Pichai, 'AI at Google'.

has aptly observed.[32] Ethicizing algorithms aims to render relations between self and others devoid of dissensus.

Algorithms are now made through ethics, which pre-empts dissensus over what and who counts in the distribution of people and things. In 'aligning the creation of AI/AS [autonomous systems] with the values of its users and society',[33] ethical codes efface both dissensus over what these values are and frictions over the creation of digital technologies. By imagining engineers as the locus of ethical codes and their implementation, ethics as a technique of government can be debilitating for the political subjects who live through the consequences of others' decisions. Ethics makes algorithms governable by conducting the conduct of engineers and technologists. Many of the ethical guidelines proposed by different institutions formalize rules that are subsequently to be implemented by engineers, developers, and companies. Ethics thus becomes 'institutionalized as a set of roles and responsibilities, and operationalized as a set of practices and procedures'.[34]

Bringing attention to the uncertainty, ambiguity, and even the opacity of decision-making is not sufficient to address the effects of ethics in rendering invisible and debilitating those who are to have 'no part' in the world designed for ethical technologies and ethical engineers. Yet, the 'part of no part' only becomes visible through dissensus over the collective distribution of the sensible. This is even more difficult given the supra-sensible and infra-sensible algorithmic operations we discussed in Chapter 2. Moreover, privileging engineers, computer scientists, and technologists as the subjects of ethics reframes the relation between humans and machines, people and things, ethical subjects and algorithmic objects, to which the section 'Public things' turns.

Public things

'Ensure that AI is human-centric', enjoins the European Commission's High-Level Expert Group.[35] In these invocations of ethics, humans and AI are set in opposition. If there is any conflict that appears in the report, it is in this opposition between an abstract human and a general machine, not in the ethical codes themselves. This relation is imagined on a model of the machine taking over decisions, autonomy, and sovereignty from the abstract human

---

[32] Amoore, *Cloud Ethics*, 10.
[33] IEEE, 'Ethically Aligned Design'.
[34] Metcalf, Moss, and boyd, 'Owning Ethics', 451.
[35] European Commission's High-Level Expert Group on Artificial Intelligence, 'Draft Ethics Guidelines for Trustworthy AI', ii.

subject. Moreover, ethics is oriented towards a seemingly abstract human as evinced in the injunction to be 'human-centric' or 'design for all'.[36] Indeed, ethical responses to the questions raised by emerging digital technologies and their extension into the fabric of everyday life have 'overwhelmingly sought to reinstate the human as the proper figure of sovereignty, its executive decisions bound by juridical and ethical codes of conduct'.[37] Google's ethics principles include a commitment that '[o]ur AI technologies will be subject to appropriate human direction and control'.[38] The discourse of human control is often replicated in the literature that proposes to develop ethical guidelines and starts from the assumption that decisions previously made by humans are 'increasingly delegated to algorithms'.[39]

As we noted earlier, two categories of subjects inhabit the world of ethics. On the one hand, the subjects whom the IEEE calls 'technologists' or 'anyone involved in the research, design, manufacture or messaging around AI/AS including universities, organizations, and corporations making these technologies a reality for society'.[40] The technologists are the experts who are called upon to enact meaningful control over machines, and to make algorithms ethical. The other subjects are the unspecified humans—people or users—who can become objects and potential victims of algorithms. It is in relation to this assumption of vulnerability that the ethics of big data, algorithms, and AI has focused on privacy and data protection. The GDPR was hailed as a watershed for privacy and protection and has led to numerous changes in privacy terms and complex statements about cookies and privacy on each website. Some websites became unavailable in Europe. The GDPR appeared to bring an ethical constraint on the big users of technology and build some form of responsibility and transparency in these systems for vulnerable users.

Yet, the model of an autonomous human voluntarily choosing a contract or taking control has always been false, and even more so for algorithmically constituted relations.[41] Relations between tech companies and users are asymmetrically mediated by algorithmic objects and digital platforms. One day, one of us received an email from Booking.com alerting us to an update in the company's privacy policy. Such emails and alerts have been so common in Europe since the GDPR entered into force that many probably do not even notice

[36] Ibid.,
[37] Amoore and Raley, 'Securing with Algorithms', 7.
[38] Pichai, 'AI at Google'.
[39] Mittelstadt et al., 'The Ethics of Algorithms'.
[40] IEEE, 'Ethically Aligned Design'.
[41] The GDPR also enacts boundaries between citizens and non-citizens, given that Article 23 restricts the application of rights when national security, public security, defence, or public interest are considered (General Data Protection Regulation, 'Regulation (EU) 2016/679').

them anymore. Booking.com has been particularly well known for providing an interface for finding hotel accommodation. The email alerted users that the company would start sharing information between the different companies that are affiliated with Booking Holdings Inc. to create new services, develop new brands, and prevent and detect fraud.[42] The company emphasizes that data sharing is about personalization and experience:

> In short, it means a better experience for you across all Booking Holdings brands. We'll be able to offer you exactly the kind of accommodation that's right for you, along with providing a much more inclusive service when it comes to booking your next trip. This will be done through website personalisation, more personalised communications and improvements to our products and services.[43]

The email points out the importance of transparency, as mandated by GDPR. It ends, however, on a cautionary note: 'Sad but necessary bit: If you disagree with this Privacy Statement, you should discontinue using our services.'[44] The updated Privacy Statement is based on a stark binary: acceptance and loss of rights or privacy rights but forced self-exclusion from service. There is no autonomous human who can voluntarily choose a transaction, but a human entangled with practices of law, commodification, and governing.

Communication scholar Mike Ananny has rightly drawn attention to these limitations of ethical codes and guidelines and enjoins us to consider the 'unit of ethical analysis … that is not a code or a human action on code but, rather, an intersection of technologies and people that makes some associations, similarities, and actions more likely than others'.[45] A similar approach is taken by the AI Now Institute, when they argue that what is needed to move beyond the current ethical orientation is 'infrastructural thinking'.[46] For them, infrastructural thinking entails extending attention to how technologies are 'entangled in social relations, material dependencies and political purposes'.[47] As we have shown in Chapter 4, digital platforms rely on intricate workflows that are both social and technical and working through the small and dispersed to bring

---

[42] Email from booking.com to Claudia Aradau, 6 February 2019.

[43] Email from booking.com.

[44] Booking.com, 'Privacy Statement'.

[45] Ananny, 'Toward an Ethics of Algorithms', 97.

[46] Infrastructural thinking is one of the seven elements listed by the institute as a way to advance AI ethics. They also include 'From fairness to justice', 'Accounting for hidden labour in AI Systems', 'Deeper interdisciplinarity', 'Race, Gender and Power in AI', 'Strategic litigation and policy interventions', and 'Research and organizing: an emergent coalition' (Whittaker et al., 'AI Now Report 2018').

[47] Ibid., 33.

the outside in and take the inside out. Ethics guidebooks render the relations between people and technologies, humans, and algorithms as relations of mastery and control. From the mastery of technology, ethics reimagines the human as a sovereign who can mould material objects and algorithms at will or passive subjects who are controlled by technologies and AI. Action thus remains unencumbered by power, materials, objects, instruments, devices, and bodies. The abstract human of ethics reveals itself as an engineer or technologist, the professional body replacing the public body.

How can ethico-political interventions hold together materiality as both embodiment and technology? Political theorist Bonnie Honig has proposed to recast political action as mediated by public things.[48] Moving beyond the 'object turn' in social studies, she argues that we need to pay attention not just to relations between humans and things, but more specifically to *political* things, the things that mediate democratic political action. For Honig, a public thing does not mean that it is opposed to the private. Rather, a public thing constitutes a public, as it assembles a collectivity around a thing and 'bind[s] citizens within the complicated affective circuitries of democratic life'.[49] If public things have often been associated with the infrastructures of democracy, Honig extends this understanding to objects around which citizens constellate in political life. 'Public things', she argues, 'depend on being agonistically taken and retaken by concerted action'.[50] Public things are constitutive of democratic life, which otherwise would be reduced to 'procedures, polling, and policing'.[51] Democratic politics entails the redistribution of the sensible, the disruption of arrangements of people and things.

Public things assemble a collective, they require action in concert and move us away from anthropocentric ethics. Contra Latour's contention that political theory has excluded things, Honig reclaims 'public things' from the perspective of political theory and democratic politics. As she puts it, '[w]ithout public things, action in concert is undone and the signs and symbols of democratic life are devitalized'.[52] The commitment to public things needs to be understood

---

[48] Honig, *Public Things*.

[49] Ibid., 7.

[50] Ibid., 91.

[51] Ibid., 4.

[52] Ibid., Honig's analysis resonates with Latour's proposal for an 'object-oriented democracy'. However, Latour's understanding of politics and democracy in *Dingpolitik* does not account for the redistribution of the sensible through action in concert. Rather, objects are seen to offer occasions for concern, and even difference and dispute. However, this is a rather minimal understanding of democracy at work, as '[e]ach object may also offer new ways of achieving closure without having to agree on much else' (Latour, 'From Realpolitik to Dingpolitik', 5). We return to the different vocabularies of contestation and their relation to democratic politics in the Conclusion of this book.

in the context of the neoliberal transformation of public things into private things. Honig thinks about the inattention to the infrastructures of public phones in relation to the private phone, or the demand for private energy generators in the wake of Hurricane Sandy. Public things—from small devices to infrastructures—are constitutive of relations between individuals and between self and other. The things that Honig is concerned about are either invisible—background infrastructures—or become visible in moments of crisis or due to collective protest. These things require maintenance, care, and repair, as the literature on infrastructures and materiality has shown.[53] By making action in concert possible, public things add a material dimension to Rancière's politics of dissensus and the redistribution of the sensible.

Honig's proposal to rethink public things as constitutive of democratic action in concert also resonates with critical insights on the limits of privacy in addressing the challenges of government through and of algorithms. Media theorist Wendy Hui Kyong Chun articulates this blurring of the public and the private in the formula: 'Subjects act publicly in private or are "caught" in public acting privately'.[54] We have also seen that the protection of personal data and privacy are limited in an algorithmic space defined by political and economic asymmetries. Digital anthropologist Payal Arora cautions us against an ethnocentric and exoticizing approach to privacy and data protection, which does not account for the needs for visibility, speaking up against oppression, and activism in the Global South.[55] In their report on ethics and algorithms, AlgorithmWatch researchers have argued that algorithmic discrimination does not necessarily affect individual rights, as 'discrimination only becomes visible when comparisons are made between different collectives'.[56] Nevertheless, privacy keeps being repeated as one of the key ethical requirements in institutional guidelines and frameworks, although researchers have cautioned that asymmetric big data analytics does not depend on an 'identifiable individual'.[57] Chun urges us to refuse the binary of private–public in favour of 'creating and inhabiting public spaces online and offline'.[58] Rather than just 'making things public', as Latour would say, authors like Chun and Honig enjoin us to 'make public things political'.

---

[53] Graham and Thrift, 'Out of Order'; Aradau, 'Security That Matters'.

[54] Chun, *Updating to Remain the Same*, 95. In his 1980 volume, Anders had already diagnosed the 'obsolescence of privacy' with the rise of mass media, because we are increasingly 'at home' in the public. Anders cautions that 'the public sphere has also lost its singularity', as the home is no longer private. The public sphere is 'often understood only as an extension of the private sphere'. Anders, *The Obsolescence of Man*, 57.

[55] Arora, 'Decolonizing Privacy Studies'; Arora, 'General Data Protectection Regulation'.

[56] Jaume-Palasi and Spielkamp, 'Ethics and Algorithmic Processes', 14.

[57] Mittelstadt et al., 'The Ethics of Algorithms'.

[58] Chun, *Updating to Remain the Same*, 95.

Can algorithms or datafications become political things? In their dispersion and heterogeneity, algorithms are elusive objects for action in concert, while their opacity and complexity render them difficult objects of dissensus. Yet, action in concert can remake algorithms into scenes of friction, it can work to reconfigure rights and subjectivity, politics and ethics, the private and public. The section 'Little tools of friction' will now explore two such scenes of friction that attempt to materialize dissensus. One scene emerges around the Google employees' petition against the weaponization of AI and another around a scene of collective hacking.

Little tools of friction

A letter to Google

In 2018, the *New York Times* published a letter written by thousands of Google employees and engineers in protest at Google's involvement in Project Maven.[59] Project Maven planned to develop an AI surveillance technology for image recognition of vehicles and other objects in motion. The petition, which initially appeared on Gizmodo, deploys ethical and normative language: 'We believe that Google should not be in the business of war'.[60] The petition also mentions 'growing fears of biased and weaponized AI', the difficulties that Google would encounter in attracting talent and the risks of joining the ranks of companies working for the US Department of Defense (DoD). The Google employees state that building technology 'to assist the US government in military surveillance—with potentially lethal outcomes—is not acceptable'.[61] They have foreseen the rapid development of AI for military purpose. Only two years later, AI-empowered targeting is thought to have made a decisive difference in the Second Nagorno-Karabakh War between Azerbaijan and Armenia. Azerbaijan successfully deployed 'loitering munitions, so-called "kamikaze drones"', which once launched are meant to 'loiter' in a target area and then more or less autonomously identify and destroy a target.[62]

The Google petition is underpinned by a normative anti-war stance. Yet, this is not the ethics of consensus we discussed earlier. The normative principles that the Google employees invoke are neither enshrined in international law nor generally accepted. The Pentagon used the language of war and protection

<hr />

[59] Shane and Wakabayashi, '"The Business of War"'.
[60] Menegus, 'Thousands of Google Employees Protest'.
[61] Ibid.,
[62] Deutsche Welle, 'Germany Warns: AI Arms Race Already Underway'.

to justify its development of AI in a digital arms race with China. The letter-turned-petition disturbs the distribution of the sensible and what is given to take a position that at first sight would appear impossible. The petition stands for acting in concert, and particularly acting in concert in one of the undemo-cratic sites of democracy—the workplace. The force of the petition was the force of emerging collective subjects as public actors. Initially signed by 3,100 employees, the numbers rapidly rose to over 4,000 employees who remained publicly anonymous. The petition also politicized the use of targeted killings by the US government. The US drone programme not only operates outside established legal frameworks and definitions of war, but it has also been beset by 'credible allegations of unlawful killings'.[63]

The petition has subsequently assembled further publics beyond the num-bers internal to Google. More than 1,000 researchers working on digital technologies signed an open letter in support of the Google employees. Their letter reiterates some of the points of the employees' petition, including the request not to be involved in the development of military technologies. Most significantly, it draws attention to the politics of US targeted killings:

> With Project Maven, Google becomes implicated in the questionable practice of targeted killings. These include so-called signature strikes and pattern-of-life strikes that target people based not on known activities but on prob-abilities drawn from long range surveillance footage. The legality of these operations has come into question under international and U.S. law.[64]

At the beginning of 2019, the Arms Control Association announced that the 4,000 Google employees were voted arms control persons of the year.[65]

However, if Rancière's politics of dissensus was focused on the redistribu-tion of the sensible, the petition limits this reconfiguration to 'weaponized' AI, thus leaving unquestioned the work of 'normal' AI. In that sense, we speak of frictions as actions that slow down, try to move in a different direction, or otherwise produce hindrances in the 'smooth' distribution of the sensible. Friction depends upon the materiality of things constitutive of political action in concert.[66] Google employees are not making claims to rights, yet they open a scene for political action in concert. They produce frictions by creating publics around Project Maven. It is thus not surprising that, in the wake of Google's

[63] Rahim, 'Why Project Maven'.
[64] Suchman et al., 'Open Letter'.
[65] Arms Control Association, 'Google Employees Voted Arms Control Persons of the Year'.
[66] We extend the understanding of friction in science and technology studies (STS) as that which 'resists and impedes' to slowing down, inflecting in a different direction, and unfolding differently. For an overview of the uses of 'friction' in STS, see Edwards et al., 'Science Friction'.

decision to stop cooperating with the Pentagon on Project Maven and other military AI, the Defence Innovation Board was tasked with developing ethical principles for the use of AI by the military. Led by the former chairman of Alphabet and Google, Eric Schmidt, the board released ethical guidelines in June 2019, which were in line with 'existing legal norms around warfare and human rights'.[67]

Reading the letter as a little tool of friction does not mean that Google's withdrawal from the direct 'business of war' in Project Maven spells the end of Google's (or other tech) involvement in the business of war. Rather than proposing a form of 'pure' ethics or politics, the letter initiates frictions that open a democratic scene of dissensus. The Silicon Valley companies remain part of the military–industrial–media–entertainment complex both in the US and internationally.[68] As Google withdrew from further collaboration with the DoD, they also dropped their application for providing integrated cloud services, the Joint Enterprise Defense Infrastructure (JEDI) project, which we introduced in Chapter 4. The JEDI contract was initially awarded to Microsoft. After the contract award, Oracle filed a complaint against the DoD for its biased specifications that privileged a single vendor—Amazon Web Services (AWS)—despite Congressional and other concerns and the direct involvement of individuals with links to AWS.[69] AWS similarly started a lawsuit against the DoD alleging undue political influence on the award. As we discussed in Chapter 4, the Pentagon withdrew the contract in 2021, following this extensive litigation. However, the contract looks likely to be reissued and awarded to a consortium rather than single companies.

Other frictions emerged as the scene opened by the letter unfolded. Following a commitment to AI principles, Google set up an ethics advisory board only to dissolve it a week later over public criticisms about the choice of board members.[70] Later on, Google forced out Timnit Gebru, co-lead of the Ethical AI team and an internationally renowned researcher in the field of ethics and AI. She was the co-author of a paper criticizing very large language models, which we take up in Chapter 7.[71] While it was reported that the paper passed internal research reviews, 'product leaders and others inside the company had

---

[67] Edwards, 'Ethical Guidelines for Use of AI in Warfare'.

[68] The military–industrial–media–entertainment complex was theorized in Der Derian, *Virtuous War*.

[69] *Oracle America Inc v The United States and AWS Inc*, 'Pre-Award Bid Protest'. McKinnon, 'Ending JEDI Cloud Project'.

[70] Statt, 'Google Dissolves AI Ethics Board'.

[71] Bender et al., 'On the Dangers of Stochastic Parrots'.

deemed the work unacceptable'.[72] Since then, Google has totally transformed its Ethical AI research division and appointed Marian Croak, a software engineer, as its lead. In a Google blog, Croak, who had previously been vice president of engineering, outlined her vision and subtly shifted from 'ethical AI' to 'responsible AI', while promising to overcome dissensus and 'polarizing' conflict in the company.[73]

A year after the public debate around the Google employees' letter on Project Maven, the Intercept disclosed an internal email at Google that showed that Google continues to cooperate with the DoD on other AI projects.[74] Based on further internal emails at the company the Intercept also revealed that the infamous AI contribution to Project Maven relied on low-skilled workers or so-called 'data labellers'.[75] In order for algorithms to recognize objects in the drone video footage, they need to be trained on datasets that accurately separate different types of objects and people. This work is often crowdsourced and done by people around the world who can be paid as little as 1$/hour to correctly label images.[76] The ethics of algorithms and AI does not extend into the hidden abodes of digital capitalism we discussed in Chapter 5. It does not account for the invisibilized labour of making data processable by algorithms, and it does not disrupt the international asymmetries that foster exploitation and extraction, as data labellers are drawn from the poor around the world. Yet, this does not mean that the letter to Google has simply failed. A scene does not succeed or fail, it is not felicitous or infelicitous, but it continues to unfold. The frictions around AI continue to unravel and unsettle distinctions between ethics and politics, human and nonhuman, consensus and dissensus.

Hacking in concert

As we have seen in this chapter, ethical algorithms exclude the 'part of no part' by locating ethical subjectivity with the engineers and putting technologists in charge of 'responsible AI'. Subjects targeted by algorithms do not have to be relegated to ethical invisibility or passivity if, instead, we start with 'how subjects are making rights claims by blocking and filtering, encrypting communications, creating multiple and anonymized and shared identities, deploying bots, gaming trending algorithms, and so on'.[77] To put it differently,

[72] Simonite, 'When Google Ousted Timnit Gebru'.
[73] Moghadam, 'Marian Croak's Vision'.
[74] Fang, 'Google Won't Renew Its Drone AI Contract'.
[75] Fang, 'Google Hired Gig Economy Workers'.
[76] Ibid.,
[77] Madsen et al., 'Big Data', 286.

little tools of friction can be as mundane as a letter or a petition or as high tech as encryption or hacking. What counts is how these tools take hold of and render algorithmic operations intelligible, how they insert frictions that slow down, hinder, or redirect the movements of technology. Yet, the little tools of friction can also risk producing their own asymmetries and exclusions, through differential distributions of techno-political capacity. For instance, encrypting communications relies on digital expertise that is not equally shared but enacts asymmetries between the more or less tech savvy. 'Hacking' technology is similarly an act that can produce algorithmic frictions. Yet, the figure of the 'hacker' has been a highly individualized one—hackers are rightly or wrongly imagined as male virtuosos—even as they 'live this individualism through remarkably cooperative channels'.[78] Yet, what about those who do not have—or do not want to acquire—the skills for intimately engaging with technology?

Moving on from the figure of the hacker, 'hacking' as action in concert can become a scene of taking hold of algorithms collectively by rendering their operations intelligible. We turn from the figure of the hacker as an individual or small group of hackers as 'high-tech guilds' to the act of hacking.[79] Originally developed by Silicon Valley companies with a focus on technical solutions and creating competitions for new coding talent, 'hackathons', also called 'hack days' or 'hack fests', have recently been taken up in the context of social and educational interventions. Unlike the hackathons aimed at the production of more and better technologies, these hackathons can become collective socio-technical scenes which take hold of algorithms as public things. Since algorithms are human–nonhuman composites, hackathons allow us to collectively explore the materiality of friction by interfering with digital things, as they compose collectivities of humans and machines, while binding individuals to a temporary collective where capacities are assembled in more symmetrical ways to jointly take hold of algorithms.

We have employed hackathons and hacking as scenes that bring together collectives of humans and devices and strive to turn algorithms into things to be held in common. They can be apt little tools of friction, which 'express the possibilities and potentials of action'.[80] Digital users can act in concert in hackathons to explore how algorithms can afford political enactment of what sociologist Noortje Marres has called 'material participation'. Material participation is a 'device-centred perspective' with attention to 'how things mediate

---

[78] Coleman, *Coding Freedom*, 210. See also Kelty, 'Hacking the Social?'.
[79] Coleman, 'High-Tech Guilds'.
[80] Lodato and DiSalvo, 'Issue-Oriented Hackathons', 555.

publics'.[81] In our configuration, coders and non-coders would work together during the hackathons in smaller groups to target technical details of their technology use and discuss the frictions they discovered in a recomposition of the whole group. Our focus was less the development of technical skills than the attempt to co-research technical details and their socio-economic tensions, together with those who are otherwise rendered as non-political 'users'.

One such collaboration was undertaken with Young Rewired State, an organization dedicated to supporting young persons' interest in coding.[82] Through Young Rewired State, a group of teenagers could come together to experience what happens to the data they produce while using their phones. The hackathons organized with Young Rewired State engaged teenagers as co-researchers to generate a collective understanding of the data produced daily within the global mobile ecosystem, independent of their level of technological skills. Hackathons can 'potentially facilitate … practices for those who do not have the same technological expertise'.[83] During the hackathons, participants could take hold of algorithmic operations through collective coding; they could research how they are datafied by their mobile devices, who has access to data from the mobiles, and how that data could be used to extract value. Participants also helped design a workshop programme exploring empirical and conceptual implications of mobile datafications. This work transformed hackathons from technical instruments focused on innovation and finding solutions to socio-technical arrangements to explore big data and algorithms as public things.

The hackathons were carefully configured: twenty participants between fourteen and seventeen years old were given smartphones with a six-month data bundle. Together with researchers on the project, they worked on an app called MobileMiner, which was developed at King's College London, and which could dynamically trace mobile communications and detect data recordings on Google's Android operating system.[84] Google's Android does not make it easy to access ingoing and outgoing communications on its phones. Yet, MobileMiner was developed to record both network activity and a log of the app's notifications. Network activity recorded by MobileMiner included, for instance, connections to cell towers, which makes it possible to

[81] Marres, *Material Participation*, 23.
[82] This collaboration was part of the project 'Our Data Ourselves'. Blanke et al., 'Mining Mobile Youth Cultures'. For another example, see Chapter 4's discussion of mobile apps in digital humanitarianism; following the methodology developed in Aradau, Blanke, and Greenway, 'Acts of Digital Parasitism'.
[83] Pybus, Coté, and Blanke, 'Hacking the Social Life of Big Data'.
[84] Blanke et al., 'Mining Mobile Youth Cultures'.

understand what location information apps track about their users.[85] Action in concert was mediated not only by big tech platforms and algorithms, but also by MobileMiner as a little tool of friction.

MobileMiner is designed to require as few user permissions as possible. For instance, the movements of a mobile phone user can be tracked based on the cell towers they connect to, without requesting permission for the phone's location systems. To this end, MobileMiner queries the Android API for information on communications with the cell towers by individual apps.[86] The data is converted into approximate location data using the gazetteer of cell tower locations provided by opencellid.org. This allowed the hackathon participants to experiment with visualizations of frequently visited locations using OpenStreetMaps. Another approach developed for MobileMiner permanently surveys the Android filesystem to determine the port, IP address, and protocol of each network socket for each app. This enables the detection of activities on the Chrome Web browser, for instance, along with those of apps such as Facebook, Skype, Foursquare, Spotify, and many game apps on the mobile phones. In making these invisible and smooth processes of algorithmic datafication visible, the hackathon rendered digital technologies and their algorithmic operations intelligible in a collective setting.

The hackathons focused on creating MobileMiner and also on what could be done with the mobile data through predictive algorithms. As data-gathering devices, mobiles are vital sources for algorithmic prediction. They intensify the uneven distributions of power and capacity, as they are increasingly oriented towards possibilities of action. Using crowdsourced information from OpenCellID and the data from MobileMiner, participants drew on clustering techniques to explore the datafication of their everyday actions.[87] A simple cluster analysis identified several regular patterns in mobile data. For instance, one participant was present in three UK cities on two days. The cities are known as locations of major universities, and a subsequent discussion confirmed that they attended the open days of the universities and then potential interviews. This kind of data extraction can produce value for digital marketers, as it reveals patterns and interests. What matters for them is not the 'truthfulness' of conscious doing, but the patterns that emerge without the conscious involvement of individuals and the meanings they attach to these actions.

[85] Pybus, Coté, and Blanke, 'Hacking the Social Life of Big Data'.
[86] Blanke et al., 'Mining Mobile Youth Cultures'.
[87] Greenway et al., 'Research on Online Digital Cultures'.

Mobile data-based exploration confronted the hackathon participants with the power of algorithms to construct predictions largely based on mobile location information. It interpellated them as actors rather than generalized tech users:

> Far too many people don't understand quite how much they are giving to companies and how much this data is worth to them especially when the privacy policies are shady at best. And when you can't have members of the public check what the Facebooks and Googles are doing inside of these apps and with the data behind closed doors then it becomes very easy for them to exploit the user.[88]

Hackathons are temporary scenes, which can be mediated through specific tools, whose development has been made possible by collaborations between academics and developers. The hackathons also turned algorithmic operations, and particularly predictive analytics, into a matter of action in concert and investigated them through the frictions they produce. Participants could experience algorithms as public things and explore the possibilities for interfering in digital worlds.

Neither the Google employees' public petition nor the hackathons with young people organized in a university have stopped the production of AI for military purposes or the extraction of data by tech companies. Yet, as these scenes unfold, the little tools of friction they introduce produce new forms of intelligibility and foster collective subjectivity by holding things in common. A letter to Google might have started as a banal and rather mundane object, but it helped create public debate about the role of algorithms. Even if it has not led to redistributions of the sensible or abolished military uses of AI, the little tools of friction have had public reverberations and have created memories of collective interventions. A later statement about the unionization of Alphabet workers highlighted past mobilizations by workers: 'Organized workers at the company forced executives to drop Project Maven, the company's artificial-intelligence program with the Pentagon, and Project Dragonfly, its plan to launch a censored search engine in China'.[89] Hackathons might have been usually reserved for the high-tech coders of the digital age. Yet, action in concert reconfigures them as shared material participation into the extraction of data for predictive purposes. Rather than interpellating 'users', hacking becomes a collective site of holding algorithms as public things in common.

---

[88] An anonymized hackathon participant quoted in Pybus, Coté, and Blanke, 'Hacking the Social Life of Big Data'.

[89] Koul and Shaw, 'We Built Google'.

These scenes of materializing dissensus recompose relations between subjects and objects, as they unsettle understandings of political action and who counts as a political subject.

If ethical algorithms and AI render the 'part of no part' invisible and pre-emptively disactivate democratic dissensus, ethico-political interventions that work with little tools of friction help unfold scenes where action in common upon algorithmic operations becomes possible. In these scenes, the ethical focus on the self—embodied by technologists and engineers—is disturbed through motley collectives of workers, researchers, and citizens. In Chapter 7, we show how calls for ethicizing algorithms have been supplemented by calls to render algorithms accountable by setting these within social and political relations where an account of algorithmic operations can be given publicly. Making algorithms accountable catalyzes another type of scene, which we call 'scene of refusal'.

7

Accountability

As Amazon's facial recognition system, Rekognition, was being increasingly marketed to public and security agencies in the US, the American Civil Liberties Union (ACLU) conducted a test to match US members of Congress with 25,000 publicly available arrest photos using the same software. The ACLU reports that 28 Congresspersons have been incorrectly identified as persons who had been arrested for a crime.[1] The ACLU attorney Jacob Snow points out that the incorrect matches were 'disproportionately of people of color, including six members of the Congressional Black Caucus'.[2] Academic research has also shown how algorithmic bias in datasets is translated into high error rates for certain categories of people. An analysis of three commercial gender classification systems—Microsoft, IBM, and Face+++—by researchers at MIT Media Lab discovered that darker-skinned women were the most misclassified group, with error rates of up to 34.7% compared to error rates of up to 0.8% for lighter-skinned men.[3]

In the light of the Black Lives Matter movement, Amazon placed a moratorium on the use of its facial recognition technology by the police, while IBM stopped developing facial recognition systems. Even though several cities such as San Francisco, Berkeley, and Oakland in the US have banned the use of facial recognition by government agencies, facial recognition algorithms are employed by an increasing range of public and private actors. While calls to ban facial recognition are increasingly heard in Europe as well, the technology has also been speedily rolled out at European Union's borders.[4] According to a report by the civil liberties organization Big Brother Watch in the UK, facial recognition systems used by the police were wrong nine times out of ten.[5] Still they continue to be seen as an essential tool of policing and border control.

[1] Snow, 'Amazon's Face Recognition'.
[2] Ibid.,
[3] Buolamwini and Gebru, 'Gender Shades'.
[4] FRA, 'Facial Recognition Technology'.
[5] Big Brother Watch, 'Face-Off Campaign'.

Algorithmic Reason. Claudia Aradau and Tobias Blanke, Oxford University Press.
© Claudia Aradau and Tobias Blanke (2022). DOI: 10.1093/oso/9780192859624.003.0008

Facial recognition systems have been most present in public debates about discriminatory algorithms and biased data. Many of the public controversies around facial recognition have focused on the problems of training data, particularly the scrapping of facial images on the Internet. To create training datasets, public and private actors have taken 'images manually culled and bound together from sources as varied as university campuses, town squares, markets, cafes, mugshots and society-media sites such as Flickr, Instagram or YouTube'.[6] In 2021, Google made it illegal to collect content from YouTube and identify a person without their consent.[7] This move adds pressure on companies like Clearview AI, which allows law enforcement agencies to search billions of images in its database of 10 billion faces, scraped from the Internet, including from YouTube videos. Since its practices have become known, privacy activists and data protection organizations have started several legal challenges against Clearview AI in the US and Europe, given public concern about 'the end of privacy as we know it', as the *New York Times* puts it.[8] While facial recognition has rallied most concern globally, its contestation has also tended to reproduce geopolitical lines and forms of othering, with countries such as China assumed to develop advanced facial recognition unimpededly.

In this chapter, we analyse how accountability has been enacted in these controversies over facial recognition algorithms and systems. Initial disclosures of the extensive experimentation with facial recognition by law enforcement in Europe and the US has led to calls for algorithmic accountability through tools such as auditing. Algorithmic and data audits have been proposed as public instruments of accountability. They target 'inclusive benchmarks' and balanced training data.[9] In the UK, the Information Commissioner's Office is developing a method for auditing algorithms.[10] The AI Now Institute in New York proposed to cultivate algorithmic impact assessments for public accountability.[11]

We argue that facial recognition exposes a particular enactment of algorithmic accountability through auditing error. To render algorithms accountable

---

[6] Murgia, 'Who's Using Your Face?'.
[7] Clark, 'YouTube's Updated Terms of Service'.
[8] Hill, 'The Secretive Company That Might End Privacy as We Know It'. Following a joint investigation by the UK Information Commissioner's Office (ICO) and the Office of the Australian Information Commissioner, ICO announced its intent to fine Clearview AI over £17 million for breaches of UK data protection law. ICO, 'ICO issues provisional view to fine Clearview AI'.
[9] Buolamwini, 'Response: Racial and Gender Bias in Amazon Rekognition'.
[10] Peakin, 'ICO Appoints Researcher'.
[11] Reisman et al., 'Algorithmic Impact Assessments'.

entails 'putting them to the test' by making visible their errors, resulting in bias and discrimination. This enactment of accountability requires professional practices and devices for internal or external verification. More recently, a second mode of accountability has emerged as 'Explainable AI', where algorithms are asked to give an account of their decision-making. 'Explainable AI' has even been lauded as democratizing accountability, given that it does not require a class of professionals to 'reverse engineer' and audit algorithms.

Error analysis and explainability have been key sites for claims of algorithmic accountability, but have also given rise to global scenes of controversy about how to make algorithms governable. Calls to ban facial recognition or otherwise refuse its deployment enact accountability differently, which we call 'accountability through refusal'. Refusal disturbs the hierarchies of error optimization and trust in algorithmic explanations. In January 2020, the city of Moscow launched what was claimed to be to be the largest facial recognition system worldwide. The system was employed during the Covid-19 pandemic to target 'quarantine breakers'.[12] At the time of writing, privacy activist Alyona Popova took a law case against Moscow's Department of Technology, which manages the video surveillance, to the European Court of Human Rights.[13] A similar case concerning facial recognition had been filed in the UK against the South Wales Police force.[14] At about the same time, China also had its first lawsuits against facial recognition technologies, as we will discuss later.[15] We understand refusal as a continuum that ranges from mundane ways of saying 'no' to extended practices of litigation and mobilizations to ban the development or use of facial recognition in certain cases.

The chapter proceeds in four steps. We start with a discussion of accountability as a subject of scholarly and public controversy. Is accountability another technology in the bureaucratic toolbox or can accountability become a device of contestation? In the first two sections, '(Un)accountable algorithms' and 'Accouting for error: politics of optimization', we unpack the emergence of 'accountability through error' and 'accountability through explanation' and their respective politics of optimization and trust. In the final section, we draw on dispersed practices that open scenes of 'accountability through refusal'. We show how refusal disrupts optimization and trust.

---

[12] Roussi, 'Resisting the Rise of Facial Recognition'.
[13] For a discussion of the cases, see Bacchi, 'Face for Sale'.
[14] *R (Bridges) v CCSWP and SSHD,* 'Judgment'; *R (Bridges) v CCSWP and SSHD,* 'Judgment in the Court of Appeal'.
[15] Lee, 'China's Facial Recognition Regulations'.

(Un)accountable algorithms

Accountability has become a ubiquitous term and practice, responding to the increasing complexity and distance of decisions, actors, and operations away from the institutions of representative government. Accountability carries the promise of democratizing sites and practices where democracy appeared rarefied—at a distance from the electorate or detached from existing mechanisms of democratic control. Therefore, it is perhaps not surprising that algorithmic accountability has emerged as a rallying call against the perceived opaque hold that algorithms have upon our social and political lives. Yet, despite its democratic and positive aura, accountability has also been criticized as a neoliberal technology bringing about an 'audit society'.[16] As technologies of auditing are transferred from the financial sector to other spheres of social life, accountability has been a central element of neoliberalism, control, and responsibilization of individuals at work.[17] Moreover, auditing enacts 'a relationship of power between scrutinizer and observed: the latter are rendered objects of information, never subjects in communication'.[18]

As with ethics, we can understand accountability as a technique of government, in that it proposes to 'conduct the conduct' of algorithms. It mobilizes new forms of management, the creation of new institutions and professionals of accountability. This can take the financial form of auditing or broader forms of giving an account of one's work and actions. Accountability involves operations of quantification and verification, which can reduce the space of narrative justification and professional expertise. Thus, accountability does not just foster suspicion and distrust, but it renders practices calculable and makes subjects quantifiable. In a seminal edited collection exposing the effects of accountability in higher education, anthropologist Marilyn Strathern enjoins us to 'acknowledge the need for accountability while being critical of the kinds of social processes it often seems to put in train'.[19] The contributors to the edited book trace undesirable effects of formalization, bureaucratization, loss of autonomy, distrust, and coercion that accountability implies.

Demands for algorithmic accountability have been voiced again and again, suggesting the creation of new professions such as the 'algorithmists' proposed by Mayer-Schönberger and Cukier, who would 'fill a need similar

---

[16] Power, *The Audit Society*; Power, 'The Audit Society—Second Thoughts'.
[17] Rose, 'Government and Control'.
[18] Shore and Wright, 'Coercive Accountability', 59.
[19] Strathern, 'Introduction: New Accountabilities', 14.

to the one accountants and auditors filled when they emerged in the early twentieth century to handle the new deluge of financial information.'[20] If for them algorithmists follow the formalism and bureaucracy of internal financial auditors, others have seen auditing algorithms as an external accountability mechanism. Christian Sandvig and colleagues have acknowledged the difficulties of auditing algorithms and have proposed the development of new methods 'to ascertain whether they are conducting harmful discrimination by class, race, gender'.[21] The AI Now Institute focuses on algorithmic impact assessments, which are largely modelled on risk assessment.[22]

Although algorithmists have not yet been fully established as a separate profession, we can already find elements of their work in contemporary efforts by researchers and companies. The focus is often on auditing data, where bias is more easily quantifiable. A typical IBM research audit on facial recognition data traces the kinds of facial features missing from widely used training data and argues that in order to achieve 'facial diversity', more datasets that reflect global and local differences in faces are required.[23] Lack of diversity is a common issue with facial recognition data. One such famous example is CelebA, a facial dataset that helped to produce excellent recognition rates of well over 90%, but less than 15% of its records show darker skin colours. CelebA is a dataset of celebrity faces, considered to be in the public domain. Microsoft has produced another facial dataset MS Celeb, which contained more than 10 million images of nearly 100,000 persons harvested from the Internet using a flexible definition of celebrities, which included journalists and academics. The individuals in MS Celeb were not asked for their consent and privacy audits led to an attempt to remove of the data, which turned out to be arduous. Although Microsoft tried to delete the database, several copies had already been in circulation, and it was difficult to stop its distribution by community sites such as GitHub.[24] While MS Celeb was originally planned for academic use, companies such as IBM, but also Chinese companies such as Alibaba and SenseTime, used the database. SenseTime's facial recognition technology is suspected to be part of the Chinese government's surveillance of the Uyghur population.

In the wake of the public controversy over its racialized and gendered bias in facial recognition data, Microsoft reported on its AI blog that it had assessed

[20] Mayer-Schönberger and Cukier, *Big Data*, 180.
[21] Sandvig et al., 'Auditing Algorithms', 6.
[22] AI Now, 'Algorithmic Accountability Policy Toolkit'.
[23] Merler et al., 'Diversity in Faces'.
[24] Harvey and LaPlace, 'Microsoft Celeb'.

its data and algorithms and made changes to reduce problems of classifying gender across skin tones. The company claimed it was able to 'reduce error rates for men and women with darker skin by up to 20 times'.[25] Microsoft's reporting of its challenges has been translated in the media as 'Microsoft says its racist facial recognition tech is now less racist'.[26] However, Microsoft researchers acknowledge that reducing error rates through algorithmic and data audits is not simply a technical challenge but a difficult political issue of how and when to 'mitigate AI systems that reflect and amplify societal biases not because of dataset incompleteness or algorithmic inadequacies, but because human societies are biased'.[27]

Focused on societal biases, audits might reveal the past and present of power relations. Accounting for the training data of facial recognition algorithms can unravel histories of data extraction, racialization, and criminalization. Databases of facial images have historically started with mugshots held in police files and therefore focused on the figure of the criminal.[28] As Ruha Benjamin has argued, audits can become abolitionist tools, which disrupt bureaucratization and disciplining.[29] Accountability can modify power relations through contestation and collective agency. It could thus shift from what the authors of *Data Feminism* have called concepts that 'secure power' to concepts that 'challenge power'.[30] In avoiding the pitfalls of 'bad actors' and 'bad algorithms', accountability can question the 'very hierarchical logic that produces advantaged and disadvantaged subjects in the first place'.[31] More recently, Latin American digital rights activists Joana Varon and Paz Peña have proposed a feminist toolkit to question AI systems, which challenges dominant discourses of accountability, inclusion and transparency by highlighting several dimensions of domination:

Is a particular A.I system based on surveilling the poor? Is it automating neoliberal policies? Is it based on precarious labor and colonial extractivism of data bodies and resources from our territories? Who develops it is part of the group targeted by it or it's likely to restate structural inequalities of race, gender, sexuality? Can the wider community have enough transparency to check by themselves the accuracy in the answers to the previous questions?[32]

---

[25] Roach, 'Microsoft Improves Facial Recognition'.
[26] Epstein, 'Microsoft Says Its Racist Facial Recognition Tech Is Now Less Racist'.
[27] Roach, 'Microsoft Improves Facial Recognition'.
[28] Aradau and Blanke, 'Algorithmic Surveillance and the Political Life of Error'.
[29] Benjamin, *Race after Technology*.
[30] D'Ignazio and Klein, *Data Feminism*, 60.
[31] Hoffmann, 'Where Fairness Fails', 901.
[32] Varon and Peña, 'Building a Feminist Toolkit'.

A feminist lineage of accountability places it in relation to political questions about what or who counts, who does the counting, and what comes not to count.[33] Can accountability challenge power rather than secure asymmetric power relations and neoliberal technologies of quantification and verification? In the rest of this chapter, we analyse enactments of accountability through three controversies that have emerged around facial recognition. We start with accountability as giving an epistemic account of algorithmic wrongdoing that surfaced through errors.

Accounting for error: politics of optimization

'Optimization does not mean perfection.'
—Donna Haraway, *Simians, Cyborgs, and Women:*
The Reinvention of Nature (1991), 64

Facial recognition has come under increased public scrutiny given its failures, errors, and fallibilities. As one of the most widely deployed AI applications, the errors of facial recognition appear frequently in public debates. Many researchers have tried to connect algorithmic errors to social questions of discrimination and oppression. Facial recognition for law enforcement has too high error rates, highlights Big Brother Watch in a case against the Metropolitan Police in London. Errors are systematic rather than accidental, revealing underlying patterns of bias and discrimination. The US Technology Policy Committee of the Association for Computing Machinery (ACM), a high-profile association of computer scientists, acknowledges that, 'when rigorously evaluated, the technology too often produces results demonstrating clear bias based on ethnic, racial, gender, and other human characteristics recognizable by computer systems'.[34] However, in computer science, making algorithmic errors visible through such 'rigorous evaluation' relies on particular assessment indicators, which need to be computable. Therefore, such errors can only surface certain forms of bias or discrimination. The same association of computer scientists adds that '[facial recognition] technology is not sufficiently mature and reliable to be safely and fairly utilized without appropriate safeguards against adversely impacting individuals, particularly those in vulnerable populations'.[35] They recommend its temporary suspension rather than

---

[33] Haraway, *Simians, Cyborgs, and Women*; Singleton, 'When Contexts Meet'.
[34] ACM U.S. Technology Policy Committee, 'Statement on Principles and Prerequisites for the Development, Evaluation and Use of Unbiased Facial Recognition Technologies'.
[35] Ibid.,

an indefinite ban, in light of a future where errors can be corrected, and facial recognition can become 'unbiased'.

The ACM Technology Policy Committee's statement comes in the wake of activist and scholarly work to make errors of facial recognition visible. Yet, there is also a split between civil society calls to ban facial recognition, particularly for use by law enforcement and decision-making by public and private actors, and professional demands to just reduce, if not eliminate, bias. We see a dual professionalization of the work of algorithms: that of auditing as well as the work of optimizing the performance of algorithms. Data scientists themselves have suggested that auditing algorithms will 'become the purview of a learned profession with proper credentialing, standards of practice, disciplinary procedures, ties to academia, continuing education, and training in ethics, regulation, and professionalism.'[36] The author of *Weapons of Math Destruction* set up her own consultancy to audit algorithms.[37] O'Neil wants companies to open their data and algorithms to outside reviews that determine their fairness. Auditing involves checking for correspondence with 'real life' and leads to a seal of approval, which she sees as equivalent to the label 'organic' for food production. Auditing algorithms becomes a way of ordering and ranking and not just correcting algorithms.

For auditors and computer scientists, algorithmic errors and failures are often indicators that AI systems are not yet good enough and do not reveal fundamental issues. When information studies scholar Safiya Noble investigated Google's search engine, she argued that 'search engine results perpetuate particular narratives that reflect historically uneven distributions of power in society.'[38] While Noble focuses on the representation of Black girls in Google search engine results, the intersection between opaque algorithms, commercial interests, and the effacement of multiple perspectives through 'ranking' has not only harmful, but also anti-democratic effects. Noble's analysis shows that racist and sexist results are the effects of an algorithm shaped by advertising requirements as well as existing structures of racism and sexism. In the conclusion to her book, she acknowledges that Google made modifications to the algorithm in the wake of her earlier article that highlighted the pornification of Black girls and that Google hid certain search results.[39] In a typical algorithmic auditing move, Google treated Noble's findings as errors to be corrected. Through error correction, Google has computationally optimized the

[36] Guszcza et al., 'Why We Need to Audit Algorithms'.
[37] O'Neil Risk Consulting & Algorithmic Auditing, 'It's the Age of the Algorithm'.
[38] Noble, *Algorithms of Oppression*, 71.
[39] Ibid.,

algorithm but has not addressed the wider political consequences for public and democratic life that Noble highlights.

As public demands for accountability have focused on the errors of algorithms, there has been less attention to the discussion of error optimization in the machine-learning community. Google could react directly to accusations of racist and sexist rankings by treating racism and sexism as errors. Error analyses such as Google's optimization of its own rankings are key to making an algorithm 'work' in specific domains. While errors are publicly rendered in terms of 'mis-takes', the implication is that the algorithm can lead to a correct 'take'. In 2016, Richard Lee, a New Zealand citizen of Asian descent, was blocked from renewing his passport by a robot, because his eyes were identified as closed. He was asked to change the passport picture.[40] Lee's answer to the algorithmic failure to renew his passport shows the trust in an algorithmic corrective epistemology: 'It was a robot, no hard feelings. I got my passport renewed in the end.'[41]

Since the epistemic transformation of AI from logical to statistical models, artificial intelligence work has mainly focused on building models that can solve particular problems by iteratively adjusting and reducing the remaining error.[42] The 'winter of AI' was related to an over-reliance on logical models to simulate human reasoning and their subsequent failure. Computer scientists wanted to create an artificial intelligence that replicated human intelligence but was separate from humans. Peter Norvig, former Director of Research at Google, explains an epistemic transformation from logical models to statistical models, which 'have achieved a dominant (although not exclusive) position' since the 1980s.[43] Unlike earlier logical models, statistical models focus on associations of humans and machines that can learn from data by iteratively adjusting what has already been learned using calculated error rates. These can be measured by comparing what has been learned with what had been expected to be learnt. Modelling becomes a workflow of increased algorithmic performance through error optimization, which compares effects in data with expected inputs and outputs in a finite number of iterations.

When we attended an exhibition dedicated to AI and Big Data in London in 2019, logical models of AI were hardly mentioned but error played a prominent

---

[40] Reuters, 'New Zealand Passport Robot'.

[41] Ibid.,

[42] At the time of writing, the latest AI success was AlphaFold, DeepMind's application of deep neural network techniques to determine the 3D shape of a protein from its amino-acid sequence. Models like AlphaFold are developed within complex workflows of human–computer interaction, starting with large testbeds to tune algorithms so that they can be constantly evaluated for their effectiveness through a well-defined error analysis.

[43] Norvig, 'On Chomsky'.

role as a key question for algorithmic operations in what computer scientists call 'the wild'. 'The wild' stands for the moment an algorithm is taken out of its experimental development and released as an application into a world full of imperfect data, new confusing relations, etc.[44] At the expo, a data scientist from Microsoft presented error 'tweaking' as central to the deployment of machine learning. For many data scientists, finding an 'optimal' error rate for the task at hand is key.[45] Yet, what exactly counts as optimal error continually eludes computer scientists, as optimization depends on different social meanings, political questions, and economic imperatives. Ng tackles this question in his book *Machine Learning Yearning*:

How do we know what the optimal error rate is? For tasks that humans are reasonably good at, such as recognizing pictures or transcribing audio clips, you can ask a human to provide labels then measure the accuracy of the human labels relative to your training set. This would give an estimate of the optimal error rate. If you are working on a problem that even humans have a hard time solving (e.g., predicting what movie to recommend, or what ad to show to a user) it can be hard to estimate the optimal error rate.[46]

Optimizing errors is therefore linked to human–machine relations and epistemological situations that are difficult to solve even for humans. What counts as optimal error depends not only on social meaning, but equally on economic value.

As errors are linked to optimizations of algorithms 'in the wild', they receive extensive attention in the applied computer science literature. A co-authored book by Clarence Chio and David Freeman, research engineer at Facebook working on integrity and abuse and formerly at LinkedIn, expounds algorithmic optimization at social media companies. The authors see false positives—in this case, the number of social media users wrongly identified as non-authentic—as undesirable, because they can 'block a user that didn't already have an established relationship with your site. Such a user will most likely give up rather than complain to your support team'.[47] To differentiate 'authentic' users from bots, LinkedIn assigns a 'reputation score' to browsers, IP addresses, etc. based on the level of disruption seen from these in the past.[48]

---

[44] Digital technologies have increasingly blurred the distinction between testing or experimentation and implementation. Digital technologies, from mundane devices to AI systems, are now tested in real life directly. See Bunz, 'The Calculation of Meaning'; Aradau, 'Experimentality, Surplus Data and the Politics of Debilitation'.
[45] Research Notes, 15 April 2019, https://www.ai-expo.net/global/.
[46] Ng, *Machine Learning Yearning*, 46.
[47] Chio and Freeman, *Machine Learning and Security*, 259.
[48] Freeman, 'Data Science vs. the Bad Guys'.

Then, machine-learning techniques are deployed to combine the reputation score into a final risk score. This happens either almost instantaneously with a minimal set of features or on historical data with a much larger set of features and more complex models. As LinkedIn does not want to lose users, it remains conservative in its assessment and rather misses out on some true positives in order to avoid too many false positives. 'How can we stop bad activity without making good members unhappy?' would be the question that LinkedIn asks of its algorithms.[49]

As Chio and Freeman explain, machine-learning errors are optimized according to a company's understanding of economic value.[50] Achieving higher accuracy can be very expensive and depends on available resources. A 1% increase in accuracy can be much more expensive than a 20% increase, depending on the starting point and available resources. These kinds of social and economic considerations are repeated in almost all AI applications 'in the wild'. Whereas Facebook and LinkedIn require errors optimized on avoiding false negatives, this is different for security applications such as the facial surveillance of public places. Optimization translates here into how to predict very few faces of interest against an unhappy public that is indiscriminately targeted. In the UK, a legal case against the use of automated facial recognition by the South Wales Police highlighted how high false positive rates can become acceptable in order to not miss out on faces of interest in a crowd, as small groups are targeted in much larger populations.[51]

Training security applications is both difficult and expensive, as they need to overcome the 'accuracy paradox', which means that the model with the highest numerical accuracy is not always also the best model. In a public crowd of, say, 10,000, there might be ten known thieves. In such a situation, any algorithm would easily achieve 99.9% accuracy by simply predicting that there are no thieves in the crowd, but the algorithm would not be useful. Calibrating this situation and getting the error optimized can only be done through an expensive process of trial and error, where data scientists target the ten entries of thieves with specific modulations of what counts as error. For instance, they might optimize the algorithm by over-rewarding the prediction of faces by thieves and over-penalizing missing out on them. Auditing algorithmic error does not account for the distinction between optimization and perfection noted in the quote introducing this section. There can be no perfect algorithm; they can always be tweaked depending on what is considered an optimized

---

[49] Ibid.,

[50] Chio and Freeman, *Machine Learning and Security*, 259.

[51] *R (Bridges) v CCSWP and SSHD*, 'Judgment'.

error. Once an optimal error is decided, optimization also becomes a demar-
cating line for accountability, as errors can be corrected only if optimization is
not affected.

Accountability has been enacted through error when different publics have
encountered algorithmic malfunctions, misrecognitions, glitches, failures, or
other fallibilities. In this sense, claims to algorithmic accountability are entangled with a politics of optimization. They all imply that there is a correct or
valid application of AI waiting on the other side of failure and discrimination
that can be found after a system upgrade or further beta testing. These forms
of accountability through error enact algorithmic systems as fallible but ultimately correctable and therefore always desirable. Errors become temporary
malfunctions, while the future of algorithms is that of indefinite optimization.

While these public controversies over the errors and biases of facial recognition unfolded, Timnit Gebru, the co-lead of Google's ethical AI team, was
forced out by the company. As we briefly discussed in Chapter 6, she had
co-authored a paper arguing that extremely large text processing by Google
makes it very hard if not impossible to address sexist and racist language.[52]
The paper raised doubts about the fundamental limits of Google's approach
to assemble larger and larger data to create new tools and ever better error
optimization. While Google had no problems correcting the ranking of sites
related to Black girls, as it considered it to be just another error like any other
example of delivering unwanted results, Gebru's co-authored paper was a more
fundamental critique of the company and its algorithms. It started to ask the
question what should and should not be done with algorithms, which might
lead to the unpredictable refusal to do it. This attracted Google's ire in comparison to errors that can be indefinitely corrected and do not challenge the
logic of optimization.

Self-accountable algorithms: explainability and trust

Confronted with public pressure about algorithmic errors, bias, and discrimination, computer scientists have promoted another form of accountability
through explainability. The international working group on Fairness, Accountability, and Transparency in Machine Learning (FAT-ML) has defined
explainability as the principle which '[e]nsures that algorithmic decisions
as well as any data driving those decisions can be explained to end-users

---

[52] Bender et al., 'On the Dangers of Stochastic Parrots'.

and other stakeholders in non-technical terms'.[53] AI explainability emerged particularly in relation to critiques of algorithmic opacity and 'black boxing' of algorithmic decisions. As we discussed in Chapter 2, algorithmic decisions are dispersed workflows which operate both beneath and beyond the threshold of human perception.

Making algorithms accountable through explainability has fostered a new research and business field across computing, economics, and philosophy. 'Explainable AI' (XAI) aims to generate trust that AI decision-making is fair and similar to what a human would have come up with.[54] In XAI terms, to explain an algorithm and its underlying model means to relate its input to its output so that humans can trust the generated relations. AI models are generally chosen based on optimal technical performance. As we have seen, error optimization is primary in this process, and not whether humans can also follow the reasoning. XAI adds a new requirement to balance out accuracy with explainability. XAI has become a field that considers what humans should think about how they are treated by algorithms.

XAI is already widely used and referenced. In their evidence submitted to the UK House of Commons inquiry into algorithmic decision-making, IBM argued for the importance of accountability so that the algorithms 'that underpin AI systems need to be as transparent, or at least as interpretable as possible. In other words, they need to be able to explain their behaviour in terms that humans can understand'.[55] DARPA, the Defense Advanced Research Projects Agency, started a programme on 'Explainable AI', as explainability is seen as 'essential if users are to understand, appropriately trust, and effectively manage these artificially intelligent partners'.[56] A review of the XAI landscape has identified FAT and DARPA as some of the most prominent actors in this research area, while many companies—both start-ups like H2O.ai and big tech companies like Microsoft and IBM—have turned 'Explainable AI' into a business model.[57] In the EU, the GDPR has made explanation of algorithmic decision-making a legal requirement by including a right to request an account of the 'logic' involved in automated decisions and 'the significance and the envisaged consequences of such processing for the data subject'.[58] The GDPR, however, remains vague about what the 'meaningful information' about this logic is.

---

[53] FAT-ML, 'Fairness, Accountability, and Transparency in Machine Learning'.
[54] Miller, 'Explanation in Artificial Intelligence'.
[55] IBM, 'Written Evidence'.
[56] Gunning, 'Explainable Artificial Intelligence'.
[57] Adadi and Berrada, 'Peeking inside the Black-Box'.
[58] General Data Protection Regulation, 'Article 15. Right of Access by the Data Subject', Article 15.1(h). See Goodman and Flaxman, 'European Union Regulations'.

Explainability supplements error by focusing not on algorithmic 'wrong-doing' but on algorithmic 'truth-doing'. Algorithms are expected to give an account of their operations. Yet, the growing importance of XAI needs to be understood not just in epistemic terms, but also supporting what Peter Denning, a pioneer of American computer science, has posed as one of the fundamental questions of computer science: '[W]hat can be (efficiently) automated?'[59] Machine learning and AI are fundamentally motivated by this computer science desire for automation. Historian of science Stephanie Dick reminds us that this move towards automation is simultaneously the move to 'make human behavior more machine-like'.[60] The field of XAI attends to computerized automation and building user trust in what is otherwise an automated, machine-like process. Explainable AI is not an epistemic account of algorithmic action, but part of this process of automation. It is therefore not surprising that XAI has been taken up by all major providers of AI systems, as it allows them to push for ever more automated and complex AI models.

Explainability has been proposed by AI providers as a means to make algorithms self-accountable. Considering the increased use of neural networks in AI, giving an account of algorithmic operations has been increasingly problematic. Neural networks have been called the 'dark secret' of AI,[61] as their operations are difficult to follow even for their own designers. Much of the discussion on algorithmic explainability has highlighted concerns with such opaque algorithms that are not accountable, as their inner workings are not open either because they are too complex or because they are proprietary.[62] These models often combine complexity with proprietary constraints, as more complex models are more expensive to produce, require more data, and are therefore locked away by companies.[63] The XAI community has reacted by creating so-called model-agnostic ways for algorithms to explain their operations, which do not require access to the underlying algorithm and which allow for complex neural networks to be deployed. Model-agnostic methods have developed separate explanation algorithms that are run to explain the output of machine-learning algorithms.

With neural networks, facial recognition has hugely advanced its performance in its core objective of 'one-to-many' identifications. This task compares

---

[59] Denning criticizes this principle as 'too austere', as 'it only hints at the full richness of the discipline' (Denning, 'Computer Science: The Discipline').

[60] Dick, 'Artificial Intelligence'.

[61] Knight, 'The Dark Secret at the Heart of AI'.

[62] Rudin, 'Stop Explaining Black Box Machine Learning', 2. On the larger question of opacity in machine learning, see Burrell, 'How the Machine "Thinks"'.

[63] Rudin, 'Stop Explaining Black Box Machine Learning'.

one person's photo with N registered photos and predicts the person with the highest degree of similarity. Facial recognition has been increasingly deployed at the European Union's borders with a growing number of databases and capacities. The EU Agency for the Operational Management of Large-Scale IT Systems (eu-LISA) describes how deploying one-to-many facial identification at borders 'requires both significant processing power and highspeed network connectivity to ensure high quality and speed of biometric recognition and identification'.[64] One-to-many identification is furthermore used in criminal investigations, where algorithms detect faces from security cameras and compare them with a database of known faces to identify suspects.

As facial identification is so widely deployed, it has attracted strong interest in XAI. A DARPA-funded project extends the definition of XAI to Explainable Face Recognition (XFR).[65] XFR is about identifying regions in the digital picture of a face, which work best to determine similar faces and distinguish dissimilar ones. It does not aim to establish an explanation of facial recognition as such, but to convince non-experts of 'truth-doing': that the right regions of the face are activated for identification purposes.[66] Many popular explanatory techniques in AI-based facial recognition highlight regions in the facial image that made the machine decide that a face is identified and why that face is different from other faces. However, such 'attention maps'[67] only visualize facial identities and differences and require further explanations. Just because a system identifies a part of an image that is important to facial matches correctly, it does not mean that these matches are also correct. On the contrary, self-accounting of algorithms through visualizations is known to instil over-confidence. Human–computer interaction research has shown that visualizations like attention maps led to a tendency to 'over-trust' the outcomes of the algorithms by their designers.[68] Explainability results in the opposite of explanations and gives rise to an 'automation bias' or the faulty confidence in the designers that the system gets it right.

Researchers from the US National Institute of Standards and Technology (NIST) have also begun to work on the principles of XFR in the context of the US justice system, where XFR would compete with human 'forensic facial recognizers'.[69] These experts prepare detailed reports within the US justice

[64] eu-LISA, 'Artificial Intelligence in the Operational Management of Large-Scale IT Systems', 16.
[65] Williford, May, and Byrne, 'Explainable Face Recognition', 249.
[66] Rudin, 'Stop Explaining Black Box Machine Learning'.
[67] Lin et al., 'An Explainable Cosine Metric'.
[68] Kaur et al., 'Interpreting Interpretability'.
[69] Phillips and Przybocki, 'Four Principles of Explainable AI'.

system and 'explain' facial recognition decisions following standards such as the ones by Facial Identification Scientific Working Group (FISWG).[70] Their explanations leverage known pre-defined facial features such as scars or other identifying marks and target specific users in the justice system and are thus inherently explainable. Measured against the experts, current XFR systems still fall well short of what is required by the best practices of facial examiners and by US courts.[71] Their visualizations are not powerful enough to explain the complex work of opaque and/or proprietary algorithms and often lead to confirmation bias.

Against the high aim that algorithms give an account of their operations, XAI and XFR both disappoint. However, XAI and XFR have fostered an accountability bureaucracy equipped with toolkits that allow AI systems to be run without interrupting their infra-sensible and supra-sensible processes. Algorithms can continue to be neural networks, remain proprietary, and nonetheless appear accountable. While XAI and XFR might not explain algorithms, they promise to quell the anxiety of algorithmic subjects, while continuing to use advanced algorithmic reasoning that can be automatized as far as possible.[72] Human-readable outputs of XAI and XFR turn citizens into trusting consumers of an automated algorithmic accountability. They do not need to fully understand how AI operates, but only 'trust' that it corresponds to their existing expectations and needs.[73]

The XAI intervention by DARPA we mentioned earlier is intended for soldiers and their 'artificial intelligence partners'. There is no promise to explain reality, but to make military users and consumers trust complex AI systems and their algorithmic operations even in situations like the battlefield. XAI is then not so much an epistemological intervention that proposes to reconfigure knowledge asymmetries, but a bureaucratization of algorithms and business models for the tech industry, as it relies on producing more models by experts who then proffer trust in the algorithms. 'Trust', sociologists Luc Boltanski and Ève Chiapello remind us, 'is what makes it possible to relax control while banking on a form of self-control that is cheap for an organization.'[74]

Rather than an epistemological challenge, AI explainability is more about trust that the algorithms get it right in the end. XAI is deemed to 'engender greater understanding and trust' in those generally affected by AI and

[70] FISWG, 'Facial Identification Scientific Working Group'.
[71] Phillips and Przybocki, 'Four Principles of Explainable AI'.
[72] Diakopoulos, 'Accountability in Algorithmic Decision Making', 60.
[73] Doshi-Velez and Kim, 'Towards a Rigorous Science of Interpretable Machine Learning'.
[74] Boltanski and Chiapello, *The New Spirit of Capitalism*, 390.

should aim to respond to the 'basic, emotional needs to understand and trust [algorithms].'[75] Those with such 'basic, emotional needs' are generally not those who understand the complex relations of error rates and algorithmic performance. Data scientist Cynthia Rudin has criticized the field of XAI for serving an AI industry that has an interest in keeping models opaque and away from the public.[76] The field lacks in quality of explanations, which can be less-than-satisfactory and even misleading. Refusing these developments, Rudin promotes the focus on models that can be more expensive to produce, as they require more human labour and are specific to certain domains, but are 'inherently interpretable' rather than just 'explainable'.[77] Interpretable models allow designers and users to understand why a model has made a prediction.[78]

Making self-accountable algorithms is addressed to non-expert consumers of algorithmic optimization and not active algorithmic citizens. As we have shown, rather than an epistemic account of algorithmic operations, explainability becomes economized as part of an automation move to reduce human–machine interactions. As error is optimized according to the socio-economic logics of different domains of implementation, explainability enacts a politics of trust in algorithms. However, accounting for error and giving an account by explaining are not the only forms of accountability, although they have been often mobilized in both expert and public controversies. In the section 'Accountability through refusal', we show how accountability has been enacted through refusal in ways that subvert and disrupt error optimization and the trust in the truth-doing of Explainable AI.

Accountability through refusal

Controversies over facial recognition have emerged not only in the US and the UK, but also in China and Russia. China is rarely mentioned in the earlier discussions of algorithmic accountability. As with other digital technologies, China's use of facial recognition is seen as a dystopian present of inescapable surveillance and often set in opposition to Western developments in AI and facial recognition. Chinese citizens can use facial recognition to pay for food, unlock their homes, or check in at airports. The Chinese government plans

---

[75] Hall, Ambati, and Phan, 'Ideas on Interpreting Machine Learning'.
[76] Rudin, 'Stop Explaining Black Box Machine Learning'.
[77] Ibid.,
[78] Miller, 'Explanation in Artificial Intelligence'.

for a comprehensive system of facial recognition cameras that is 'fully networked, always working and fully controllable'.[79] China already has almost two hundred million public surveillance cameras that can spot anybody in a crowd.[80]

The Carnegie Endowment for International Peace reports that facial recognition has become a worldwide export for China's technology companies.[81] They list many examples of countries around the world where the Chinese company Huawei, for instance, provides facial recognition technologies for surveillance. In Algeria, they have installed an 'intelligent video surveillance system'. Huawei have also supported a Serbian 'safe city' initiative with a thousand cameras and 800 locations in Belgrade. In Kenya, a similar system helped police the visit of Pope Francis in 2015. Advances in Chinese facial recognition have been linked with the surveillance of the Uyghur minority and widely denounced as 'first known example of a government intentionally using artificial intelligence for racial profiling'.[82]

As China has become a world leader in facial recognition, representations of dystopian surveillance have been intensified in the media and Western states' discourses. The extensive report by the US National Security Commission on AI is largely motivated by a perceived political and technological threat from China. Setting the picture of a global 'AI arms race', it renders China as a strategic threat in the global AI competition, but also as the 'other' of a democratic AI presumably characteristic of the US. The report's authors draw stark lines between liberty and repression, surveillance and democracy:

> China's domestic use of AI is a chilling precedent for anyone around the world who cherishes individual liberty. Its employment of AI as a tool of repression and surveillance—at home and, increasingly, abroad—is a powerful counterpoint to how we believe AI should be used.[83]

China becomes the authoritarian counterpart to the US democratic regime and use of technology. Yet, as we saw in Part I of this book, democracy and surveillance are tightly connected in the government of individuals and populations, while liberty and repression become blurred in the government of difference. Moreover, not only does the othering of China re-enact warlike imaginaries of global politics, but it effaces the controversies over and

---

[79] Feldstein, 'The Global Expansion of AI Surveillance'.
[80] Lakshanan, 'China's New "Super Camera"'.
[81] Feldstein, 'The Global Expansion of AI Surveillance'.
[82] Mozur, '500,000 Face Scans'.
[83] NSCAI, 'Final Report', 2.

refusals of these technologies in China as well as other countries around the world.

We propose to attend to refusal as dispersed practices of contesting facial recognition and holding to account through refusal. Refusal, as anthropologist Carole McGranahan has suggested, is not just saying 'no'. It 'marks the point of a limit having been reached: we refuse to continue on this way'.[84] Refusal is not synonymous to resistance, as it is not contesting relations of subordination or domination, but is defining relations within a 'plane of equivalence'.[85] We will return to refusal as constitutive of democratic scenes alongside other vocabularies and practices of contesting and disrupting technology in the book's Conclusion. Here, we take refusal to cover a continuum of reversing, rebuffing, refuting, and rejecting. Widely acclaimed mobilizations to 'ban' facial recognition need to be supplemented by more mundane forms of refusal which reverse, rebuff, refute, or reject.

China has recently had its first privacy lawsuit filed by Guo Bing, law professor at Zhejiang Sci-Tech University, against the Hangzhou Safari Park and their facial recognition system to identify visitors.[86] Guo Bing had an annual admissions card, which had previously required only the use of fingerprints. As the park 'upgraded' their system from fingerprints to facial recognition, Guo Bing accused the park of violating consumer protection law. In an interview with *Sixth Tone*, Guo complains that '[i]t was completely messed up. The staff was just using their phones to scan people's faces. Isn't it crazy?'[87] According to surveys by the Beijing News Think Tank, Chinese citizens are growing more and more concerned by the extensive use of facial recognition.[88] They also reported that almost 46.27% of the most popular mobile apps in China do not ask for clear consent from users for using facial recognition, which might add to growing disquiet.

The case received widespread media coverage in China, as Guo appealed the decision of local courts to the Fuyang District People's Court, then the Hangzhou Intermediate People's Court, and in 2021 the Zhejiang High People's Court. While all courts decided in his favour and asked the park to delete his facial data and repay membership fees, Guo has continued his appeal. He wanted to see addressed 'whether a zoo has the right to gather people's facial information and whether the park is qualified to require facial

---

[84] McGranahan, 'Theorizing Refusal', 320.
[85] Prasse-Freeman, 'Resistance/Refusal', 113.
[86] Zhong, 'First Lawsuit against Use of Facial Recognition Technology'.
[87] Ye, 'A Professor, a Zoo, and the Future'.
[88] Borak, 'Facial Recognition Is Used in China for Everything'.

recognition in the contract.[89] Guo's lawsuit was also followed by other cases against facial recognition. Another law professor, Lao Dongyan, said 'no' to the installation of facial recognition technology for access to her residential buildings.[90] While these cases received wide coverage in Chinese (social) media, reports in Western media often minimized their impact and claims. The Economist Intelligence Unit, for instance, reported that 'Mr Guo … has said he is happy to submit to facial scans by the government that are in the public interest. All he wants is his money back on his season ticket.'[91]

In 2020, China published the first draft of its new Personal Information Protection Law (PIPL), which advances the protection of personal data in China.[92] The law came into effect in late 2021. PIPL is seen to have similarities with the EU's GDPR given their common limitations on data processing and similar terminologies of 'consent' or 'lawful processing.'[93] 'Personal information rights' are subject to particular protections, although there are notable differences to the GDPR. PIPL seems to be less specific on these rights as 'it lacks more precise GDPR language addressing such rights, including where certain restrictions or exemptions may apply.'[94] Like in the West, regulations in China are the result of a growing public contestation of big data and AI technology. In spring 2021, China released a draft of security standards for facial recognition data, which suggests among other things that '[i]ndividual authorization is required for collecting facial recognition data.'[95] Against unified representations of techno-dystopia in China, sociologist Chuncheng Liu has urged us to examine the 'exclusions, inconsistencies, and contradictions they [algorithms] foist upon social life without falling into an oversimplified fatalist narrative.'[96] Bias and failures of algorithmic systems have received wide public attention in China. Facial recognition technology is here particularly visible because it is so much part of everyday life.

There is by now a long list of errors and failures of everyday algorithmic surveillance in China. Chinese facial recognition systems have been widely used not just for law enforcement, but also to detect 'public nuisances' like jaywalkers. Businesswoman Dong Mingzhu was shamed as a jaywalker after a facial recognition system had identified her and displayed her image publicly on a large screen. However, the system had mistaken the reflection

[89] Yin, 'Focus Tightens on Facial Recognition'.
[90] Liu and Ren, 'A Rights Defense by a Law Professor'.
[91] The Economist Intelligence Unit, 'China Regulations'.
[92] Owen, 'China's Draft Personal Information Protection Law'.
[93] Xu, 'Analyzing China's PIPL'.
[94] Ibid.,
[95] China Law Translate, 'Facial Recognition Standards Overview'.
[96] Liu, 'Seeing Like a State, Enacting Like an Algorithm'.

of an advertisement featuring her on the side of a bus as her jaywalking.[97] The police admitted to the error, but subsequently claimed that an upgrade to the system fixed the problem. In another example, primary school children from Jiaxing in eastern China's Zhejiang province demonstrated on social media how they could hack the facial recognition locks used by Hive Box, a Chinese smart locker company, by simply displaying a printed photo of their owners.[98] Hive Box responded that the facial recognition system was still in beta testing and would soon be improved. China is also becoming more and more alarmed by a quickly developing black market for facial data to pass personal identification checks.[99]

While not all these examples entail refusals of facial recognition, they show how refusals can build upon and intersect with errors and failures. Rather than trusting explanations, Chinese citizens enact socio-technical distrust. Guo refuses to allow the zoo to run facial recognition systems, while the Zhejiang school children experiment with the limits of one-to-many facial recognition. Attending to refusal illustrates how accountability cannot be limited to a politics of optimization and trust. It also disrupts readings of algorithmic surveillance as geopolitical techno-dystopia, which reinforces lines between non-democratic and democratic regimes. The first ever case against facial recognition brought before the European Court of Human Rights (ECHR) is the one from Russia, referenced at the start of this chapter, where rights activist Alyona Popova had challenged the use of facial recognition against protestors. As Moscow's Department of Information Technology held that Popova could not provide proof that she had been identified by facial recognition during her arrest at a demonstration against sexual violence, the District Court declined the lawsuit and Popova took the case to the ECHR.

As we have seen, enactments of accountability are shaped by and produce power relations. With auditing, algorithms become part of increasingly professionalized worlds divided into experts and non-experts. It is the experts who develop assessment indicators and produce reality through what is quantifiable. Gender, for instance, can be made computationally readable and thus auditable, while other types of oppression or domination cannot be directly computed. Explainable AI takes hold of the 'account' and produces algorithms that can give an account of themselves in order to support a growing AI industry's interest in complex, proprietary algorithms. However, it can also drive

---

[97] Liao, 'Chinese Facial Recognition'.
[98] Yujie, 'Facial Recognition Smart Lockers'.
[99] Liu, 'Face Recognition Black Production'.

a new form of interdisciplinary collaboration between computer science, social science, and philosophy. Attending to refusal as practices of holding to account can expand the scenes of algorithmic politics. Scenes of refusal disrupt an unjust social order through both small rebuttals and public rejections.

In Chapter 8 of this book, we explore a third technique of making algorithms governable by rebordering the domestic and the international. As algorithmic operations are increasingly deployed globally, states try to govern their activities by redrawing boundaries, reterritorializing their activities, and extending the reach of national law through digital citizenship. Yet, concentrating on the power struggles between states and companies has obscured the forms of resistance that do not reproduce the borders between the domestic and the international.

8

International

In 2017, the *Guardian* newspaper in the UK published an article about Facebook's Free Basics, a project to bring affordable access to selected Internet services to India. Entitled "'It's digital colonialism!' How Facebook's free Internet project has failed its users', the article drew on a report by Global Voices that showed how—under the mantra of free access to the Internet—users in India were given access to a selected few prominent US companies rather than the whole Internet.[1] The project was heavily criticized for privileging Facebook's own services, and later Facebook had to withdraw from it in India. Free Basics controlled access to an Internet focused on the Facebook platform without charging customers. In India, Internet activists and tech workers mobilized in support of net neutrality and against the extension of Facebook's platforms.

In the Western media, Free Basics had become a paradigmatic example of a new form of economic colonialism through platforms. The *Atlantic* compared Facebook with the East India Company and circulated the diagnosis of a new digital colonialism.[2] Marc Andreessen, who was on the Facebook board of directors, tweeted that anti-colonialism had been a catastrophe for Indian people, for which he later apologised.[3] Andreessen inadvertently confirmed a link between Facebook's activities in the Global South and colonialism that has since become a staple of the critique of platforms. Pointing out the neo-colonial aspects of a Silicon Valley company claiming 'to understand the complex problems of underprivileged Indian people', cultural theorist Nishant Shah highlighted the challenge to the very idea of net neutrality that Free Basics entailed: 'Here was an organisation, which was also being front-end to a massive social media network private company, which was saying that they will decide what information is good for you and you cannot hold them accountable for it'.[4] Zuckerberg defended the project in an article for the *Times of India*

---

[1] Solon, "'It's Digital Colonialism'".
[2] Lafrance, 'Facebook and the New Colonialism'.
[3] Ibid.,
[4] Luchs, 'Free Basics by Facebook', 4.

Algorithmic Reason. Claudia Aradau and Tobias Blanke, Oxford University Press.
© Claudia Aradau and Tobias Blanke (2022). DOI: 10.1093/oso/9780192859624.003.0009

claiming that Free Basics will achieve 'digital equality for India'.[5] He could not understand how anybody could be against this project. In fact, Free Basics was rolled out in more than 60 countries of the Global South.[6]

Free Basics was meant to be an app downloadable on a mobile phone. Facebook would strike deals with local mobile providers so that users could have access to certain parts of the Internet for free. The Internet that users could access would be closed and encircled by Facebook's definition of acceptable websites. The story of Free Basics highlights the constitutive role of encircling, borders, and (re)bordering for international politics in the digital age. It also brings to the fore struggles over these borders and technology as an empirical question. States and markets, private and public have been historically 'commingling', with commingling understood to be either an extension of statecraft or a dismantlement of sovereign power.[7] In their analysis of data colonialism, sociologists Nick Couldry and Ulises Mejias underscore that 'powerful corporations operating *in collaboration* with powerful states ... are defining the new colonial geographies and constructing a different social and economic order'.[8] As we saw in Chapter 4, big tech companies and digital platforms are frequently analysed as contemporary forms of companies such as the East India Company, having the power to order international politics. Yet, these hierarchical and ordering sets of relations characteristic of imperial and colonial power have been challenged by historical accounts of empire.[9] At the same time, the victory of the 'Save the Internet' campaign in India was made possible through a 'practice of technopolitics that resonated within the broader narrative of technocultural nationalism championed by the current ruling party'.[10] The borders between the domestic and the international are differently imagined and politicized by the actors in the controversy over Free Basics.

If Free Basics conjures a joint imaginary of imperial power of companies that are datafying the world and sovereign tech nationalism, another discourse of the international has been framed in terms of war. 'Buying Huawei technology [is] "like buying Chinese fighter planes"', warned a *Forbes* article, using one of the tropes most associated with international politics, that of war.[11] '[T]he Kremlin has attempted to interfere in numerous electoral processes around the

[5] Zuckerberg, 'Free Basics Protects Net Neutrality'.
[6] Kwet, 'Digital Colonialism'.
[7] Fourcade and Gordon argue that the question of whether public–private relations 'extend or weaken the state's capacity and authority' is an empirical one (Fourcade and Gordon, 'Learning Like a State', 79).
[8] Couldry and Mejias, *The Costs of Connection*, 39 (emphasis in text).
[9] For a discussion, see Ogborn, *Indian Ink*, 2-5.
[10] Prasad, 'Ascendant India, Digital India', 415.
[11] Doffman, 'Buying Huawei Technology'.

world in recent years', cautioned the European Union in launching a new site, EU vs Disinfo, to combat disinformation, and reactivating imaginaries of Cold War and great power politics.[12] These stories about election interference, manipulation, propaganda, and information warfare are supposed to alert citizens but are also warnings directed at the tech companies that they are involved in this war, because they provide the digital platforms making the production and viral circulation of digital content possible and accessible across the world. For policy makers, digital platforms play a role in recasting international politics into a new form of digital power politics almost analogous to the Cold War. Interference and meddling are indicative of an imaginary of the international centred around state sovereignty and territorial borders, while military power through digital technology reproduces the trope of a globally expanding war.

These imaginaries of international politics underpin calls upon the state to make digital platforms and their algorithmic operations governable. In this chapter, we analyse how the international is rendered governable through borders and boundaries. How are increasingly global platforms and algorithmic operations governed, through which modes of bordering and rebordering? What is absent or unknown in these processes? Our empirical scene in this chapter is the struggle between Facebook and states, Facebook and its users, and finally Facebook and its workers on bordering and rebordering the digital. We will see how tensions like those that defined the Free Basics controversy are repeated in struggles about sovereignty over content and citizen protection, user relations, and worker rights. The Facebook scenes of this chapter showcase how social media companies have produced different modes of governing and have become entangled with states in international practices. We argue that, in producing the figure of the citizen and the user of digital platforms, states and companies at the same time erase the figure of the worker in international politics.

To shed light on the erasure of work and workers in these controversies, we start by analysing how borders enable different modes of governing between public and private, markets and states, domestic and international, global, and local. Secondly, we consider controversies between states and social media companies around the algorithmic circulation of content. A legislation proposed in Germany for the regulation of hate speech on digital platforms, known as NetzDG, requires social media companies with more than two million users to remove unlawful content from their platforms or face a fine of

---

[12] European External Action Service, 'EU vs Disinfo'.

up to EUR 50 million.[13] This legislation has been widely hailed as a prime example of how to regulate big tech companies, to be emulated by other states and organizations such as the European Union. We propose 'borders' and 'thresholds' as techniques of two different arts of governing by states and companies, respectively. We argue that states rely on drawing boundaries, assigning responsibilities, and holding juridical subjects accountable, while social media companies have promoted novel modes of governing through thresholds, which are not directly antagonistic to sovereign power. Thirdly, we analyse how these arts of governing rely upon and foster the subjectivity of the citizen and user. Finally, we examine a class action by content moderators against Facebook, which both discloses and critiques this emergent mode of governing. Brought by three former content moderators who suffered psychological and traumatic health effects because of their work on the Facebook platform, the class action reconfigures questions of critique. As the class action transforms a scene of controversy into one of resistance, it both invokes and attempts to displace the modes of governing developed by digital platforms.

(Re)bordering the international

Borders conjure imaginaries of fences, walls, barriers, and checkpoints. An archipelago of technologies that stop and filter has come to shape both internal and external borders in Europe and beyond. Borders produce legible zones of governing, they prepare some for being stopped, confined, or even killed, while speeding up the circulation of others. On the one hand, borders separate the domestic from the foreign, the national from the international, the local from the global. They are also the limit of democracy, as they contradict the principle that 'democracy is a possibility for citizens to directly or indirectly control the authorities and powers to which they obey, … in fact this is [not] the case on the borderline — neither for foreigners nor for the nationals themselves'.[14] On the other hand, borders are 'complex social institutions, which are marked by tensions between practices of border reinforcement and border crossing'.[15] They are techniques of ordering by separating different forms of politics and its subjects. Thus, borders are not just directly visible zones and technologies. As international relations theorist R. B. J. Walker outlines, boundaries draw distinctions and connections 'in ways that disturb many familiar assumptions

[13] Heldt, 'Reading between the Lines and the Numbers'.
[14] Balibar, 'Reinventing the Stranger', 30.
[15] Mezzadra, 'The Proliferation of Borders', 128.

about where politics is supposed to occur and consequently what political life is supposed to involve, who is supposed to engage in it and under what conditions.[16]

Alongside the proliferation and dispersal of borders, bordering encompasses the practices that render certain populations governable, that foster hierarchies of life between those who can move and those to whom the right to mobility is withdrawn. The terminology of bordering renders the policing and control of difference, with the border being 'a principal organising mechanism in constructing, maintaining, and controlling social and political order'.[17] Through bordering and rebordering, differential subjects are produced for the arts of government. Barry Hindess reminds us that borders are key to governing as '[t]he modern art of government has thus been concerned with governing not simply the populations of individual states but also the larger population encompassed by the system of states itself'.[18] Walker adds another international/imperial dimension, as the boundaries of political life 'are articulated not only at the territorial boundaries of the modern state, as almost all modern critical political analysis has tended to assume, but at the boundaries of the modern international, even though it is far from clear where, or when, these boundaries are supposed to be'.[19] He locates two tropes that articulate these boundaries: the spatial trope of friend–enemy and the temporal trope of civilized–barbarian.[20] While the former is activated through state practices of bordering and rebordering, the latter relies on colonial and imperial power.[21]

Walker's formulation of the 'double outside' helps make sense of the apparent contradiction between antagonism and alliance in governing algorithms and their operations globally. This chapter shows that the antagonism between state and tech companies—enacted through territorialization and enclosure—is underpinned by the sovereign imaginary of friend–enemy and the tensions between political and economic sovereignty. The alliance of state and companies in the fight against disinformation, terrorism, and extremism has resonances of the civilized–barbarian distinction, which enacts not only the boundaries of civilization, but also the line beyond which 'the brutishness of civilization is therefore permitted, where violence may be freely and

---

[16] Walker, *Out of Line*, 1.
[17] Yuval-Davis, Wemyss, and Cassidy, *Bordering*, 5.
[18] Hindess, 'Politics as Government', 407.
[19] Walker, 'The Double Outside of the Modern International', 59.
[20] Ibid., 68.
[21] Postcolonial scholars have reinforced that 'sovereignty in the colonies was never what it was in the metropole' (Barkawi and Laffey, 'Retrieving the Imperial', 120).

legitimately exercised'.[22] Walker argues that the 'double outside' of the state and of the system of states leads to a paradox of both conceptualization and action. The double reverts upon itself, and social movements are caught within these imaginaries, as their alternatives can be plagued by 'either imperial pretensions (one world) and/or a new set of distinctions ... between acceptable and unacceptable forms of human being (two worlds)'.[23]

Recent work by political theorist Wendy Brown has drawn attention to how borders are rendered more blurred and dispersed through the neoliberal economization of social relations, but also through the mobilization of 'familialism' in conjunction with markets as a mode of neoliberal governmentality. For Brown, neoliberalism displaces democratic procedures and processes through the 'perfect compatibility' between markets and traditional morality. Traditional morality is that of the 'familial', personal sphere, where '*diktat* is the basis of household authority, and *force* is how it legitimately defends itself against intruders'.[24] Brown's analysis alerts us to a reconfiguration of markets and morals, where traditional and familial morality is neither a relic nor an incidental or opportunistic supplement to neoliberalism. The compatibility between neoliberalism and 'heteropatriarchal Christian familialism' constitutes the specificity of the present according to Brown.[25]

While political theorists have shown how bordering and rebordering enable and are underpinned by different rationalities of government, there has often been less attention to the multiplication of struggles over borders and boundaries and not just the multiplication of bordering mechanisms.[26] If Walker attends to how borders and boundaries are enabled and enable particular modes of politics, Brown highlights the blurring of borders, which separate economics and politics, private and public action. However, the struggles and modes of resistance over practices of bordering and rebordering are less present in their analyses. Walker's theorization of the international focuses on distinctions between citizens and humans, states and empires, universal and particular, which ultimately 'traps' the imaginaries of social movements. Brown's analysis of neoliberalism highlights important alliances between domesticity and neoliberalism, markets and morals, but does not attend to the

---

[22] Brown, *Walled States, Waning Sovereignty*, 45–46.
[23] Walker, *Out of Line*, 8.
[24] Brown, 'Neoliberalism's Frankenstein', 68. On the compatibility between markets and traditional morality, see Brown, *In the Ruins of Neoliberalism*.
[25] Brown, *In the Ruins of Neoliberalism*, 114.
[26] For an analysis of borders as sites of struggle over power relations, see Squire, *The Contested Politics of Mobility*.

multiplicity of struggles that challenge these distinctions, and the forms of violence their entanglements entail.

As Latin American scholar Verónica Gago has pointed out, Brown risks an 'idealization of democracy', by eluding both the violence that gave rise to neoliberalism and the 'repressive violence' that persists within contemporary democracy.[27] To understand neoliberalism as political rather than non-political, Gago turns to an insight of feminist scholars: that of the materiality of labour and struggle. Feminist scholars have long drawn attention to how waged labour and productive labour rely on the invisibilization of other forms of labour, such as women's domestic and reproductive labour. As we have seen in Chapter 5, in the 1970s, feminist Marxists reformulated the question of domestic labour and analysed the specific exploitation of women in capitalism. They challenged boundaries between private and public, paid and unpaid work, citizens and non-citizens, and struggled against the nationalism of the state. Feminist scholars painstakingly connected the exploitation of women's labour with the 'exploitation of difference' in capitalism.[28] Their work helps us attend to an absence in the discussions and imaginaries of international politics presented in this section. Even as different arts of government emerge between states and tech companies, these reproduce the absence of work and workers. To render these absences visible, the section 'Arts of governing: borders and thresholds' outlines how both states and companies have developed distinct techniques to make algorithmic operations governable. Subsequently, we attend to what these arts of governing render as the 'part of no part', those who interrupt the 'order of domination', and the implications for resistance and rights across and beyond borders.[29]

Arts of governing: borders and thresholds

In 2018, the German government passed the Network Enforcement Act, known as NetzDG. According to the law, social media companies have twenty-four hours to remove content from the Web that has been reported to them and is obviously in contradiction to the German law ('manifestly unlawful content'). If it is not a clear violation ('unlawful content'), the platforms have seven days to remove content. Furthermore, they have to produce half-yearly reports on their removal activities and make these public. Social network

[27] Gago, *Feminist International*, 203.
[28] Ibid.,
[29] Rancière, *Disagreement*, 11. See also Chapter 6 in this book.

providers are defined under NetzDG as those platforms that allow sharing of content by users, with some exceptions such as journalistic platforms, where there is editorial control over published content, or professional networks like LinkedIn. Alongside the usual social media suspects such as Facebook, Twitter, YouTube, and Instagram, this originally also included surprising members like Change.org, an online petition site.[30]

To comply with the law, social network providers have to offer their users in Germany a means of reporting potentially unlawful content. If the platforms are based outside of Germany, they need an authorized representative within Germany.[31] In one of the first NetzDG reports in summer 2018, Twitter stated that it had removed 260,000 posts, YouTube 215,000 entries, and Facebook only 1,704. By 2019, Facebook had caught up and had removed 160,000 pieces of content, where 70% of this content had been discovered by content moderators rather than Facebook users.[32] Google runs a live dashboard on the content it deletes under NetzDG.[33] In the latter half of 2020, it had erased more than 70,000 pieces of content from its YouTube site. Over 88% of the content had been removed within twenty-four hours of the complaint being received, in most cases globally, as not only NetzDG was violated but also YouTube's community guidelines.

The NetzDG legislation has been widely hailed as an advance for the regulation of digital platforms, their algorithms, and social media companies more broadly, with several other states wanting to follow Germany and develop their own regulation laws.[34] The legislation first drew widespread media attention following a high-profile case against Facebook in 2019, which led to a EUR 2 million fine, due to 'incomplete information provided in its published report on the number of complaints received about unlawful content.'[35] Moreover, the 'form used to file a complaint under NetzDG was harder to find on Facebook than other social media sites.'[36] Public reporting emphasized the symbolic value of the fine given the overall amount of money linked to Facebook, while highlighting a double antagonism between states and companies, on the one hand, and Europe and America, on the other:

> The fine is a small amount compared with Facebook's first-quarter revenues of more than $15 billion. But it has symbolic weight, marking the first time

---

[30] For Change.org, '[t]he expense of implementing NetzDG was high' (Pielemeier, 'NetzDG').
[31] Wessing, 'Germany's Network Enforcement Act'.
[32] Facebook, 'NetzDG Transparency Report'.
[33] Google, 'Removals under the Network Enforcement Law'.
[34] France, for instance, had plans to adopt a similar law.
[35] Bundesamt für Justiz, 'Fine against Facebook'.
[36] Barton, 'Germany Fines Facebook $2.3 Million'.

that a European country has sanctioned an American social media giant for failing to be transparent about the way it handles hate speech.[37]

The reporting's double antagonism over techniques of governing obscures the entanglements and alliances between states and companies, the EU and the US, as it is read through the lens of sovereignty. In fact, NetzDG is about resetting the boundaries between state and companies, between law and community standards. It is about sovereignty as 'boundary marker' and 'form of power',[38] which organizes the inside and outside of its borders. The German state purports to render global platforms governable by reterritorializing companies so that they are accountable to national laws. In so doing, it turns digital platforms into judges of lawful speech within their borders, which have to remove content before any state official has ever been able to see it. Law and territory become reconnected, while the international is rebordered through the opposition between lawful and unlawful content.

Yet, the lens of sovereignty and the focus on bordering through territorialization does not account for another art of governing that social media companies produce and that does not work in the register of sovereign power. Facebook has recently set up its own 'supreme court', a group of independent experts reviewing content moderation practices within the company, which can even overrule Mark Zuckerberg. While the name 'supreme court' reminds us of sovereign power, it is only the most high-profile instrument to govern content based on Facebook's own 'community standards'.[39] These standards apply globally and not just in Germany and should enable people to communicate 'safely' on the platform, ensuring communicative reason. Within the standards, the boundaries of community remain fluid, its outsides undefined compared to the reterritorialization that NetzDG attempts.

Creating community standards is the job of Facebook's 'operations team', who can adjust them according to political or legal developments. While Facebook's supreme court captivates the public eye, its content machineries rely on workers who interpret its content rules and how they can be applied to different pieces of content. For instance, during heightened attention to migration in Europe, special protections were extended to migrants.[40] The hate speech policy update against migrants went live in April 2016 and recognized migrants as a vulnerable group that needed special protection against 'dehumanizing

[37] Deckler, 'Germany Fines Facebook €2m for Violating Hate Speech Law'.
[38] Brown, *Walled States, Waning Sovereignty*, 52.
[39] The community standards in German are available at https://de-de.facebook.com/communitystandards/.
[40] Hoppensted, 'Facebooks Löschzentrum'.

speech'.[41] They were added to a special 'quasi-protected category', which allowed for a general discussion of migrants but not their dehumanization. The difference was less discernible in practice, as posts like 'deport the migrants' were allowed, while posts like 'migrants are scum' were removed.

Between NetzDG and community standards, Facebook's content review process entails two steps, procedurally prioritizing its community over national law.[42] Having received a user complaint, a Facebook content worker first checks whether the content violates its own community standards. If that is the case, the content is taken down immediately. If that is not the case and if the content also received a complaint under NetzDG provisions, the German NetzDG rules are applied. Google also has two policies on removal which are based on the global–national opposition. If the content violates Google's own YouTube community guidelines, then it is removed globally. If it just violates the German Criminal Code as required by NetzDG, then it is only restricted locally.[43] Finally, Facebook's Instagram is similarly explicit that in the choice between NetzDG and community guidelines, the latter come first.[44] If the community standards are violated, the content is removed 'globally' and 'immediately'. If the content does not violate the in-house community guidelines, it is reviewed for national 'legality'. If the content is not in violation of the community standards but is unlawful under NetzDG, only users in Germany have the content disabled. This applies to everything that can be seen in Germany, as NetzDG does not define extraterritorial applications and what happens with Instagram content that was created outside of Germany.

The scene of controversy around NetzDG makes visible two arts of government. On the one hand, the sovereign power of the state aims to delimit territory, wield the power of law, and govern the 'double outside of the modern international'.[45] On the other hand, the platforms' governmentality is deployed by means of global community guidelines and standards for governing speech. Social media companies invoke global communication and a global community of users in order to create acceptable thresholds for digital content circulation. Foucault famously thought of biopolitics as 'a matter of organizing circulation, eliminating its dangerous elements, making a division between good and bad circulation, and maximizing the good circulation by diminishing the bad'.[46] In producing community standards, Facebook adds a

---

[41] Facebook Files, 'Hate Speech and Anti-Migrant Posts'.
[42] Heldt, 'Reading between the Lines and the Numbers'.
[43] Google, 'Removals under the Network Enforcement Law'.
[44] Instagram, 'What's the Difference between NetzDG and Instagram's Community Guidelines?'.
[45] Walker, 'The Double Outside of the Modern International'.
[46] Foucault, Security, Territory, Population, 18.

more peculiar dimension to the organization of circulation. Only content that is illegal according to local (i.e., national) legislation is removed from circulation, while other content that might be in breach of community standards is first deprioritized. For instance, while hate speech may become the object of removal, Facebook does not directly remove other content. As it explains in its community standards, it aims to 'significantly reduce its distribution by showing it lower in the News Feed'.[47]

These techniques of governing the circulation of content are not about drawing boundaries between inside and outside, or about filtering good and bad circulation, delimiting friends from enemies and barbarians from the civilized. They are about modulating thresholds of transition, in-between zones of transformation, where good and bad circulation are not mutually exclusive as in Foucault's biopolitics. Rather than lines or spaces of inclusion–exclusion, thresholds are associated with differences of intensity and magnitude. As critical theorist Walter Benjamin has noted, thresholds 'protect and mark the transitions'.[48] They transform sovereign borders, limits, and enclosures. According to Benjamin, '[t]he threshold must be carefully distinguished from the boundary. A *Schwelle* [threshold] is a zone. Transformation, passage, wave action are [all] in the word *schwellen*, swell, and etymology ought not to overlook these senses'.[49] Thresholds are not about separation, but about transition, passage, and transformation. They mark out zones of ambiguity, where subjects and objects belong to intermediate categories and are not necessarily categorized as inside or outside, friend or enemy, civilized or barbarian. Thresholds mean that the relation between national law and global community guidelines is not mutually exclusive or antagonistic, but it becomes reconfigured as a transitional one. One does not exclude or annul the other.

The scene opened by NetzDG shows how two different arts of government work through borders and thresholds. Spatiotemporal bordering entails sovereign territorialization, boundaries of lawfulness, and demarcations of citizenship. Although some criticisms of NetzDG have highlighted the ambiguity of its provisions, as categorizations of 'manifestly unlawful' and 'unlawful' content are not explained, it determines twenty-one categories of unlawful content according to German law. Independent of their vagueness, the various categories imply prohibition, which is differentiated temporally, depending on how egregiously unlawful the content under consideration is. By contrast, Facebook's community guidelines create thresholds rather

---

[47] Facebook, 'Community Standards'.
[48] Benjamin, *The Arcades Project*, 88.
[49] Ibid., 494.

than draw boundaries. As we have seen, thresholds imply ambiguity and zones of transition, they work through intensification and (de)amplification. More/less formulations are typical of thresholds rather than boundaries. Borders pertain to the categories of either/or. The introduction of a threshold avoids the setting of an opposition, an unsurpassable limit, or a sovereign boundary.

Thresholds enact a different form of control, one which transcends the binaries of either/or, inside/outside. When platforms need to engage in the policing of users' actions, their own actions are rendered in both proximity of and distance from law enforcement. Take Facebook's explanation of their own policing practices:

> The consequences for breaching our Community Standards vary depending on the severity of the breach and a person's history on the platform. For instance, we may warn someone for a first breach, but if they continue to breach our policies, we may restrict their ability to post on Facebook or disable their profile. We may also notify law enforcement when we believe that there is a genuine risk of physical harm or a direct threat to public safety.[50]

Facebook's community standards modulate here a series of relations—from the intimacy of personalized histories on the platform to the distancing of physical harm towards law enforcement. Their policing is mediated through the ambiguity of 'may' rather than sovereign 'will'.

Facebook's policing is also not subordinated to rationalities of risk governance that categorize populations according to propensities for risky behaviour and profile certain groups for the purposes of prevention or pre-emption.[51] The 'may' or 'may not' makes action hover on the threshold. Ambiguity is explicitly incorporated into the standards and global guidelines that companies produce: 'Our policies may seem broad, but that is because we apply them consistently and fairly to a community that transcends regions, cultures and languages.'[52] The ambiguity that emerges is expressed as a relation between the spirit and letter of law. Facebook argues that the company applies standards in the spirit rather than letter of the law. It focuses on its community of users and eschews the language of citizenship. How does the distinction between citizens and users come to matter and how does it rework

---

[50] Facebook, 'Community Standards'.
[51] For a discussion of risk governance in international politics, see Aradau, 'Risk, (In)Security and International Politics'.
[52] Facebook, 'Community Standards'.

the intersections between the two arts of government? What distribution of the sensible is enacted through borders and thresholds?

Making up citizens and users

Community guidelines emerged in relation to urgent questions of governing conduct on the Internet and attributions of legal responsibility, as platforms come to mediate social and political relations between states and citizens. They create new governmental arrangements of people and things. In his extensive analysis of community guidelines across different social media companies, media scholar Tarleton Gillespie has attended to the governmental aspects of the guidelines and has highlighted a tension between the representation of companies as 'community keepers' and the need to police the fragile boundaries of the company.[53] In 2019, Zuckerberg promised to reorder these fragile boundaries and create a 'digital living room' shifting people from public to private conversations.[54] Zuckerberg's intention of moving from a 'digital town' to a 'digital living room' came under the guise of integrating Instagram, WhatsApp, and Facebook. His promise was one of recasting relations, this time between the town and the living room, as the spaces of privacy versus publicity.

This domesticized and intimate governmentality of digital platforms blurs boundaries and produces a moralizing international politics of familialism, domesticity, and personal relations. Through relations of personalization and practices of domestication, social media platforms can seemingly distance themselves both from sovereign law and from accusations of being overly market driven. Moreover, the proximity and intimacy of personalized relations make these appear as unmediated—user to user and user to Facebook. Unmediated relations seem devoid of algorithms, data infrastructures, institutions, and human labour. Zuckerberg's call for a global 'digital living room' is a call to generalize the domestic bond, to personalize all relations, including international relations on the model of dependence, proximity, familiarity, and trust.[55] Facebook's response to the breach of its community guidelines is modulated by these relations of dependence and trust. In claiming to be attuned to domesticized demands of personalization, authenticity, loyalty, and

[53] Gillespie, *Custodians of the Internet* 49.
[54] Isaac, 'After Facebook's Scandals'.
[55] There is still a network logic at work in the Facebook model. Drawing on Luc Boltanski and Ève Chiapello's *The New Spirit of Capitalism*, Rider and Murakami Wood have argued that Zuckerberg's earlier Facebook manifesto is an expression of such a connexionist world (Rider and Murakami Wood, 'Condemned to Connection?').

discretion, Facebook enacts a mode of governing different from sovereignty. Like Facebook, social media platforms carefully guard themselves from the charge of excluding users or of punishing them. When Snap Inc. claims discretion, it is not in the sense of sovereign decision, but in the sense of 'try[ing] to do what we think best reflects these values in each situation'.[56]

Internationalized domesticity implies a personalization of relations of dependence and trust. Users do not enter digital platforms as citizens or rights holders. If NetzDG extends the reach of sovereign law by rebordering digital worlds through the presence of citizens to be protected, there are no borders and boundaries for users. Users are imagined as coexisting globally and governed through a careful modulation of thresholds. They enter digital platforms one by one rather than collectively. Gillespie has observed that Facebook tries its best to avoid any collectivization—for instance, when groups mobilize to flag up content on Facebook as a result of 'collective political indignation'. Such 'organized flagging' is not prohibited explicitly, but it is seen as 'an unseemly use of the site's reporting tools'.[57] The accusations of such organized flagging have been largely associated with conservative groups and raise questions about the role of political vocabularies of rights and wrongs, justice and injustice. The 'users' in their unmediated relations reproduce 'the seductive fiction that the network is a *hospitable platform*'.[58] Forms of collectivity may become threatening to this hospitality as they inspire collective agency.

The subjectivity of the citizen underpins formulations in the NetzDG law and enables its reach within and beyond borders. The user dominates the practices of social media platforms. The complaint forms by Facebook, YouTube, Instagram, and others under the requirements of NetzDG target 'users in Germany'. By shifting from citizens to users, community standards and guidelines do not just transform international politics but 'may productively substitute for various other forms of authoritative rule'.[59] The user of social media is 'used' by the companies which turn sociality into data so that it can be valorized.[60] To be a user is to enter a relation to an object that can be exploited, a relation of use, associated with 'usefulness' rather than a claim. The articulation of users is dependent on that of use, which renders digital platforms as mundane things to use rather than public things to work on in common. A community of users is not about action in concert but about rendering relations between

---

[56] Snap Inc., 'Community Guidelines'.
[57] Gillespie, *Custodians of the Internet*, 92–3.
[58] Fisher, 'User Be Used', 384 (emphasis in text).
[59] Timmermans and Epstein, 'A World of Standards', 71.
[60] Fisher, 'User Be Used'.

'users' as personalized, proximate, and unmediated, which mainly serves the datafication processes of the social media company.

Furthermore, the category of users enacts subjectivity and enables certain forms of action and experience. Users have a long history in technology production and design, as they are configured in their difference from technology producers. In the 1970s at the Massachusetts Institute of Technology the term 'luser' was used to distinguish users from implementors (hackers).[61] User relations to the machine are largely prescribed before they even get in contact with it.[62] Users work with a computer rather than make it; they operate a machine while being excluded from the details of its internals. At most, users report issues with social media content or appeal a platform decision, but they are not entrusted with doing anything about it. The vocabulary of the user enables individualized and intimate agency, while foreclosing other forms of agency. The user appears as a 'threshold' category to the extent that anyone—citizens, migrants, refugees, women, etc.—can become a user as long as they comply with company guidelines. There are otherwise no explicit limits and no boundaries. If the German law on the regulation of hate speech aims to stabilize the boundaries of community and citizenship, social media platforms render these boundaries into ambiguous threshold zones. Digital platforms do not preventively exclude, but they respond to users who flag up content that breaches community standards.

Individualized user complaints domesticate action in concert. What they produce can be understood as 'community without citizenship'. At first sight, 'community without citizenship' might appear devoid of the problem of exclusion and of boundary-drawing. After all, as political theorist Engin Isin has succinctly put it, '[c]itizenship is a bounded concept. It is bound up with the state if not the nation that signifies its authority and limits.'[63] Citizenship is operative as a category of both internal and external exclusion. Citizenship enacts internal exclusions through hierarchies of 'second class' citizens or citizens who might have *de jure* status but are in practice excluded from rights. Externally, citizenship enacts the exclusion of those who are not—or not yet— citizens in a world of sovereign states. Citizenship has been a technology for the international management of world populations, which 'operates by dividing that population into a series of discrete subpopulations and setting them against each other.'[64]

[61] The Jargon File, "'Luser'".
[62] Kushner, 'The Instrumentalised User', 3–4.
[63] Isin, *Citizens without Frontiers*, 5.
[64] Hindess, 'Citizenship in the International Management of Populations', 1495.

However, despite appearing to lack borders and boundaries, the platformed 'community without citizenship' is not devoid of its own exclusions. While the ambiguity and generic format of users seems indefinitely inclusive in contrast to exclusionary boundaries of citizenship, the category of users eschews the Facebook workers who produce, clean, or filter data. Facebook's domestication of users into seemingly global communities is also the invisibilization of the conditions of production of its digital infrastructures by those who do not enter them because they would want to be part of the community. It reproduces the myth of 'disintermediation' as direct connections between platforms and users.[65] The community of users ignores the distributed labour of humans and machines mobilized in the practices of content moderation on digital platforms. To comply with NetzDG requirements, Facebook started to operate two deletion and content surveillance centres in Germany together with local partners. Salaries are around the minimum wage, while each moderator needs to check 2,000 pieces of content per day on average.[66] Only a few seconds are given to moderators to make decisions on whether to delete videos for violation of the content rules. Finally, Facebook content moderators need to sign Non-Disclosure Agreements (NDAs) to protect the company.

From Germany, content moderators do not just deal with German language content. In fact, many employees are specialized in Arabic, Turkish, Italian, and other languages. A report by the UK's Digital Culture, Media, and Sport Committee of the Parliament on Misinformation and 'Fake News' notes that after NetzDG 'one in six of Facebook's moderators now works in Germany, which is practical evidence that legislation can work.'[67] NetzDG might resurrect the spectre of 'waning sovereignty',[68] but it does not support Facebook workers. Their work is a far cry from the image Silicon Valley likes to promote, where employees work on campuses modelled on university research environments and have extensive benefits. According to a 2019 investigation, workers in a Phoenix centre for Facebook content moderation made less than $30,000 a year and were permanently micromanaged with only short breaks allowed, while a median Facebook employee earned $240,000 a year.[69] Facebook reacted to bad press on content moderation by slightly increasing the content moderators' wages, especially for those exposed to the worst images.[70]

---

[65] Srinivasan and Oreglia, 'The Myths and Moral Economies', 222.
[66] Krause and Grassegger, 'Inside Facebook'.
[67] DCMS, 'Disinformation and "Fake News": Final Report', 13.
[68] Brown, *Walled States, Waning Sovereignty*.
[69] Newton, 'The Trauma Floor'.
[70] Fisher, 'Facebook Increases Pay'.

Yet, most content work does not take place in the Global North, and it does not afford workers these kinds of conditions. Digital platforms employ a dispersed force of microworkers around the world,[71] and even public outcry does not seem to improve their conditions. The Philippines are probably the largest hub of the global call centre industry and have thus also become a global centre of content moderation for social media platforms:

> Unlike moderators in other major hubs, such as those in India or the United States, who mostly screen content that is shared by people in those countries, workers in offices around Manila evaluate images, videos and posts from all over the world. The work places enormous burdens on them to understand foreign cultures and to moderate content in up to 10 languages that they don't speak, while making several hundred decisions a day about what can remain online.[72]

Information studies scholar Sarah Roberts has argued that the outsourcing of content moderation to the Global South is 'a practice predicated on long-standing relationships of Western cultural, military, and economic domination that social media platforms exploit for inexpensive, abundant, and culturally competent labor'.[73] Unlike the intimacy and proximity of user-to-user relations, microworkers are rendered invisible through both proliferation and dispersion across the world. Yet, as we will see in the section 'Resistance beyond borders', microwork and microworkers have enabled forms of resistance by recasting intimacy and dependence, and challenging borders and boundaries. We propose to understand their resistance as opening up a scene of internationalism, which is transversal rather than bound by borders and nationalism.

Resistance beyond borders

In 2019, three former content moderators working on the Facebook platform filed a class action in the court of San Mateo, California, to ensure that Facebook ceases 'unlawful and unsafe work practices' and sets up a 'medical monitoring fund for testing and providing mental health treatment'.[74] The three content moderators accused Facebook of being the cause of post-traumatic

[71] Irani, 'The Cultural Work of Microwork'.
[72] Dwoskin, Whalen, and Cabato, 'Content Moderators See It All—and Suffer'.
[73] Roberts, *Behind the Screen*, 18.
[74] *Scola et al. v Facebook Inc.*, 'Amended Complaint and Demand for Jury Trial', §9.

stress disorder (PTSD) and trauma, given intense exposure to graphic content and extreme violence. The main claim of unlawfulness against Facebook is that the company created standards for the well being and resilience of content moderators as part of the Technology Coalition but failed to implement them. The case brought together work, citizenship rights (the content moderators speak in the name of 'California citizens' who perform content moderation), and action in concert (class action).

Firstly, the three Facebook workers recast the domesticized and intimate governmentality that Facebook has produced for 'users' but not 'workers'. The lawsuit is traversed by tensions between rights claims and work conditions, on the one hand, and domestic logics of trust, dependency, and protection, on the other. The plaintiffs' complaint describes working conditions as dismantling human subjectivity through the randomness, speed, and stress that the Facebook content moderation algorithms create:

> The moderator: in the queue (production line) receives the tickets (reports) randomly. Texts, Pictures, Videos keep on flowing. There is no possibility to know beforehand what will pop up on the screen. The content is very diverse. No time is left for a mental transition. It is entirely impossible to prepare oneself psychologically. One never knows what s/he will run into. It takes sometimes a few seconds to understand what a post is about. The agent is in a continual situation of stress. The speed reduces the complex analytical process to a succession of automatisms. The moderator reacts. An endless repetition. It becomes difficult to disconnect at the end of the eight hour shift.[75]

By starting a class action, the three former content moderators reclaim public roles and renounce the duty of loyalty and discretion. As Sarah Roberts has noted, 'a key to their [the content moderators'] activity is often to remain as discreet and undetectable as possible'.[76] They are to remain discreet, which is enforced through non-disclosure agreements, and undetectable by being dispersed globally, their microwork not surfacing in the publicized personalized relations between users or between users and platforms. In 2021, Irish MPs began to move against these non-disclosure agreements, after a group of outsourced Facebook employees in Ireland gave evidence against them.[77] Such agreements violate workers' right to assemble and are leveraged by companies to force complaints into silence.

---

[75] Ibid., §60.
[76] Roberts, *Behind the Screen*, 1.
[77] Bernal, 'Facebook's Content Moderators Are Fighting Back'.

In their claim, the California content moderators reintroduce the category of workers and that of citizens. This is a citizenship with a twist, because the class action is filed in the name of 'California citizens'. California citizenship is not a legal status, but we can read it as a claim to action in concert for everyone in the Silicon Valley company, because the three former content moderators include the 15,000 content moderators for Facebook around the world. As a non-existent legal category, California citizens reverses the Facebook community of users as 'community without citizenship' into what the philosopher Étienne Balibar has called 'citizenship without community'. In contrast to the view that links citizenship and national community, Balibar argues that citizenship without community entails 'confrontation with different modalities of exclusion' and the questioning of what is given as common identity or the unity of the community.[78] Work, particularly precarious and dangerous work, becomes a challenge to bounded categories of citizenship.

The class action is poised between the different claims to human and workers' rights, on the one hand, and domestic dependency, trust, and loyalty, on the other. The workers' complaint formulates work relations as relations of trust, as 'thousands of contractors … are entrusted to provide the safest environment possible for Facebook users'.[79] Moreover, labour conditions resulting in psychological trauma and other health problems can be rendered in terms of both rights and dependency. The class action resists the domestic governmentality of digital platforms through the combined agency of worker-citizens. At the same time, it mobilizes domestic relations and morals to make a claim for care against Facebook. While Facebook asserts that employees have sufficient access to 'resiliency and wellness resources', the moderators often feel left alone with the stress from child pornography, murder, or animal cruelty content that is posted on Facebook.[80]

In 2020, Facebook agreed to settle the class action for $52 million. The payment 'may be used for medical screening for injuries resulting from exposure to potentially graphic or disturbing material in the course of work as a Content Moderator'.[81] In the settlement, Facebook clearly articulates its response in terms of domesticized care and dependency. It asks its vendors to provide clinicians during shift hours and extends practices of 'resilience pre-screening', coaching, and wellness sessions.[82] An anonymous Facebook whistle-blower hotline is set up for content moderators to raise issues of

---

[78] Balibar, *We, the People of Europe?*, 76.
[79] *Scola et al. v Facebook Inc.*, 'Amended Complaint and Demand for Jury Trial', §1.
[80] Silver, 'Hard Questions'.
[81] *Scola et al. v Facebook Inc.*, 'Plaintiffs' Renewed Notice of Motion', 1.
[82] *Scola et al. v Facebook Inc.*, 'Settlement Agreement and Release'.

settlement non-implementation. There is, however, no external oversight, and the settlement remains a matter of internal company practices. Moreover, the settlement extends only to content moderators working for Facebook vendors in California, Arizona, Texas, and Florida.[83] The dispersed microworkers of the Global South remain outside the settlement. The content moderators' class action cannot directly redress international asymmetries of work and citizenship, even as the litigation mobilizes the vocabularies of dependency, trust, and care. Differences between populations across the world 'serve as membranes through which unequal social relations occur and across which new socialities are formed and imagined.'[84]

Despite this, by drawing attention to the effects that the labour of content moderation has on workers, the class action renders their work and presence visible globally and problematizes the effects that digital platforms have, in terms of both the conditions of labour and the imagined global community of users. The class action resists the discourse of the community of users and enacts a reversal of Facebook's domesticized governmentality. At the same time, the class action is set at a distance from state initiatives on regulation, which maintained the boundaries of state and citizens. Its transnationalism contrasts with what we earlier observed about the attempts by states to regain sovereignty through legislation.

As we have seen, the German legal initiative NetzDG aims to hold a range of digital platforms accountable for the circulation of content on their platforms. For some, it stood for the reclaimed sovereignty of states against an increasingly global world governed by the sovereignty of capital. For others, it shifted state responsibilities for regulation to private companies and made them into judges of what is allowed and what not. Even worse, NetzDG was seen to promote censorship of online content and to violate obligations to respect free speech. In their submission on the introduction of the Social Media and Oversight Bill in the UK, Big Brother Watch used NetzDG as an example of undesirable legislation that has created an antagonistic relation to freedom of speech.[85] Human Rights Watch complains that platforms can become 'no accountability zones',[86] as NetzDG does not specify how a legal person can appeal against the platforms' decisions. Unlike NetzDG, the platforms' community guidelines allow users to challenge blocked content through an appeal process. NetzDG endows the citizens only with the limited power of flagging content

[83] *Scola et al. v Facebook Inc.*, 'Proposed Settlement'.
[84] Vora, *Life Support*, 23.
[85] Big Brother Watch, 'Big Brother Watch's Briefing on the Social Media Service Providers'.
[86] Human Rights Watch, 'Germany: Flawed Social Media Law'.

and thus renders relations between platforms and states as antagonisms over law and sovereignty. All these concerns and interventions efface the scenes of resistance that unfold through class actions in the name of all social media content moderators. While NetzDG stands for the problems of attempts by states to regain sovereignty and leave the global work of digital platforms untouched, the class action disrupts the domesticized governmentality of social media companies.

Bordering matters in international politics, as it turns categories of inside/outside, domestic/foreign, national/international into resources for governing by social media companies and states. This chapter has argued that social media companies aim to 'conduct the conduct' of users globally through relations of dependency, trust, authenticity, and the proliferation of thresholds rather than borders. This does not imply that geopolitical borders are no longer relevant for social media platforms. Geopolitical borders are entangled with sovereign law and remain very real as companies tackle regulations and taxes. In 2008, for instance, Facebook moved its European headquarters to Ireland to take advantage of low corporate tax. Once the EU General Data Protection Regulation (GDPR) came into force, Facebook argued that it should only apply to its users in the EU, thus taking 1.5 billion Facebook users in Africa, Asia, Australia, and Latin America out of the purview of the legislation.[87] While the power of states over very large tech companies is undeniable, state rebordering and reterritorialization of tech companies also remains limited by the emerging art of government through thresholds. These two arts of government configure citizens and users as their respective political subjects.

Rather than a struggle over sovereignty or a new form of private–global colonialism, we have shown how social media companies deploy techniques of governing through thresholds and community guidelines. States have not stood by and discovered the advantages of Facebook's fluent global community of users. While their public discourses lament the extension of big tech companies beyond sovereign boundaries, they use the formation of a different international and the 'foreign' as a resource for their own state practices. In a case brought by Big Brother Watch and a coalition of NGOs against the UK security agencies' practices of mass surveillance, the distinction internal/external makes possible the intensification of state surveillance.[88] What counts as 'external communication' enables the extension of surveillance into spheres that would

[87] McCarthy, 'Facebook Puts 1.5B Users on a Boat'.
[88] *Big Brother Watch and Others v the UK*, 'Grand Chamber Judgement'.

be prohibited if they counted as 'internal communications' within sovereign borders. In the Big Brother Watch case, UK officials explained that 'a person in the United Kingdom who communicated with a search engine overseas was engaging in an external communication, as was a person in the United Kingdom who posted a public message (such as a tweet or Facebook status update), unless all the recipients of that message were in the British Isles'.[89] This assumption takes advantage of global platforms and tends to make more or less all digital communication with Google or Facebook external, removing legal limits to surveillance.

The arts of government that deploy borders and thresholds erase workers and the socio-technical work of production and reproduction from international politics. The *Scola et al. v Facebook Inc.* class action stands for a disruptive intervention over the distribution of the sensible, which resists both the discourse of the community of users in Facebook's domesticated governmentality and that of state citizens protected by state boundaries. The class action repositions workers within a transversal scene of resistance, where the boundaries of citizenship, the territorial borders of the state, and invisibilization of workers by the community of users are simultaneously resisted. Even as borders and thresholds are difficult to undo, resistance operates through a series of reversals and levers on power asymmetries. Resistance adds a third dimension to the scences of friction and refusal we have analysed in Chapters 6 and 7. Friction, refusal, and resistance are all practical and analytical interventions, which recompose ethics, accountability, and the international. In the Conclusion, we situate these interventions through friction, refusal, and resistance within a conceptualization of contestation, controversy, and democratic politics.

[89] Ibid., §75.

Conclusion

Democratic scenes

Big Data World, AI & Big Data Expo, and AI Cloud Expo are some of the exhibitions of digital products, software, and hardware that take place regularly in cities around the world, from Singapore and Hong Kong to Madrid and London. At a Big Data and Artificial Intelligence exhibition, participants promised to unleash the big data revolution, avoid 'data drudgery', and 'shoot for the moon'.[1] The expo brought together data scientists, engineers, developers, lawyers, and sales representatives to discuss the challenges and promises of big data, AI, and machine learning. Despite the 'hype' around these technologies, many of the talks in the AI Lab Theatre, which we attended, started by diagnosing the problems of AI. Drawing on public controversies, from the ProPublica research on racism in predictive policing to Apple's gender-biased credit card limits, engineers and data scientists engaged with the social and political diagnoses of their own work. This awareness of bias and discrimination was widespread among the audience, who put their hands up when prompted to express recognition of these controversies. Professional and public controversies were entangled on this global scene of digital capitalism.

Following these diagnoses, engineers and scientists proceeded to offer solutions, often in the form of yet another technological development. For instance, one speaker criticized algorithms for giving a flat view of things and recommended to contextualize them in order to reach a better understanding of data. Context became equivalent to engineering challenges of knowledge graphs and Linked Data. Another talk proposed to address questions of bias and ethics and alerted participants to the range of devices available for implementing 'ethical' AI. The IBM AI Fairness 360 toolkit is an 'open-source toolkit of metrics to check for unwanted bias in datasets and machine

[1] Big Data LDN, 'To Intelligence ... and Beyond'.

Algorithmic Reason. Claudia Aradau and Tobias Blanke, Oxford University Press.
© Claudia Aradau and Tobias Blanke (2022). DOI: 10.1093/oso/9780192859624.003.0010

learning models, and state-of-the-art algorithms to mitigate such bias'.[2] The EU's High-Level Expert Group Guidelines on Trustworthy AI were also mentioned, alongside other policy and academic resources to address algorithmic discrimination and bias. These talks were paralleled by other engineering-oriented talks focusing on optimizing processes, producing more value from data through real-time, millisecond analytics, and data processing with various cloud platforms. A 'strategy theatre' dedicated to governance and mobile device management had a line-up of talks on the EU's General Data Protection Regulation (GDPR), data privacy, and delivering value while ensuring compliance.

The exhibition ended with a keynote session with Chris Wylie, the Cambridge Analytica whistle-blower, who was interviewed by the *Times* journalist James Hurley. The keynote session most explicitly tackled political and democratic issues, which otherwise hovered on the margins of the two-day exhibition. 'Do you believe that people are easy to manipulate?', asked the journalist at the start of the conversation. From questions of manipulation, the acumen of data, and the power of big tech companies and regulations, this leading question barely hid its implications that the role of Cambridge Analytica in Brexit and US elections had been over-hyped. Hurley went on to focus on the lack of understanding of the average person, the use of the same technologies by the Obama and not just the Trump campaign, and then to questions of regulation and the tension between national regulators and international platforms.

Wylie persuasively started by deconstructing the assumptions in his interlocutor's questions and then proceeded to explain his understanding of the political effects of the technologies and methods deployed by Cambridge Analytica. He reframed the question of manipulation from the assumption of lack of agency in the initial question of manipulation into one of asymmetry of information. The implied continuity between the Trump and the Obama campaigns became a comment about the political entanglements of targeting technologies. The Obama campaign was open about the ads it produced and presented them as such. It also tried to increase rather than suppress voting. Wylie acknowledged that Cambridge Analytica targeted a 'small subset of the population' but suggested not to underestimate its impact, framing his arguments by a particular understanding of subjectivity and action, and working through the small. He pointed out that the Cambridge Analytica skills were honed as part of the Strategic Communication Laboratories group, Cambridge Analytica's parent company, working with the military on the spread

[2] Varshney, 'Introducing AI Fairness 360'.

of radicalization online, and proceeded to use the analogy of radicalization to explain the effects of social media today and the rise of the alt-right. As Wylie reiterates in his memoir, published around the time of the exhibition and quickly becoming one of the top-ranked books on Amazon in the categories of current events and international security, '[t]he concentration of power that Facebook enjoys is a danger to American democracy'.[3]

Unlike earlier expos we had attended, this exhibition was not only driven by promises of deploying big data and AI to tackle social, economic, health, and political issues. It was traversed by intensifying concerns with bias, ethics, accountability, state, and law, in short with how to render data, algorithms and AI governable. While remaining a place of 'pilgrimage to the fetish Commodity',[4] the expo helps highlight a key argument that we have made in this book. Algorithmic reason materializes by means of professional and public controversies, it is traversed by frictions, refusals, and resistances. The expo was not just a commercial scene of digital capitalism, but also a scene of controversy and dissensus. By entering various scenes in which algorithms are becoming objects of controversy, this book proposed to understand the political rationalities that hold together situated, multiple, and heterogenous algorithmic operations, which have been inserted into the government of self and other. We wanted to avoid dystopian views of technologies, catastrophic anticipations of the end of democracy, or diagnoses of generic colonialism that risk effacing contestations or that relegate them to an indefinite future to come.

Algorithmic Reason has proposed a different perspective on the heterogeneous practices governing our lives through data and algorithmic operations. Algorithmic reason names the rationalities that have turned language, bodies, and actions into data that can be processed by computers. These rationalities promise to revitalize governing practices by transcending binaries of small/large, population/individual, speech/action, and self/other. The conceptualization of algorithmic reason helps us understand how things are held together in their heterogeneity. While recent critical work has drawn attention to the need to study the 'everyday life' of algorithms,[5] we have argued that it is important to understand how these heterogeneous practices deploy and circulate specific political rationalities. As Brown has remarked about neoliberal reason, it is 'globally ubiquitous, yet disunified and nonidentical with itself

---

[3] Wylie, *Mindf*Ck*, 18. Rankings on http://www.amazon.co.uk as of 29 November 2019.
[4] Benjamin, "'Paris, the Capital of the Nineteenth Century'", 7.
[5] Neyland, *The Everyday Life of an Algorithm*.

in space and time.'[6] Algorithmic reason is similarly global and heterogeneously distributed, remaking the practices and techniques of governing. It is not only the responsibility of engineers with their interests in automation and optimization, but it has come to shape societies and how we can understand them.

Taking algorithmic rationalities seriously allows us to understand how algorithms have become so deeply entwined with governmental practices. Governing entails the problematization of the behaviour of individuals and populations, how to 'conduct the conduct' of multiplicities and singularities, and how to deal with the boundaries between self and other. These oppositions of self/other and individual/population have shaped social and political thought and have led to different techniques of governing. The individual body and the population required different techniques and modes of knowledge to be made governable.[7] As we have shown in Chapter 1, statistical knowledge could move from the individual to the population by producing aggregates and averages, but found it hard to move back again.

The promise of governing both individuals and populations remained inevitably limited. The problem of government is that of individualization and totalization—how to govern the individual while at the same time governing the whole population; how to govern the self at the same time as governing the other. This dual problematization has been at the centre of this book. Algorithmic reason promises to move from self to other, from populations to individuals and back, as we discussed in Part I ('Rationalities'). In the Conclusion, we bring together some of the implications of the government of self and other we have unpacked in this book through 'Materializations' (Part II) and 'Interventions' (Part III).

In attending to the emergence of algorithmic reason, we do not suggest that it is a replacement of other political rationalities like 'neoliberal reason'. We do not make a claim to totality with the term 'reason'. Tensions between individualization and totalization continue to underpin neoliberal reason, as it aims to 'economize all features of existence, from democratic institutions to subjectivity'.[8] Totalization through market relations is juxtaposed to individualization by producing responsible, self-governing subjects. Despite multiple crises and tensions, neoliberal reason continues to shape practices of governing and subjectivation. It can align itself with a range of other political projects and circulates globally exactly because of its multiplicity. But it also has a certain

[6] Brown, *Undoing the Demos*, 21.
[7] Foucault, *Security, Territory, Population*.
[8] Brown, *In the Ruins of Neoliberalism*, 11.

coherence through 'the *combination* of a logic of market rationality, a conception of personhood (centered on, but not exclusive to, human individuals), a calculating framework of efficiency, and a view of authority as a fundamental political and social bond'.[9] Algorithmic reason sits beside neoliberal reason and does not substitute it anymore than it does statistical reason.

As we have argued in this book, algorithmic reason aims to datafy the world and make it algorithmically actionable: institutions, subjects, experiences, relations, everything becomes ready for algorithms. Algorithmic reason recasts the question of how knowledge can be produced in order to govern populations and individuals, self and other. It generates relatively new forms of knowledge and decision and therefore relatively new techniques of governing self and other, while providing a coherence to dispersed practices and enabling the transmission of methods and circulation of devices.

Unfolding controversies

We have proposed that the methodology of the scene developed in the book makes it possible to attend to how controversies unfold in relation to algorithms, and their latest instalments as big data and AI. Unfolding means to open from the folds, but also to expand and to disclose. In that sense, scenes are neither events nor situations, but contain elements of both. As scenes unfold, we can trace how arguments, tools, and practices are entangled and contested across social worlds. Scenes are socio-temporal arrangements where heterogeneous subjects and objects co-appear and give rise to varied contestations. These scenes materialize differently around the world, but they are also transversal operations and concerns. Security agencies attempt to develop capacities globally to find the anomalous needle in the data hay. Digital humanitarianism operates transnationally by being interlinked with digital platforms. Demands for accountability of facial recognition technology are shared in the US, across many European countries, and China. Digital platforms have led to new kinds of worker associations across borders.

Scenes are incisions in the world where conflicts play out over what is perceivable, what garners political value, and what becomes infra-sensible, supra-sensible, or imperceptible in some way. By focusing on scenes and their controversies, we have adopted a polymorphous approach to contestation. Controversies have an interdisciplinary history, from scientific

---

[9] Clarke, 'Living with/in and without Neo-Liberalism', 141 (emphasis in text).

to socio-technical controversies in science and technology studies (STS). As Noortje Marres explains in the context of digital controversies, these include three approaches that can be characterized as demarcationist, discursivist, and empiricist. If demarcationists want to distinguish legitimate from illegitimate positions, discursivists and empiricists are interested in the 'composition of controversies' and 'the entangling of epistemic and political dynamics'.[10] Our analysis of controversies could be seen as a mixture of discursivist and empiricist approaches, although we did not seek to 'minimize ontological assumptions', as Marres defines empiricist approaches. Our methodology of the scene meant that we selected and analysed controversies that were disruptive for the distribution of the sensible.

Finally, we approached controversy as a specific mode of contestation where an element of publicity is present. This entails what sociologist Cyril Lemieux has called a triadic structure of contestation, referring not just to the actors involved in a controversy, but to the public of peers or non-peers it convenes.[11] In that sense, controversies are different from languages of struggle, agonism, and antagonism, which configure conflict and dissensus as dyadic structures, in that the resolution emerges from these very structures. Controversies do not rely just on the actors themselves but require a third structural element such as a public, a judge, a committee, and so on. Controversies have been understood as 'unfolding "moments" in which issues arise that are resistant to settlement by an extant apparatus'.[12] While an element of publicity has been important to our analyses of controversies—from the Cambridge Analytica scandals to the expert publics of patents—we have also shown how scenes of controversy can morph into other modes of dissensus, from friction to refusal to resistance. For us, the distinction between the dyadic structure of conflict and the triadic structure of controversy works as a heuristic device that helps distinguish and connect varied forms of contestation.

Therefore, each chapter started with a a scene of contestation or controversy, where different participants problematize the practices, knowledge, and effects of algorithmic reason. Scenes bring together heterogeneous actors. They include not just professionals and experts or parliamentarians, politicians, big tech companies, and NGOs but a whole range of different roles and people. Controversies happen in often mundane sites such as the trade expo we mentioned earlier, but also in law courts, in the media, and

[10] Marres, 'Why Map Issues?', 661–3.
[11] Lemieux, 'À quoi sert l'analyse des controverses ?'. See also Jackiewicz, 'Outils notionnels pour l'analyse des controverses'.
[12] Schouten, 'Security as Controversy', 26.

in workplaces. As science and technology studies scholars have pointed out, controversies include materials and technologies as elements of their unfolding and not just 'human collectives'.[13] The methodology of the scene has connected governmentality and politics.[14] It has required transdisciplinary concepts and collaboration that mean we needed to take engineers, developers, data scientists, and computer scientists seriously as political and epistemic subjects. We have used scenes to attend not just to the messiness, heterogeneity, and effects of algorithms, but also to draw out the conditions of possibility of multiple and varied algorithmic practices. Algorithmic reason is what holds them together both spatially and temporally.

The first two chapters of the book unpacked algorithmic reason through its rationalities that reconfigure individuals and populations, speech and action, self and other. As we have seen in Chapter 1, algorithmic reason works through decomposing and recomposing the small and large and thus recasting the political relationship between individuals and populations. The shift from the small to the large requires a recasting of subjectivity and of the relation between speech and action, as well as what we can know about the whole and the parts through data. Bruno Latour and his colleagues have provocatively suggested that, with digital traces, '[t]he whole is always smaller than its parts', or that '*there is more complexity in the elements than in the aggregates*'.[15] In our analysis of microtargeting and the Cambridge Analytica controversy, we have shown how this view is at least optimistic and generally does not reflect the granularity of algorithmic operations. The incessant recomposition of the small and the large is always fragile and does not scale smoothly but produces frictions at all levels.

If the humanities and social sciences placed epistemic limits and methodological constraints on how the part and the whole could be made knowable and how the knowledge on individuals and populations could be combined, algorithmic reason makes it possible to move between small and large data and back again. Data is simultaneously smaller and larger than an individual. The small and the large introduce a vocabulary for governing actors and practices, which is different from the whole and the part, the individual and the population, the people and the citizen, as they have been mobilized in other arts of government, from sovereignty to discipline and biopolitics.

---

[13] Marres, *Material Participation*; Barry, *Material Politics*. As we saw in Chapter 6, Bonnie Honig challenges the reading of political theorists as not attending to the materialities and objects of political contestation and agonistic democracy.

[14] William Walters has argued that work on governmentality has at times 'eclipsed a proper consideration of politics' (Walters, *Governmentality*, 5).

[15] Latour et al., '"The Whole Is Always Smaller Than Its Parts"', 591 (emphasis in text).

Vocabularies of the citizen and the people as well as the transformation of the many into one have shaped understandings of sovereign power. The 'social physics' of nineteenth-century statistics and biopolitical forms of governmentality are both based on knowledge of the whole and the parts as well as aggregating individuals into population groups. Therefore, going back from aggregates and statistically produced groups to the individual became hard, if not impossible, to do.

Algorithmic reason transcends such impasses through the potentially infinite recompositions of small and large data. This does not mean that algorithmic reason moves from non-knowledge to knowledge, as big data and AI enthusiasts have argued. It also does not mean that we move from knowledge to non-knowledge, as the motto 'correlation is not causation' would seem to suggest. We have shown that algorithmic knowledge emerges in confrontation with statistical and testimonial knowledge. We started from the promise of algorithmic reason to recompose the large and the small and traced how these recompositions go hand in hand with the idea that speech and action can be recast as acts of truth-doing against the tension between wrongdoing and truth-telling. The digital space is celebrated for being seemingly replete with datafied nonconscious acts that transcend the binary of speech and action.

Chapter 2 turned to the government of difference and analysed how algorithmic reason makes differences through partitioning and 'cutting' through a world as data. By 'following' an algorithm developed by a predictive policing company, we could show how algorithms divide a city permanently into suspicious and nonsuspicious places through infra-sensible partitioning of abstract feature spaces. Algorithms pertain neither to decisionism nor to bureaucratization, but they work through mundane data decompositions and workflows, operating beyond the dimensions of what any human subject might be able to perceive. Algorithms can decompose and recompose data points indefinitely so that the lines of decision as partitioning of feature spaces are indefinitely drawn and redrawn. Producing knowledge through recompositions of the small and the large and making decisions by means of partitioning, algorithmic reason transforms the contours of political realities in ways that reproduce and recast power relations.

Given that partitioning lies at the heart of their rationality, it is not surprising that algorithms are often shown to create new exclusions and amplify existing discriminatory effects. Big data and AI have been situated in the continuity of colonialism, racism, and patriarchal capitalism. Yet, rather than tracing an uninflected line from colonialism to digital colonialism, we have argued that we need to follow the details of the recompositions of power and its effects in the present. This allows us to understand how historical bias is not just transmitted or amplified by data, as critics of the racializing effects of digital technologies have argued. There are many additional factors such as how targets of algorithms are determined away from white-collar crime suspicions in Manhattan, how algorithmic input is justified against diverse features that record places in heterogeneous ways, or how algorithms focus on some data at the expense of other data. Chapter 2 has illustrated how neural networks and decision trees are set to concentrate on different features. Algorithms are not simply devices of 'self-fulfilling prophecies' of historically discriminating data.

The second part of the book, 'Materializations', has unpacked the practices of decomposition, recomposition, and partitioning across three scenes of controversy: over targeting in war, digital humanitarian action, and valorization by tech companies. Through these scenes, we have traced different aspects of governing through algorithms: the production of dangerous others, the power of digital platforms, and the valorization of data. In Chapter 3, we have shown how security agencies are producing dangerous 'others' by reconstituting them algorithmically as anomalies, where small details draw the line between what is conceived as regular and what is irregular. Anomaly detection relies on the continuous composition and recomposition of subjects as data points so that calculations of distance can produce differences between data. Anomalous others are unlike enemies, criminals, and other risky suspects as these have been the targets of governmental interventions historically.

Drawing on materials from the Snowden archive and computer science literature on anomaly detection, we have argued that security practices of contact-chaining to find new suspects are transformed into detecting different types of network anomalies where a suspect does not need to be in any known relationship with other suspects. In fact, the greatest promise of anomaly detection with machine learning is that suspicious behaviour can be extended to digital traces like the length of a telephone call, which are otherwise not known to induce suspicion. As anomaly detection can entail 'the premature exposure to death and debility that working with or being subjected to digital technologies accelerates',[16] these modes of racialization are indicative of a relatively new form of nanoracism, a racism that remains at the threshold of the perceptible even as its effects are deadly. It is possible that a target can be simultaneously a well-known journalist and a dangerous other because anomalies could potentially be both, without any tension or contradiction.

---

[16] The Precarity Lab, *Technoprecarious*, 2.

Recompositions of the small and the large have also remade societal and technical infrastructures. Algorithmic reason has materialized in platforms and enabled their global expansion. As discussed in Chapter 4, platforms are composites of small and large forms; it is this composition and recomposition that makes their plasticity possible and leads to concerns about their imperial reach, global surveillance, and economic monopoly. While digital platforms extract, appropriate, and extend, we have argued that they also break up and decompose. Their material history shows how algorithmic reason can effectively internalize externals and externalize internals through processes of recomposition. Using distributed services like application programming interfaces, platforms pull in outside parts, while cloud technologies offer platform elements outside. Through the dual move of taking the inside out and bringing the outside in, a few platforms have become the building blocks of most things digital. In dispersing the various elements of platforms and re-embedding them, they constitute a new form of micropower. We have analysed the effects of platform micropower for humanitarian action and organizations. Humanitarian actors have been late comers to the digital world, but they have embraced many of the digital technologies, particularly biometrics and other technologies of data extraction. They also connect on all levels to platforms, as these promise global instantaneous reach. Digital platforms have been much less visible in discussions of humanitarianism, but insidiously produce humanitarianism as control.

The third materialization of algorithmic reason we investigated is that of economic value. We do not claim to develop a new theory of digital economy but investigate the political effects of widely debated analyses of economic value. By taking the patents of Internet companies as the place where controversies over value production play out, new forms of valorization emerge, which focus on the recomposition of smaller and smaller details. In academic and non-academic apprehensions of digital economies, labour-centric political critiques of economies are complemented by controversies about the universality of surveillance and monopolies of platform capitalism. These concerns are often followed by political desires for states to regulate, protect, and organize. Yet, other new forms of valorization present in patents might be ignored.

Like other platforms, Spotify places its users more and more under capitalist surveillance and uses network effects to cement its platform power in order to appropriate and circulate music products from around the world. Its patents, however, also tell the story of a growing anxiety that this might not be enough because of a limited ability to produce new content and the angst to fail at consumption. Spotify's patents display a new form of valorization through the combination of small details that render existing products as new by connecting them to potentially infinite situated actions of its users. While this becomes especially notable in the patents of a music company, it is also a trend for other Internet companies and raises new questions of subjectivity and agency, when confronted with personalized predictions that keep the 'consumerist continuum' going. The patents set the scene for permanently recreating apparently new products and subjects, enjoined to consume through machine-learning targeting. New modes of personalization were created by featurizing users' movement speed, which was enough to choose new music, not unlike in earlier chapters, where suspicious others were formed through featurizing city locations or telephone behaviour.

In its materializations of anomalies, platform power, and value, algorithmic reason incessantly produces relations between self and other and multiplies differences. Rather than a data double or a behavioural subject, algorithmic reason fosters multiplicities of subjects in varied combinations of relations, which are not simply about doubling the original but about making it algorithmically relevant. Individual and organizational selves are altered and adjusted to become big data organizations and algorithmically governable. Anomalous others emerge as potentially dangerous, while vulnerable others like refugees are targeted with promises of more efficient processing based on a combined feature set that includes data from governments, NGOs, and companies.

The algorithmic government of self and other raises difficult questions about the role of the individual, of agency, as well as the limits of privacy and data protection. As we saw in Chapter 3, an anomaly is not simply an individual, even though anomaly detection makes it possible to identify a journalist, Ahmad Zaidan, as a suspicious 'other', potentially targeted for lethal action. An anomaly is the result of compositions and recompositions of data points to create new partitions between self and other. Through continual partitioning as well as infra-sensible and supra-sensible recompositions, forms of collective subjectivity are increasingly difficult to imagine and construct. If algorithmic reason names the conditions of possibility of governing self and other, which transform both individual and collective subjectivity, this does not mean that it goes unchallenged.

Friction, refusal, resistance

In Part III on 'Interventions', we turned to how scenes of controversy over making algorithms ethical, accountable, and bounded are transformed through friction, refusal, and resistance. These analyses diverge from diagnoses of algorithmic governmentality, which see it as eviscerating democratic politics, spelling the end of emancipation and even of political subjectivity. How are friction, refusal, and resistance folded onto scenes of democratic politics? From the petition of Google employees protesting Pentagon contracts to the algorithmic discriminations and separations where new forms of nanoracism are hidden behind seemingly neutral ideas such as anomaly detection, the stakes could not be higher. In this part of the book, we advance the analysis of scenes of controversies by attending to the effects that these have upon governmental and anti-governmental interventions. We reconnect controversies to an expanding vocabulary of contestation, which includes friction, refusal, and resistance, where each is responding to different modes of making algorithms governable.

In Chapter 6, an ethico-politics of friction reconfigures scenes of algorithmic controversies by slowing down, interrupting, or otherwise making algorithmic operations more costly. When science and technology studies (STS) scholar Paul Edwards defines friction as 'the costs in time, energy, and attention required simply to collect, check, store, move, receive, and access data', his focus is on the work that generating data requires.[17] Friction is indicative of effort, difficulty, cost, and slowing down. For us, frictions are not just sociotechnical occurrences but can be instigated, as we show in the final part of the book. Such frictions slow down and differentially inflect the unfolding of scenes of controversy. Frictions are material as much as social, they are collective and dissensual, working towards a redistribution of the sensible. When Google employees write a petition, it is its wider circulation that leads to unexpected unfoldings and wider discussions beyond the question of AI weaponry. The unfoldings begin to recast understandings of AI technologies as social phenomena and can initiate the formation of transversal collectives.

While the Google employees' letter has at times been dismissed by critical scholars as not going far enough, the prism of friction allows us to understand the move to slow down and inflect technologies differently. In all our scenes, algorithmic operations have been presented as more similar to other human–machine labour processes than the general idea of artificial intelligence might suggest. As labour processes and workflows, they draw attention both to the mundane, unexceptional practices of algorithms, which are step-by-step operations, and to the limitations on the emergence of collective dissensus.

---

[17] Edwards, *A Vast Machine*, 84.

Algorithmic operations are often infra-sensible and even supra-sensible. Therefore, algorithms are difficult to turn into 'public things' that make democratic action in concert possible and redistribute the sensible. Algorithmic 'trouble' and 'glitches' have been proposed as concepts through which to understand the moments in which algorithms reveal their malfunctioning, errors, and failures and thus invite criticisms. Algorithmic trouble builds on Donna Haraway's invitation to 'stay with the trouble' in its etymological sense of stirring up, disturbing but also being present and 'entwined in myriad unfinished configurations of places, times, matters, meanings', while glitch draws on its uses as error and failure of computational technologies.[18] However, glitch is also an 'unintended error' that 'tends to be negligible, quickly absorbed by the larger, still-functioning system'.[19] Friction shares a disruptive orientation with glitch and trouble and requires proximity to data and its algorithmic operations. Yet, by concerted action to make these into public things, our conceptualization of friction differs from the ontological indeterminacy of trouble and the epistemic surprise of glitch.

Unlike friction, refusal as a second type of intervention sets up a fundamental opposition to algorithmic operations. As scenes of refusal unfold, we see claims for technology to be undone, redone, or even abolished and not just slowed down and redirected. In Chapter 7, we proposed to shift the scene of correcting errors and proffering explanations as dominant 'accounts' about algorithmic operations to accountability through refusal. In the global scenes of the rollout of facial recognition to surveil and make economies run faster, a new algorithmic auditing regime is offered as an answer to growing citizens' concerns. Algorithms become part of increasingly professionalized worlds divided into experts and non-experts and assessed by quantifiable indicators. Tech industries add auditing structures to the services they offer. Algorithms might even audit themselves and give their own accounts as Explainable AI to conjoin our trust with the industry's desire to automate.

Globally, scenes of accountability have also created the conditions for new forms of keeping algorithms in check. Refusals of technology are both dispersed and proliferating. They can be highly visible, as we saw in the refusals that translate into legal challenges in Europe and China, or hover at the threshold of the perceptible. This legibility is differentially distributed around the world. Refusal is a 'stoppage, an end to something, the breaking of relations', but it is also generative of public questioning of technologies such as facial

---

[18] Haraway, *Staying with the Trouble*, 1. Legacy Russell has coined the term 'glitch feminism' (Russell, *Glitch Feminism*). On algorithm trouble, see Meunier, Ricci, and Gray, 'Algorithm Trouble'.

[19] Kane, *High-Tech Trash*, 15.

recognition.[20] In that sense, refusal is different from resistance, because it 'rejects this hierarchical relationship, repositing the relationship as one configured altogether differently'.[21] In her analysis of the racializing effects and conditions of technologies, Ruha Benjamin has argued for forging an 'abolitionist toolkit' predicated on reimagined solidarity and justice rather than benevolence and charity.[22] While the abolitionist toolkit has been imagined in the particular context of US politics and social structures (and to some extent those in Europe), refusal as a motley toolkit of practices challenges imaginaries of the international and particularly the lines of war and threats that frame countries or regions such as the European Union as producers and curators of 'good tech'.

In the book's final chapter on the International, we specifically attended to how borders between the national and the international are resisted. While states aim to reterritorialize big tech companies through law and sovereign injunctions, they are also deeply entangled with these companies in governing a global digital world that is rendered as threatening, replete with 'unknown unknowns' of terror and disinformation. The German NetzDG law has not only made visible how a state reborders companies, but also how a platform like Facebook has developed competing arts of governing by working through global community guidelines and standards. Borders become thresholds, which allow national law and global community guidelines to coexist as not mutually exclusive. Yet, resistance emerges not just against the practices of big tech companies, but also against the bordering of sovereign politics. As former content moderators for Facebook accuse the company of lack of care for their workers, they mobilize different modes of subjectivity: worker and citizen. Political subjectivities are recast in relation to Facebook's domestic governmentality and identified as global. As Foucault has argued, resistance is not external to power, but it emerges from within power relations: 'It exists all the more by being in the same place as power; hence, like power, resistance is multiple and can be integrated in global strategies.'[23] Resistance emerges at the interstices of power relations. Facebook's domestication of relations and its 'community without citizenship' is challenged by claims to workers' rights and a global extension of the idea of California citizens.

Friction, refusal, and resistance reconfigure scenes of controversy and dissensus by unfolding democratic potentials. They enable the political formation

[20] McGranahan, 'Theorizing Refusal', 322.
[21] Ibid., 323.
[22] Benjamin, *Race after Technology*, 192.
[23] Foucault, *Power/Knowledge*, 142.

of algorithms as public things. While each of the three concepts is indicative of a particular mode of contestation, we have shown that algorithmic reason does not undo democracy, reflexivity, or political action. As algorithmic operations evince these combinatorial and emerging qualities, algorithmic reason oriented us to political rationalities that also have constraining or otherwise limiting effects. In her analysis of technofeminism, STS scholar Judy Wajcman asked '[c]an feminism steer a path between technophobia and technophilia'?[24] We have tried to steer such a path by unfolding scenes about what algorithms can know and do and what they cannot know and do. Between deterministic readings of technology and readings that highlight lack of determination, this book has traced a trajectory of algorithmic reason as underdetermined.

Even as the conditions of political action become more limiting, frictions, refusals, and resistances can reconfigure political interventions as antigovernmental in the sense of facing up to governing by algorithms.[25] These concepts and practices are entangled rather than mutually exclusive. They do not replace a set of concepts and practices with another set, as some authors have suggested in calling for replacing accountability with co-liberation, ethics with justice, or bias with oppression.[26] Friction, refusal, and resistance work upon and within scenes of controversy and dissensus. As controversies over algorithms, data, and AI unfold, scenes can also become worksites of democracy in the sense of what Balibar has called the 'democratization of democracy' as 'the reactivation of more radical forms of participation than had emerged in the past, or ... the invention of new forms of equality and liberty, adapted to the social conditions of the day'.[27]

---

[24] Wajcman, *Technofeminism*, 6.

[25] We use the prefix 'anti' here in the sense that Balibar has given it as 'the most general modality of the act of "facing up"' (Balibar, *Violence and Civility*, 23).

[26] See, for instance, D'Ignazio and Klein, *Data Feminism*, 60.

[27] Balibar, 'Democracy and Liberty in Times of Violence'.

References

Abbott, Dean. *Applied Predictive Analytics: Principles and Techniques for the Professional Data Analyst* (London: John Wiley & Sons, 2014).

Access Now. 'Dear Spotify: Don't Manipulate Our Emotions for Profit'. 2021. Available at https://www.accessnow.org/spotify-tech-emotion-manipulation/, [cited 28 May 2021].

Access Now. 'Spotify, Don't Spy: Global Coalition of 180+ Musicians and Human Rights Groups Take a Stand against Speech-Recognition Technology'. 2021. Available at https://www.accessnow.org/spotify-spy-tech-coalition/, [cited 28 May 2021].

ACM U.S. Technology Policy Committee. 'Statement on Principles and Prerequisites for the Development, Evaluation and Use of Unbiased Facial Recognition Technologies'. 2020. Available at https://www.acm.org/binaries/content/assets/public-policy/ustpc-facial-recognition-tech-statement.pdf, [cited 4 June 2021].

Acxiom. 'Consumer Insights Packages'. n.d. Available at https://www.acxiom.com/what-we-do/data-packages/, [cited 18 February 2019].

Adadi, Amina, and Mohammed Berrada. 'Peeking inside the Black-Box: A Survey on Explainable Artificial Intelligence (XAI)'. *IEEE Access* 6 (2018): 52138–60.

Aggarwal, Charu C. *Outlier Analysis* (New York: Springer, 2013).

Aggarwal, Charu C., and Chandan K. Reddy. *Data Clustering: Algorithms and Applications* (Boca Raton, FL: CRC Press, 2013).

Agyemang, Malik, Ken Barker, and Rada Alhajj. 'A Comprehensive Survey of Numeric and Symbolic Outlier Mining Techniques'. *Intelligent Data Analysis* 10(6) (2006): 521–38.

AI Now. 'Algorithmic Accountability Policy Toolkit'. AI Now Institute, 2018. Available at https://ainowinstitute.org/aap-toolkit.pdf, [cited 1 June 2021].

Akhgar, Babak, Gregory B. Saathoff, Hamid R. Arabnia, Richard Hill, Andrew Staniforth, and Petra Saskia Bayerl, eds. *Application of Big Data for National Security: A Practitioner's Guide to Emerging Technologies* (Amsterdam: Butterworth-Heinemann, 2015).

Akoglu, Leman, Hanghang Tong, and Danai Koutra. 'Graph-Based Anomaly Detection and Description: A Survey'. *Data Mining and Knowledge Discovery* 29(3) (2015): 626–88.

Alpaydin, Ethem. *Introduction to Machine Learning* (Cambridge, MA: MIT Press, 2014).

Amazon.com. 'News Release—Amazon.com Announces Fourth Quarter Sales up 20% to $72.4 Billion'. Amazon.com, 2019. Available at https://press.aboutamazon.com/news-releases/news-release-details/amazoncom-announces-fourth-quarter-sales-20-724-billion, [cited 24 October 2019].

Amicelle, Anthony, Claudia Aradau, and Julien Jeandesboz. 'Questioning Security Devices: Performativity, Resistance, Politics'. *Security Dialogue* 46(5) (2015): 293–306.

Amoore, Louise. *The Politics of Possibility: Risk and Security Beyond Probability* (Durham, NC: Duke University Press, 2014).

Amoore, Louise. *Cloud Ethics: Algorithms and the Attributes of Ourselves and Others* (Durham, NC: Duke University Press, 2020).

Amoore, Louise, and Volha Piotukh. 'Life Beyond Big Data: Governing with Little Analytics'. *Economy and Society* 44(3) (2015): 341–66.

Amoore, Louise, and Rita Raley. 'Securing with Algorithms: Knowledge, Decision, Sovereignty'. *Security Dialogue* 48(1) (2017): 3–10.

Ananny, Mike 'Toward an Ethics of Algorithms: Convening, Observation, Probability, and Timeliness'. *Science, Technology, & Human Values* 41(1) (2016): 93–117.

Ananny, Mike, and Kate Crawford. 'Seeing without Knowing: Limitations of the Transparency Ideal and Its Application to Algorithmic Accountability'. *New Media & Society* 20(3) (2018): 973–89.

Anders, Günther. *Burning Conscience: The Case of the Hiroshima Pilot Claude Eatherly, Told in His Letters to Günther Anders'* (London: Weidenfeld and Nicolson, 1961).

Anders, Günther. 'Theses for the Atomic Age'. *The Massachusetts Review* 3(3) (1962): 493–505.

Anders, Günther. *Die Antiquiertheit des Menschen 2. Über die Zerstörung des Lebens im Zeitalter der dritten industriellen Revolution.* 5th edition (München: C. H. Beck, 2018 [1980]).

Anders, Günther. *The Obsolescence of Man*, Vol. II: *On the Destruction of Life in the Epoch of the Third Industrial Revolution.* Translated by Josep Monter Pérez (available at https://libcom.org/files/ObsolescenceofManVol%20IIGunther%20Anders.pdf [1980]).

Anders, Günther. *Hiroshima Ist Überall* (Munich: Verlag C. H. Beck, 1982).

Anders, Günther. *Nous, fils d'Eichmann.* Translated by Sabine Cornille and Philippe Ivernel (Paris: Rivages Poche, 2003 [1964]).

Anders, Günther. *Et si je suis désespéré, que voulez-vous que j'y fasse? Entretien avec Mathias Greffrath.* Translated by Christophe David (Paris: Editions Allia, 2010 [1977]).

Anderson, Chris. *The Long Tail: How Endless Choice Is Creating Unlimited Demand* (London: Random House, 2007).

Anderson, David. 'Report of the Bulk Powers Review'. Independent Reviewer of Terrorism Legislation, 2016. Available at https://terrorismlegislationreviewer.independent.gov.uk/wp-content/uploads/2016/08/Bulk-Powers-Review-final-report.pdf, [cited 30 August 2016].

Andrejevic, Mark, and Kelly Gates. 'Big Data Surveillance: Introduction'. *Surveillance & Society* 12(2) (2014): 185–96.

Apel, Hannah, Nikhil Anand, and Akhil Gupta. 'Introduction: Temporality, Politics and the Promise of Infrastructure'. In *The Promise of Infrastructure*, edited by Nikhil Anand, Akhil Gupta, and Hannah Appel, 1–40 (Durham, NC: Duke University Press, 2018).

Apprich, Clemens, Wendy Hui Kyong Chun, Florian Cramer, and Hito Steyerl. *Pattern Discrimination* (Minneapolis: meson press, 2018).

Aradau, Claudia. 'Security That Matters: Critical Infrastructure and Objects of Protection'. *Security Dialogue* 41(5) (2010): 491–514.

Aradau, Claudia. 'Risk, (In)Security and International Politics'. In *Routledge Handbook of Risk Studies*, edited by Adam Burgess, Alexander Alemanno, and Jens Zinn, 290–8 (London: Routledge, 2016).

Aradau, Claudia. 'Experimentality, Surplus Data and the Politics of Debilitation in Borderzones'. *Geopolitics* 27(1) (2022): 26–46.

Aradau, Claudia, and Tobias Blanke. 'Politics of Prediction: Security and the Time/Space of Governmentality in the Age of Big Data'. *European Journal of Social Theory* 20(3) (2017): 373–91.

Aradau, Claudia, and Tobias Blanke. 'Governing Others: Anomaly and the Algorithmic Subject of Security'. *European Journal of International Security* 2(1) (2018): 1–21.

Aradau, Claudia, and Tobias Blanke. 'Algorithmic Surveillance and the Political Life of Error'. *Journal for the History of Knowledge* 2(1) (2021): 1–13.

Aradau, Claudia, Tobias Blanke, and Giles Greenway. 'Acts of Digital Parasitism: Hacking, Humanitarian Apps and Platformisation'. *New Media & Society* 21(11–12) (2019): 2548–65.

Aradau, Claudia, and Rens van Munster. *Politics of Catastrophe: Genealogies of the Unknown* (London: Routledge, 2011).

Arms Control Association. 'Group of 4,000 Anonymous Google Employees Urging Company Not to Be "in the Business of War" Voted 2018 Arms Control Persons of the Year'. Arms Control Association, 2019. Available at https://www.armscontrol.org/pressroom/2018-acpoy-winner, [cited 24 January 2019].

Arora, Payal. 'Decolonizing Privacy Studies'. *Television & New Media* 20(4) (2019): 366-78.

Arora, Payal. 'General Data Protection Regulation—a Global Standard? Privacy Futures, Digital Activism, and Surveillance Cultures in the Global South'. *Surveillance & Society* 17 (5) (2019).

Arthur, W. Brian. 'Increasing Returns and the New World of Business'. *Harvard Business Review*, 1996. Available at https://hbr.org/1996/07/increasing-returns-and-the-new-world-of-business, [cited 28 October 2019].

Atanasoski, Neda, and Kalindi Vora. *Surrogate Humanity: Race, Robots, and the Politics of Technological Futures* (Durham, NC: Duke University Press, 2019).

Auerbach, David. 'You Are What You Click: On Microtargeting'. 2013. Available at https://www.thenation.com/article/you-are-what-you-click-microtargeting/, [cited 10 March 2018].

Austin, Jonathan Luke. 'Security Compositions'. *European Journal of International Security* 4(3) (2019): 249–73.

AWS. 'AWS Disaster Response'. 2021. Available at https://aws.amazon.com/government-education/nonprofits/disaster-response/, [cited 19 July 2021].

Bacchi, Umberto. 'Face for Sale: Leaks and Lawsuits Blight Russia Facial Recognition'. 2020. Available at https://www.reuters.com/article/us-russia-privacy-lawsuit-feature-trfn-idUSKBN27P10U, [cited 1 June 2021].

Balibar, Étienne. *We, the People of Europe? Reflections on Transnational Citizenship* (Princeton: Princeton University Press, 2004).

Balibar, Étienne. *Violence and Civility. On the Limits of Political Philosophy*. Translated by G. M. Goshgarian. (New York: Columbia University Press, 2015).

Balibar, Étienne. 'Reinventing the Stranger: Walls All over the World, and How to Tear Them Down'. *Symploke* 25(1) (2017): 25–41.

Balibar, Étienne. 'Democracy and Liberty in Times of Violence'. In *The Hrant Dink Memorial Lecture 2018*. Boğaziçi University, Istanbul, 2018.

Balibar, Étienne. *Citizenship* (Cambridge, UK: Polity, 2019).

Balzacq, Thierry, Tugba Basaran, Didier Bigo, Emmanuel-Pierre Guittet, and Christian Olsson. 'Security Practices'. In *International Studies Encyclopedia*, edited by Robert A. Denemark (London: Blackwell, 2010).

Barkawi, Tarak, and Mark Laffey. 'Retrieving the Imperial: Empire and International Relations'. *Millenium: Journal of International Studies* 31(1) (2002): 109–27.

Barnett, Vic, and Toby Lewis. *Outliers in Statistical Data* (New York: John Wiley & Sons, 1978).

Barry, Andrew. *Material Politics: Disputes Along the Pipeline* (Chichester: Wiley Blackwell, 2013).

Barton, Georgina. 'Germany Fines Facebook $2.3 Million for Violation of Hate Speech Law'. 2019. Available at https://www.washingtonexaminer.com/news/germany-fines-facebook-2-3-million-for-violation-of-hate-speech-law, [cited 26 July 2021].

BBC. 'Amazon "Flooded by Fake Five-Star Reviews"—Which? Report'. 2019. Available at https://www.bbc.co.uk/news/business-47941181, [cited 1 November 2019].

BBC. 'Microsoft Pips Amazon for $10bn AI "Jedi" Contract'. BBC News, 2019. Available at https://www.bbc.co.uk/news/technology-50191242, [cited 13 November 2019].

Beck, Ulrich. *World at Risk* (Cambridge, UK: Polity, 2009).

Bellanova, Rocco, and Gloria González Fuster. 'Composting and Computing: On Digital Security Compositions'. *European Journal of International Security* 4(3) (2019): 345–65.

Beller, Jonathan. 'Paying Attention'. Cabinet Magazine 24(Winter) (2006). Available at http://www.cabinetmagazine.org/issues/24/beller.php.

Benbouzid, Bilel. 'On Crime and Earthquakes. Predictive Policing at the Crossroads between Science, Technology and Divining'. *Réseaux* 206(6) (2017): 95–123.

Benbouzid, Bilel. 'Values and Consequences in Predictive Machine Evaluation. A Sociology of Predictive Policing'. *Science & Technology Studies* 32(4) (2019): 119–36.

Bender, Emily M., Timnit Gebru, Angelina McMillan-Major, and Shmargaret Shmitchell. 'On the Dangers of Stochastic Parrots: Can Language Models Be Too Big?'. In Proceedings of the 2021 ACM Conference on Fairness, Accountability, and Transparency, 610–23 (2021).

Benjamin, Ruha. *Race after Technology: Abolitionist Tools for the New Jim Code.* (Cambridge, UK: Polity, 2019).

Benjamin, Walter. *The Arcades Project* (Cambridge, MA: The Belknap Press of Harvard University Press, 1999).

Benjamin, Walter. '"Paris, the Capital of the Nineteenth Century" (1935)'. In *The Arcades Project*, edited by Walter Benjamin, 3–13. (Harvard: Harvard University Press, 2002 [1972]).

Benkler, Yochai, and Helen Nissenbaum. 'Commons-Based Peer Production and Virtue'. *Journal of Political Philosophy* 14(4) (2006): 394–419.

Bennett, Colin J. 'Voter Databases, Micro-Targeting, and Data Protection Law: Can Political Parties Campaign in Europe as They Do in North America?'. *International Data Privacy Law* 6(4) (2016): 261–75.

Bennett, Jane. *Vibrant Matter: A Political Ecology of Things* (Durham, NC: Duke University Press, 2010).

Beraldo, Davide, and Stefania Milan. 'From Data Politics to the Contentious Politics of Data'. *Big Data & Society* 6(2) (2019): 1–11.

Berg, Janine, Marianne Furrer, Ellie Harmon, Uma Rani, and M Six Silberman. *Digital Labour Platforms and the Future of Work: Towards Decent Work in the Online World* (Geneva: International Labour Organization (ILO), 2018).

Bernal, Natasha. 'Facebook's Content Moderators Are Fighting Back'. *Wired*, 2021. Available at https://www.wired.co.uk/article/facebook-content-moderators-ireland, [cited 26 July 2021].

Bessner, Daniel, and Nicolas Guilhot. 'Who Decides?'. In *The Decisionist Imagination: Sovereignty, Social Science and Democracy in the 20th Century*, edited by Daniel Bessner and Nicolas Guilhot, 1–26 (Oxford: Berghahn Books, 2018).

Bhattacharyya, Dhruba Kumar, and Jugal Kumar Kalita. *Network Anomaly Detection: A Machine Learning Perspective* (Boca Raton, FL: CRC Press, 2013).

Big Brother Watch. 'Big Brother Watch's Briefing on the Social Media Service Providers (Civil Liability and Oversight) Bill 2018'. Big Brother Watch, 2018. Available at https://bigbrotherwatch.org.uk/wp-content/uploads/2018/10/Big-Brother-Watch-briefing-on-Social-Media-Service-Providers-Civil-Liability-and-Oversight-Bill.pdf, [cited 30 September 2019].

Big Brother Watch. 'Face-Off Campaign'. Big Brother Watch, 2019. Available at https://bigbrotherwatch.org.uk/all-campaigns/face-off-campaign/, [cited 27 November 2019].

Big Brother Watch, 10 Human Rights Organisations, and Bureau of Investigative Journalism and Others. 'Applicants' Written Observations'. Privacy International, 2019, available at https://www.privacyinternational.org/sites/default/files/2019-07/Applicants%27%20Observations%20-%20May%202019.pdf, [cited 6 March 2020].

Big Brother Watch and Others v the UK. 'Applications Nos. 58170/13, 62322/14 and 24960/15). Grand Chamber Judgement'. European Court of Human Rights, 2021. Available at https://www.bailii.org/eu/cases/ECHR/2021/439.html, [cited 25 May 2021].

Big Data LDN. 'To Intelligence and Beyond'. 2019. Available at https://bigdataldn.com/, [cited 22 July 2021].

Bigo, Didier. 'The Möbius Ribbon of Internal and External Security(ies) '. In *Identities, Borders, Orders. Rethinking International Relations Theory*, edited by Mathias Albert, David Jacobson, and Josef Lapid, 91–116 (Minneapolis: University of Minnesota Press, 2001).

Bigo, Didier. 'Freedom and Speed in Enlarged Borderzones'. In *The Contested Politics of Mobility: Borderzones and Irregularity*, edited by Vicki Squire, 31–50 (London: Routledge, 2010).

Bigo, Didier. 'The (In)Securitization Practices of the Three Universes of EU Border Control: Military/Navy—Border Guards/Police—Database Analysts'. *Security Dialogue* 45(3) (2014): 209–25.

Bigo, Didier, Engin Isin, and Evelyn Ruppert. 'Data Politics'. In *Data Politics: Worlds, Subjects, Rights*, edited by Didier Bigo, Engin Isin, and Evelyn Ruppert, 1–18 (London: Routledge, 2019).

Binns, Reuben, Ulrik Lyngs, Max Van Kleek, Jun Zhao, Timothy Libert, and Nigel Shadbolt. 'Third Party Tracking in the Mobile Ecosystem'. In WebSci '18 Proceedings of the 10th ACM Conference on Web Science, 23–31 (Amsterdam, Netherlands: ACM Library, 2018).

Birchall, Clare. *Radical Secrecy: The Ends of Transparency in Datafied America* (Minneapolis: University of Minnesota Press, 2021).

Blanke, Tobias. *Digital Asset Ecosystems: Rethinking Crowds and Clouds* (Oxford: Elsevier, 2014).

Blanke, Tobias, Giles Greenway, Jennifer Pybus, and Mark Cote. 'Mining Mobile Youth Cultures'. In 2014 IEEE International Conference on Big Data, 14–17 (Washington, DC: 2014).

Blanke, Tobias, and Jennifer Pybus. 'The Material Conditions of Platforms: Monopolization through Decentralization'. *Social Media & Society* 6(4) (2020): 1-13.

Boltanski, Luc, and Ève Chiapello. *The New Spirit of Capitalism*. Translated by Gregory Elliott (London: Verso, 2005).

Booking.com. 'Privacy Statement'. Booking.com, 2019. Available at https://www.booking.com/general.en-gb.html?label=37781_privacy-statement-anchor_v2-&tmpl=docs%2Fprivacy-policy&auth_success=1#policy-personal, [cited 6 February 2019].

Borak, Masha. 'Facial Recognition Is Used in China for Everything from Refuse Collection to Toilet Roll Dispensers and Its Citizens Are Growing Increasingly Alarmed, Survey Shows'. *South China Morning Post*, 27 January 2021.

Boullier, Dominique. *Sociologie du numérique* (Paris: Armand Colin, 2016).

Bousquet, Antoine. *The Eye of War: Military Perception from the Telescope to the Drone* (Minneapolis: University of Minnesota Press, 2018).

Brantingham, P Jeffrey. 'The Logic of Data Bias and Its Impact on Place-Based Predictive Policing'. *Ohio St. J. Crim. L.* 15 (2017): 473–86.

Brantingham, P. Jeffrey, Matthew Valasik, and George O. Mohler. 'Does Predictive Policing Lead to Biased Arrests? Results from a Randomized Controlled Trial'. *Statistics and Public Policy* 5(1) (2018): 1–6.

Brayne, Sarah, Alex Rosenblat, and danah boyd. 'Predictive Policing'. In Data & Civil Rights: A New Era of Policing and Justice. 2015. Available at http://www.datacivilrights.org/pubs/2015-1027/Predictive_Policing.pdf, [cited 28 July 2021].

Brown, Wendy. *Walled States, Waning Sovereignty* (New York: Zone Books, 2010).

Brown, Wendy. *Undoing the Demos: Neoliberalism's Stealth Revolution* (New York: Zone Books, 2015).

Brown, Wendy. 'Neoliberalism's Frankenstein: Authoritarian Freedom in Twenty-First Century "Democracies"'. *Critical Times: Interventions in Global Critical Theory* 1(1) (2018): 60–79.

Brown, Wendy. *In the Ruins of Neoliberalism: The Rise of Antidemocratic Politics in the West* (New York: Columbia University Press, 2019).

Bruns, Axel. *Are Filter Bubbles Real?* (Cambridge: Polity, 2019).

Bucher, Taina. *If ... Then: Algorithmic Power and Politics* (Oxford: Oxford University Press, 2018).

Bucher, Taina. 'The Right-Time Web: Theorizing the Kairologic of Algorithmic Media'. *New Media & Society* 22(9) (2020): 1699–1714.

Bueger, Christian. 'Making Things Known: Epistemic Practices, the United Nations, and the Translation of Piracy'. *International Political Sociology* 9(1) (2015): 1–18.

Bundesamt für Justiz. 'Federal Office of Justice Issues Fine against Facebook'. 2019. Available at https://www.bundesjustizamt.de/DE/Presse/Archiv/2019/20190702.html?nn=3449818, [cited 20 September 2019].

Bunz, Mercedes. 'The Calculation of Meaning: On the Misunderstanding of New Artificial Intelligence as Culture'. *Culture, Theory and Critique* 60(3–4) (2019): 264–78.

Buolamwini, Joy. 'Response: Racial and Gender Bias in Amazon Rekognition— Commercial AI System for Analyzing Faces'. Medium, 2019. Available at https://medium.com/@Joy.Buolamwini/response-racial-and-gender-bias-in-amazon-rekognition-commercial-ai-system-for-analyzing-faces-a289222eeced, [cited 22 October 2019].

Buolamwini, Joy, and Timnit Gebru. 'Gender Shades: Intersectional Accuracy Disparities in Commercial Gender Classification'. In Proceedings of the 1st Conference on Fairness, Accountability and Transparency, edited by Sorelle A. Friedler and Wilson Christo. *Proceedings of Machine Learning Research* 81: 77–91 (2018).

Bur, Jessie. 'Pentagon's "Rebel Alliance" Gets New Leadership'. C4ISRNET, 2019. Available at https://www.c4isrnet.com/management/leadership/2019/04/23/the-pentagons-tech-experts-get-a-new-leader/, [cited 30 October 2019].

Burns, Ryan. 'New Frontiers of Philanthro-Capitalism: Digital Technologies and Humanitarianism'. *Antipode* 51(4) (2019): 1101–22.

Burrell, Jenna. 'How the Machine "Thinks": Understanding Opacity in Machine Learning Algorithms'. *Big Data & Society* 3(1) (2016).

Burrell, Jenna, and Marion Fourcade. 'The Society of Algorithms'. *Annual Review of Sociology* 47 (2021): 213–37.

Butcher, Mike. 'Cambridge Analytica CEO Talks to Techcrunch About Trump, Hillary and the Future'. TechCrunch, 2017. Available at https://techcrunch.com/2017/11/06/cambridge-analytica-ceo-talks-to-techcrunch-about-trump-hilary-and-the-future/, [cited 28 February 2018].

Butler, Judith. *The Force of Nonviolence: An Ethico-Political Bind* (London: Verso, 2021).

Cadwalladr, Carole, and Emma J Graham-Harrison. 'Revealed: 50 Million Facebook Pro-files Harvested for Cambridge Analytica in Major Data Breach'. *The Guardian* (17 March 2018).

Cairncross, Frances. 'The Death of Distance'. *RSA Journal* 149(5502) (2002): 40–2.

Canguilhem, Georges. *The Normal and the Pathological* (New York: Zone Books, 1991).

Cardon, Dominique. *À quoi rêvent les algorithmes. Nos vies à l'heure des big data* (Paris: Seuil, 2015).

Casilli, Antonio. 'Automating Credulity. The Digital Labour Behind Fake News and Propaganda'. Einstein Forum Conference on Fake News and Digital Labour, 2019.

Cebula, Melanie. 'Airbnb, from Monolith to Microservices: How to Scale Your Architecture'. {Future}Stack 2017, 2017. Available at https://www.youtube.com/watch?v=N1BWMW9NEQc, [cited 15 November 2019].

Chamayou, Grégoire. *A Theory of the Drone* (New York: The New Press, 2015).

Chan, Janet, and Lyria Bennett Moses. 'Is Big Data Challenging Criminology?'. *Theoretical Criminology* 41(1) (2016): 21–39.

Chandola, Varun, Arindam Banerjee, and Vipin Kumar. 'Anomaly Detection: A Survey'. *ACM Computing Survey* 41(3) (2009): 1–58.

Cheney-Lippold, John. *We Are Data: Algorithms and the Making of Our Digital Selves* (New York: New York University Press, 2017).

China Law Translate. 'Quick Take: Facial Recognition Standards Overview'. 2021. Available at https://www.chinalawtranslate.com/en/quick-take-facial-recognition-standards-overview/, [cited 22 July 2021].

Chio, Clarence, and David Freeman. *Machine Learning and Security: Protecting Systems with Data and Algorithms* (Beijing: O'Reilly, 2018).

Choi, Hyunyoung, and Hal Varian. 'Predicting the Present with Google Trends'. *Economic Record* 88(s1) (2012): 2–9.

Chun, Wendy Hui Kyong. *Updating to Remain the Same: Habitual New Media* (Cambridge, MA: MIT Press, 2016).

Citton, Yves. *The Ecology of Attention* (Cambridge, UK: Polity, 2017).

City of Chicago. 'Crimes—2001 to Present'. City of Chicago, 2018. Available at https://data.cityofchicago.org/Public-Safety/Crimes-2001-to-present/ijzp-q8t2, [cited 30 July 2018].

CivicScape. 'CivicScape Github Repository'. CivicScape, 2018. Available at https://web.archive.org/web/20180912165306/https://github.com/CivicScape/CivicScape, [cited 30 July 2020].

Clark, Kendra. 'YouTube's Updated Terms of Service, Explained'. 2021. Available at https://www.thedrum.com/news/2021/05/25/youtube-s-updated-terms-service-explained, [cited 9 June 2021].

Clarke, John. 'Living with/in and without Neo-Liberalism'. *Focaal* 51 (2008): 135–47.

Cole, David. '"We Kill People Based on Metadata"'. *The New York Review of Books* (10 May 2014).

Coleman, E. Gabriella. 'High-Tech Guilds in the Era of Global Capital'. *Anthropology of Work Review* 22 (1) (2001): 28–32.

Coleman, E. Gabriella. *Coding Freedom: The Ethics and Aesthetics of Hacking* (Princeton, NJ: Princeton University Press, 2012).

Conger, Kate, and David E. Sanger. 'Pentagon Cancels a Disputed $10 Billion Technology Contract'. *The New York Times* (6 July 2021).

Couldry, Nick, and Ulises A. Mejias. *The Costs of Connection: How Data Is Colonizing Human Life and Appropriating It for Capitalism* (Stanford: Stanford University Press, 2019).

Craddock, R., D. Watson, and W. Saunders. 'Generic Pattern of Life and Behaviour Analysis'. Paper presented at the 2016 IEEE International Multi-Disciplinary Conference on Cognitive Methods in Situation Awareness and Decision Support (CogSIMA) (March 2016), 21–5.

Crawford, Kate. *The Atlas of AI* (New Haven, CT: Yale University Press, 2021).

Crawford, Kate. 'Can an Algorithm Be Agonistic? Ten Scenes from Life in Calculated Publics'. *Science, Technology, & Human Values* 41(1) (2015): 77–92.

Currie, T. C. 'Airbnb's 10 Takeaways from Moving to Microservices'. The New Stack, 2017. Available at https://thenewstack.io/airbnbs-10-takeaways-moving-microservices/, [cited 23 October 2019].

Currier, Cora, Glenn Greenwald, and Andrew Fishman. 'U.S. Government Designated Prominent Al Jazeera Journalist as "Member of Al Qaeda"'. The Intercept, 2015. Available at https://theintercept.com/2015/05/08/u-s-government-designated-prominent-al-jazeera-journalist-al-qaeda-member-put-watch-list/, [cited 5 July 2021].

Danaher, John. 'The Threat of Algocracy: Reality, Resistance and Accommodation'. *Philosophy & Technology* 29(3) (2016): 245–68.

Danaher, John, Michael J Hogan, Chris Noone, Rónán Kennedy, Anthony Behan, Aisling De Paor, Heike Felzmann, et al. 'Algorithmic Governance: Developing a Research Agenda through the Power of Collective Intelligence'. *Big Data & Society* 4(2) (2017): 1–21.

Daroczi, Gergely. *Mastering Data Analysis with R* (Birmingham, UK: Packt Publishing, 2015).

DARPA. 'Anomaly Detection at Multiple Scales'. Defense Advanced Research Projects Agency (DARPA), 2010. Available at https://www.fbo.gov/download/2f6/2f6289e99a0c04942bbd89ccf242fb4c/DARPA-BAA-11-04_ADAMS.pdf, [cited 26 February 2016].

Davenport, Thomas H, and John C Beck. *The Attention Economy: Understanding the New Currency of Business* (Boston: Harvard Business School Press, 2001).

Davidshofer, Stephan, Julien Jeandesboz, and Francesco Ragazzi. 'Technology and Security Practices: Situating the Technological Imperative'. In *International Political Sociology: Transversal Lines*, edited by Basaran Tugba, Didier Bigo, Emmanuel-Pierre Guittet, and R. B. J. Walker, 205–27 (London: Routledge, 2016).

Davis, Angela, and Eduardo Mendieta. *Abolition Democracy: Beyond Prisons, Torture, Empire: Interviews with Angela Davis* (New York: Seven Stories Press, 2005).

DCMS. 'Disinformation and "Fake News": Final Report'. Digital, Culture, Media, and Sport Committee (DCMS), House of Commons, 2019. Available at https://publications.parliament.uk/pa/cm201719/cmselect/cmcumeds/1791/1791.pdf, [cited 18 February 2019].

Deckler, Janosch. 'Germany Fines Facebook €2m for Violating Hate Speech Law'. Politico, 2019. Available at https://www.politico.eu/article/germany-fines-facebook-e2-million-for-violating-hate-speech-law/, [cited 20 September 2019].

Deep Mind. 'Ethics & Society'. 2019. Available at https://deepmind.com/applied/deepmind-ethics-society/, [cited 29 May 2019].

De Goede, Marieke. 'Fighting the Network: A Critique of the Network as a Security Technology'. *Distinktion: Journal of Social Theory* 13(3) (2012): 215–32.

De Goede, Marieke, and Gavin Sullivan. 'The Politics of Security Lists'. *Environment and Planning D: Society and Space* 34(1) (2016): 67–88.

Deleuze, Gilles. 'Postscript on the Societies of Control'. *October* 59(Winter) (1992): 3–7.

Dencik, Lina, Arne Hintz, Joanna Redden, and Emiliano Treré. 'Exploring Data Justice: Conceptions, Applications and Directions'. *Information, Communication & Society* 22(7) (2019): 873–81.

Denning, Peter J. 'Computer Science: The Discipline'. *Encyclopedia of Computer Science* 32(1) (2000): 9–23.

Der Derian, James. *Virtuous War: Mapping the Military-Industrial-Media-Entertainment Network* (Boulder, CO: Westview Press, 2005).

De Reuver, Mark, Carsten Sørensen, and Rahul C. Basole. 'The Digital Platform: A Research Agenda'. *Journal of Information Technology* 33(2) (2018): 124–35.

Desrosières, Alain. 'Masses, individus, moyennes: La statistique sociale au XIXe siècle'. *Hermès* 2(2) (1988): 41–66.

Desrosières, Alain. 'Du singulier au général. L'argument statistique entre la science et l'État' in *Cognition et information en société*, edited by B. Conein and Laurent Thévenot, 267–82 (Paris: Éditions de l'École des Hautes Études en Sciences Sociales, 1997).

Desrosières, Alain. *The Politics of Large Numbers: A History of Statistical Reasoning.* Translated by Camille Naish (Cambridge, MA: Harvard University Press, 2002).

Desrosières, Alain. 'Mapping the Social World: From Aggregates to Individual'. *Limn* 2 (2012).

Diakopoulos, Nicholas. 'Accountability in Algorithmic Decision Making'. *Communications of the ACM* 59(2) (2016): 56–62.

Dick, Stephanie. 'Artificial Intelligence'. *Harvard Data Science Review* 1(1) (2019).

Digital Humanitarian Network. 'Digital Humanitarian Network—History and Today'. 2021. Available at https://www.digitalhumanitarians.com/, [cited 9 June 2021].

D'Ignazio, Catherine, and Lauren F Klein. *Data Feminism* (Cambridge, MA: MIT Press, 2020).

Doffman, Zak. 'Buying Huawei Technology "Like Buying Chinese Fighter Planes", Shock Report Warns'. Forbes, 2019. Available at https://www.forbes.com/sites/zakdoffman/2019/09/25/buying-huawei-technology-like-buying-chinese-fighter-planes-shock-new-report-warns/, [cited 25 September 2019].

Domingos, Pedro. *The Master Algorithm: How the Quest for the Ultimate Learning Machine Will Remake Our World* (New York: Basic Books, 2015).

Doran, Will. 'How the Ushahidi Platform Works, and What Comes Next'. 2018. Available at https://www.ushahidi.com/blog/2018/11/05/how-the-ushahidi-platform-works-and-what-comes-next, [cited 9 June 2021].

Doshi-Velez, Finale, and Been Kim. 'Towards a Rigorous Science of Interpretable Machine Learning'. arXiv preprint arXiv:1702.08608 (2017).

Drott, Eric A. 'Music as a Technology of Surveillance'. *Journal of the Society for American Music* 12(3) (2018): 233–67.

Duguy, Michel. 'Poétique de la scène'. In *Philosophie de la scène*, edited by Michel Deguy, Thomas Dommange, Nicolas Doutey, Denis Guénoun, Esa Kirkkopelto, and Schirin Nowrousian, 145–53 (Besançon: Les Solitaires Intempestifs, 2010).

Dupré, John, and Regenia Gagnier. 'A Brief History of Work'. *Journal of Economic Issues* 30(2) (1996): 553–9.

Dwoskin, Elizabeth, Jeanne Whalen, and Regine Cabato. 'Content Moderators See It All – and Suffer'. *The Washington Post* (2018), A01.

Eberle, William, and Lawrence Holder. 'Anomaly Detection in Data Represented as Graphs'. *Intelligent Data Analysis* 11(6) (2007): 663–89.

Eckersley, Peter. 'How Good Are Google's New AI Ethics Principles?'. Electronic Frontier Foundation, 2018. Available at https://www.eff.org/deeplinks/2018/06/how-good-are-googles-new-ai-ethics-principles, [cited 23 January 2019].

Edwards, Jane. 'Defense Innovation Board Eyes Ethical Guidelines for Use of AI in Warfare'. ExecutiveGov, 2019. Available at https://www.executivegov.com/2019/01/defense-innovation-board-eyes-ethical-guidelines-for-use-of-ai-in-warfare/, [cited 28 January 2019].

Edwards, Paul N. 'Infrastructure and Modernity: Force, Time, and Social Organization in the History of Sociotechnical Systems'. In *Modernity and Technology*, edited by Thomas J. Misa, Philip Brey, and Andrew Feenberg, 185–226 (Cambridge, MA: MIT Press, 2003).

Edwards, Paul N., Geoffrey C Bowker, Steven J Jackson, and Robin Williams. 'Introduction: An Agenda for Infrastructure Studies'. *Journal of the Association for Information Systems* 10(Special Issue) (2009):364–74.

Edwards, Paul N. *A Vast Machine: Computer Models, Climate Data, and the Politics of Global Warming* (Cambridge, Mass.: The MIT Press, 2010).

Edwards, Paul N, Steven J Jackson, Melissa K Chalmers, Geoffrey C Bowker, Christine L Borgman, David Ribes, Matt Burton, and Scout Calvert. 'Knowledge Infrastructures: Intellectual Frameworks and Research Challenges'. Deep Blue, 2013. Available at http://hdl.handle.net/2027.42/97552, [cited 28 July 2021].

Egbert, Simon, and Matthias Leese. *Criminal Futures: Predictive Policing and Everyday Police Work* (London: Routledge, 2021).

Epstein, Zach. 'Microsoft Says Its Racist Facial Recognition Tech Is Now Less Racist'. BGR, 2018. Available at https://bgr.com/2018/06/27/microsoft-facial-recognition-dark-skin-tone-improvements/, [cited 16 February 2019].

Erickson, Paul, Judy L. Klein, Lorraine Daston, Rebecca Lemov, Thomas Sturm, and Michael D Gordin. *How Reason Almost Lost Its Mind: The Strange Career of Cold War Rationality* (Chicago: University of Chicago Press, 2013).

eu-LISA. 'Artificial Intelligence in the Operational Management of Large-Scale IT Systems'. eu-LISA, 2020. Available at https://www.eulisa.europa.eu/Publications/Reports/AI%20in%20the%20OM%20of%20Large-scale%20IT%20Systems.pdf, [cited 8 October 2020].

European Commission. 'Proposal for a Regulation Laying Down Harmonised Rules on Artificial Intelligence'. 2021. Available at https://eur-lex.europa.eu/legal-content/EN/TXT/?qid=1623335154975&uri=CELEX%3A52021PC0206, [cited 26 July 2021].

European Commission's High-Level Expert Group on Artificial Intelligence. 'Draft Ethics Guidelines for Trustworthy AI'. 2018. Available at https://ec.europa.eu/digital-single-market/en/news/draft-ethics-guidelines-trustworthy-ai, [cited 28 January 2019].

European Commission's High-Level Expert Group on Artificial Intelligence. 'Ethics Guidelines for Trustworthy AI'. 2019. Available at https://ec.europa.eu/digital-single-market/en/news/ethics-guidelines-trustworthy-ai, [cited 28 May 2019].

European Economic and Social Committee. 'The Ethics of Big Data: Balancing Economic Benefits and Ethical Questions of Big Data in the EU Policy Context'. EESC, 2017. Available at https://www.eesc.europa.eu/resources/docs/qe-02-17-159-en-n.pdf, [cited 19 January 2019].

European External Action Service. 'EU vs Disinfo'. East StratCom Task Force, 2019. Available at https://euvsdisinfo.eu/news/, [cited 29 September 2019].

European Parliament. 'What If Algorithms Could Abide by Ethical Principles?'. European Parliament, 2018. Available at http://www.europarl.europa.eu/RegData/etudes/ATAG/2018/624267/EPRS_ATA(2018)624267_EN.pdf, [cited 3 May 2019].

European Space Agency. 'DroneAI Solution for Humanitarian and Emergency Situations'. 2021. Available at https://business.esa.int/projects/droneAI, [cited 9 June 2021].

Ewald, François. 'Omnes et singulatim. After Risk'. *The Carceral* 7 (2011): 77–107.

Facebook. 'Community Standards'. 2019. Available at https://en-gb.facebook.com/communitystandards/, [cited 16 September 2019].

Facebook. 'Itaú'. 2021. Available at https://www.facebook.com/business/success/2-itau, [cited 5 July 2021].

Facebook. 'NetzDG Transparency Report'. Facebook, January 2019. Available at https://www.facebook.com/help/1057152381103922, [cited 10 June 2019].

Facebook Files. 'Hate Speech and Anti-Migrant Posts: Facebook's Rules'. *The Guardian*, 2017. Available at https://www.theguardian.com/news/gallery/2017/may/24/hate-speech-and-anti-migrant-posts-facebooks-rules, [cited 15 October 2019].

Fang, Lee. 'Google Won't Renew Its Drone AI Contract, but It May Still Sign Future Military AI Contract'. *The Intercept*, 2018. Available at https://theintercept.com/2018/06/01/google-drone-ai-project-maven-contract-renew/, [cited 1 June 2019].

Fang, Lee. 'Google Hired Gig Economy Workers to Improve Artificial Intelligence in Controversial Drone-Targeting Project'. *The Intercept*, 2019. Available at https://theintercept.com/2019/02/04/google-ai-project-maven-figure-eight/, [cited 1 June 2019].

Fanon, Frantz. Conduits of Confession in North Africa (2). In *Alienation and Freedom*, edited by Jean Khalfa, and Robert J. C. Young, 413–16 (London: Bloombury, 2018).

Fassin, Didier. *Humanitarian Reason: A Moral History of the Present* (Berkeley: University of California Press, 2011).

FAT-ML. 'Fairness, Accountability, and Transparency in Machine Learning'. 2019. Available at https://www.fatml.org/, [cited 29 November 2019].

Federal Trade Commission. 'Complaint against Cambridge Analytica, LLC, a Corporation. Docket No. 9383'. 2019. Available at https://www.ftc.gov/system/files/documents/cases/182_3107_cambridge_analytica_administrative_complaint_7-24-19.pdf, [cited 5 December 2020].

Federal Trade Commission. 'Statement of Chairman Joe Simons and Commissioners Noah Joshua Phillips and Christine S. Wilson in *Re Facebook, Inc.'*. 2019. Available at https://www.ftc.gov/public-statements/2019/07/statement-chairman-joe-simons-commissioners-noah-joshua-phillips-christine, [cited 5 December 2020].

Federici, Silvia. 'Social Reproduction Theory. History, Issues and Present Challenges'. *Radical Philosophy* 2.04(Spring) (2019): 55–7.

Feldstein, Steven. 'The Global Expansion of AI Surveillance'. Carnegie Endowment for International Peace, 2019. Available at https://carnegieendowment.org/files/WP-Feldstein-AISurveillance_final1.pdf, [cited 23 November 2019].

Ferguson, Andrew Guthrie. *The Rise of Big Data Policing: Surveillance, Race, and the Future of Law Enforcement* (New York: New York University Press, 2019).

Fisher, Anna Watkins. 'User Be Used: Leveraging the Play in the System'. *Discourse* 36(3) (2014): 383–99.

Fisher, Christine. 'Facebook Increases Pay for Contractors and Content Moderators'. 2019. Available at https://www.engadget.com/2019/05/13/facebook-increases-contractor-content-moderator-pay/, [cited 14 October 2019].

FISWG. 'Facial Identification Scientific Working Group'. 2021. Available at https://fiswg.org/index.htm, [cited 21 May 2021].

Fitzsimmons, Seth. 'Fast, Powerful, and Practical: New Technology for Aerial Imagery in Disaster Response'. 2018. Available at https://www.hotosm.org/updates/new-technology-for-aerial-imagery-in-disaster-response/, [cited 9 June 2021].

Floridi, Luciano. *The Fourth Revolution: How the Infosphere Is Reshaping Human Reality* (Oxford: Oxford University Press, 2014).

Floridi, Luciano. 'Soft Ethics, the Governance of the Digital and the General Data Protection Regulation'. *Philosophical Transactions of the Royal Society A: Mathematical, Physical and Engineering Sciences* 376(2133) (2018).

Fortunati, Leopoldina. 'For a Dynamic and Post-Digital History of the Internet: A Research Agenda'. *Internet Histories* 1(1–2) (2017): 180–7.

Foucault, Michel. *Power/Knowledge. Selected Interviews & Other Writings 1992-1977*. Edited by Colin Gordon (Brighton: Harvester, 1980).

Foucault, Michel. 'Questions of Method'. In *The Foucault Effect. Studies in Governmentality*, edited by Graham Burchell, Colin Gordon, and Peter Miller, 73–86 (Chicago: University of Chicago Press, 1991).

Foucault, Michel. *Discipline and Punish: The Birth of the Prison* (London: Penguin, 1991 [1977]).

Foucault, Michel. 'Omnes et singulatim: Toward a Critique of "Political Reason"'. In *Power. Essential Works of Foucault 1954-1984*, edited by James D. Faubion, 298–325 (London: Penguin, 2000).

Foucault, Michel. *Security, Territory, Population. Lectures at the Collège de France, 1977–78* (Basingstoke: Palgrave, 2007).

Foucault, Michel. *The Birth of Biopolitics: Lectures at the Collège de France, 1978–79* (Basingstoke: Palgrave Macmillan, 2008).

Foucault, Michel. *Wrong-Doing, Truth-Telling: The Function of Avowal in Justice* (Chicago: University of Chicago Press, 2014).

Foucault, Michel. *About the Beginning of the Hermeneutics of the Self. Lectures at Darmouth College, 1980*. Translated by Graham Burchell. (Chicago: Chicago University Press, 2016).

Fourcade, Marion, and Jeffrey Gordon. 'Learning Like a State: Statecraft in the Digital Age'. *Journal of Law and Political Economy* 1(1) (2020): 78–108.

FRA. 'Facial Recognition Technology: Fundamental Rights Considerations in the Context of Law Enforcement'. European Union Agency for Fundamental Rights (FRA), 2019. Available at https://fra.europa.eu/en/publication/2019/facial-recognition-technology-fundamental-rights-considerations-context-law, [cited 16 April 2020].

Freeman, David. 'Data Science vs. the Bad Guys: Defending LinkedIn from Fraud and Abuse'. SlideShare, 2015. Available at https://www.slideshare.net/DavidFreeman14/data-science-vs-the-bad-guys-defending-linkedin-from-fraud-and-abuse, [cited 22 October 2019].

Fry, Hannah. *Hello World: How to Be Human in the Age of the Machine* (New York: W. W. Norton, 2018).

Fuchs, Christian. 'The Digital Labour Theory of Value and Karl Marx in the Age of Facebook, YouTube, Twitter, and Weibo'. In *Reconsidering Value and Labour in the Digital Age*, edited by Eran Fisher, and Christian Fuchs, 26–41 (Basingstoke: Palgrave Macmillan, 2015).

Fuchs, Christian. 'Günther Anders' Undiscovered Critical Theory of Technology in the Age of Big Data Capitalism'. *tripleC: Communication, Capitalism & Critique* 15(2) (2017): 582–611.

Fuchs, Christian, and Sebastian Sevignani. 'What Is Digital Labour? What Is Digital Work? What's Their Difference? And Why Do These Questions Matter for Understanding Social Media?'. *tripleC: Communication, Capitalism & Critique* 11(2) (2013): 237–93.

Fuller, Jacquelline, and Jeff Dean. 'Here Are the Grantees of the Google AI Impact Challenge'. 2019. Available at https://crisisresponse.google/, [cited 9 March 2021].

Fumagalli, Andrea, Stefano Lucarelli, Elena Musolino, and Giulia Rocchi. 'Digital Labour in the Platform Economy: The Case of Facebook'. *Sustainability* 10(6) (2018).

Gago, Verónica. *Feminist International: How to Change Everything* (London: Verso, 2020).

Galison, Peter. 'The Ontology of the Enemy: Norbert Wiener and the Cybernetic Vision'. *Critical Inquiry* 21(1) (1994): 228–66.

Garmark, Sten, Dariusz Dziuk, Owen Smith, Lars Christian Olofsson, and Nikolaus Toumpelis. 'Cadence-Based Playlists Management System', Spotify AB Publisher. United States Patent Office, 2015.

Gawer, Annabelle, ed. *Platforms, Markets and Innovation* (Cheltenham: Edward Elgar, 2011).

GCHQ. 'HIMR Data Mining Research Problem Book'. Snowden Archive, 2011. Available at https://edwardsnowden.com/wp-content/uploads/2016/02/Problem-Book-Redacted.pdf, [cited 27 April 2016].

GCHQ. 'GCHQ Analytic Cloud Challenges'. 2012. Available at https://search.edwardsnowden.com/docs/GCHQAnalyticCloudChallenges2015-09-25nsadocs, [cited 20 February 2016].

General Data Protection Regulation. 'Regulation (EU) 2016/679 of the European Parliament and of the Council of 27 April 2016 on the Protection of Natural Persons with Regard to the Processing of Personal Data and on the Free Movement of Such Data, and Repealing Directive 95/46/EC'. *Official Journal of the European Union*, 2016. Available at https://eur-lex.europa.eu/, [cited 25 November 2019].

Gibson, Clay, Will Shapiro, Santiago Gil, Ian Anderson, Mgreth Mpossi, Oguz Semerci, and Scott Wolf. 'Methods and Systems for Session Clustering Based on User Experience, Behavior, and Interactions', Spotify AB Publisher. Unites States Patent Office, 2017.

Gillespie, Tarleton. 'The Politics of "Platforms"'. *New Media & Society* 12(3) (2010): 347–64.

Gillespie, Tarleton. 'Governance of and by Platforms'. In *Handbook of Social Media*, edited by Jean Burgess, Thomas Poell, and Alice Marwick, 254–78 (London: Sage 2017).

Gillespie, Tarleton. *Custodians of the Internet: Platforms, Content Moderation, and the Hidden Decisions that Shape Social Media* (New Haven: Yale University Press, 2018).

Gillespie, Tarleton. 'The Relevance of Algorithms'. In *Media Technologies: Essays on Communication, Materiality, and Society*, edited by Tarleton Gillespie, Pablo J. Boczkowski, and Kirsten A. Foot, 167–93 (Cambridge, MA: MIT Press, 2014).

Gilmore, Ruth Wilson. 'Abolition Geography and the Problem of Innocence'. In *Futures of Black Radicalism*, edited by Theresa Gaye Johnson and Alex Lubin, 300–23 (London: Verso, 2017).

Gitelman, Lisa. *Raw Data Is an Oxymoron.* (Cambridge, MA: MIT Press, 2013).

Goldhaber, Michael H. 'Attention Shoppers!'. *Wired* 2019(23) (1997).

Goldstein, Brett Jonathan, and Maggie Kate King. 'Rare Event Forecasting System and Method'. Civicscape, LLC Publisher, United States Patent Office, 2018.

Goldstein, Markus, and Seiichi Uchida. 'A Comparative Evaluation of Unsupervised Anomaly Detection Algorithms for Multivariate Data'. *PloS One* 11(4) (2016): e0152173.

Gonzalez, Ana Lucia. 'The "Microworkers" Making Your Digital Life Possible'. 2019. Available at https://www.bbc.co.uk/news/business-48881827, [cited 9 June 2021].

Goodman, Bryce, and Seth Flaxman. 'European Union Regulations on Algorithmic Decision-Making and a "Right to Explanation"'. *AI Magazine* 38(3) (2017): 50–7.

Google. 'Helping People Access Trusted Information and Resources in Critical Moments'. 2021. Available at https://crisisresponse.google/, [cited 5 July 2021].

Google. 'Removals under the Network Enforcement Law'. Google, 2018. Available at https://transparencyreport.google.com/netzdg/youtube, [cited 22 February 2019].

Goriunova, Olga. The Digital Subject: People as Data as Persons'. *Theory, Culture & Society* 36(6) (2019): 125–45.

Gourley, Bob, and Alex Olesker. 'To Protect and Serve with Big Data'. CTOlabs, 2013. Available at https://apo.org.au/node/34913, [cited 27 December 2015].

Graham, Mark, and Mohammad Amir Anwar. 'The Global Gig Economy: Towards a Planetary Labour Market?'. *First Monday* 24(4) (2019).

Graham, Stephen, and Nigel Thrift. 'Out of Order: Understanding Repair and Maintenance'. *Theory, Culture & Society* 24(3) (2007): 1–25.

Gray, Jonathan. 'Data Witnessing: Attending to Injustice with Data in Amnesty International's Decoders Project'. *Information, Communication & Society* 22(7) (2019): 971–91.

Giles Greenway, Pybus, Jennifer; Cote, Mark, and Blanke, Tobias. 'Research on Online Digital Cultures-Community Extraction and Analysis by Markov and k-Means Clustering'. In *Personal Analytics and Privacy: An Individual and Collective Perspective: 1st International Workshop*, PAP 2017, Held in Conjunction with ECML PKDD 2017, Skopje, Macedonia, September 18, 2017, Revised Selected Papers, edited by Riccardo Guidotti, Anna Monreale, Dino Pedreschi, and Serge Abiteboul, 110–21 (London: Springer Verlag, 2017).

Grewal, Paul. 'Suspending Cambridge Analytica and SCL Group from Facebook'. *Facebook News*, 2018. Available at https://about.fb.com/news/2018/03/suspending-cambridge-analytica/, [cited 7 December 2021].

Grossman, Lev. 'You—Yes, You—Are Time's Person of the Year'. 2006. Available at http://content.time.com/time/magazine/article/0,9171,1570810,00.html, [cited 5 November 2019].

Grothoff, Christian, and J. M. Porup. 'The NSA's SKYNET Program May Be Killing Thousands of Innocent People'. Ars Technica, 2016. Available at http://arstechnica.co.uk/security/2016/02/the-nsas-skynet-program-may-be-killing-thousands-of-innocent-people/, [cited 21 June 2016].

GSMA. 'The Data Value Chain'. 2018. Available at https://www.gsma.com/publicpolicy/wp-content/uploads/2018/07/GSMA_Data_Value_Chain_June_2018.pdf, [cited 4 February 2019].

Gunning, David. 'Explainable Artificial Intelligence (XAI). Programme Update'. DARPA, 2017. Available at https://s3.documentcloud.org/documents/5794867/National-Security-Archive-David-Gunning-DARPA.pdf, [cited 29 October 2019].

Gurstein, Michael B. 'Open Data: Empowering the Empowered or Effective Data Use for Everyone?'. *First Monday* 16(2) (2011).

Guszcza, James, Iyad Rahwan, Will Bible, Manuel Cebrian, and Vic Katyal. 'Why We Need to Audit Algorithms'. *Harvard Business Review* (28 November 2018).

Gutiérrez, Miren. *Data Activism and Social Change* (Basingstoke: Palgrave, 2018).

Haggerty, Kevin D., and Richard V. Ericson. 'The Surveillant Assemblage'. *British Journal of Sociology* 51(4) (2000): 605–22.

Hall, Patrick, SriSatish Ambati, and Wen Phan. 'Ideas on Interpreting Machine Learning'. 2017. Available at https://www.oreilly.com/radar/ideas-on-interpreting-machine-learning/, [cited 9 June 2021].

Hamon, Dominic, Timo Burkard, and Arvind Jain. 'Predicting User Navigation Events'. Google. United States Patent Office, 2013.

Han, Byung-Chul. *The Expulsion of the Other: Society, Perception and Communication Today* (Cambridge, UK: Polity, 2018).

Haraway, Donna. *Simians, Cyborgs, and Women: The Reinvention of Nature* (New York: Routledge, 1991).

Haraway, Donna J. *Staying with the Trouble: Making Kin in the Chthulucene* (Durham, NC: Duke University Press, 2016).

Harcourt, Bernard E. *Against Prediction: Profiling, Policing, and Punishing in an Actuarial Age* (Chicago: University of Chicago Press, 2008).

Harcourt, Bernard E. *Exposed: Desire and Disobedience in the Digital Age* (Cambridge, MA: Harvard University Press, 2015).

Harvey, Adam, and Jules LaPlace. 'Microsoft Celeb'. 2020. Available at https://exposing.ai/msceleb/, [cited 1 June 2021].

Hayles, N. Katherine. *How We Think: Digital Media and Contemporary Technogenesis* (Chicago: University of Chicago Press, 2012).

Hayles, N. Katherine. *Unthought: The Power of the Cognitive Nonconscious* (Chicago: University of Chicago Press, 2017).

Heldt, Amélie Pia. 'Reading between the Lines and the Numbers: An Analysis of the First NetzDG Reports'. *Internet Policy Review* 8(2) (2019).

Helmond, Anne. 'The Platformization of the Web: Making Web Data Platform Ready'. *Social Media & Society* 1(2) (2015): 1–11.

Helmond, Anne, David B. Nieborg, and Fernando N. van der Vlist. 'Facebook's Evolution: Development of a Platform-as-Infrastructure'. *Internet Histories* 3(2) (2019): 123–46.

Herrman, John. 'Cambridge Analytica and the Coming Data Bust'. *The New York Times* (10 April 2018).

Hey, Tony, Stewart Tansley, and Kristin M Tolle. *The Fourth Paradigm: Data-Intensive Scientific Discovery* (Redmond, WA: Microsoft Research, 2009).

Hibou, Béatrice. *The Bureaucratization of the World in the Neoliberal Era*. Translated by Andrew Brown. (New York: Palgrave Macmillan, 2015).

Hildebrandt, Mireille. *Law for Computer Scientists and Other Folk* (Oxford: Oxford University Press, 2020).

Hill, Kashmir. 'The Secretive Company That Might End Privacy as We Know It'. *The New York Times* (6 June 2021).

Hinchcliffe, Dion. 'Comparing Amazon's and Google's Platform-as-a-Service Offerings'. 2008. Available at https://www.zdnet.com/article/comparing-amazons-and-googles-platform-as-a-service-paas-offerings/, [cited 23 October 2019].

Hindess, Barry. 'Citizenship in the International Management of Populations'. *American Behavioral Scientist* 43(9) (2000): 1486–97.

Hindess, Barry. 'Politics as Government: Michel Foucault's Analysis of Political Reason'. *Alternatives: Global, Local, Political* 30(4) (2005): 389–413.

Hoffmann, Anna Lauren. 'Where Fairness Fails: Data, Algorithms, and the Limits of Antidiscrimination Discourse'. *Information, Communication & Society* 22(7) (2019): 900–15.

Holmqvist, Caroline. *Policing Wars: On Military Intervention in the Twenty-First Century* (Basingstoke: Palgrave, 2016).

Home Office. 'Operational Case for Bulk Powers'. UK Government, 2016. Available at https://www.gov.uk/government/publications/investigatory-powers-bill-overarching-documents, [cited 1 March 2016].

Hong, Sun-ha. *Technologies of Speculation: The Limits of Knowledge in a Data-Driven Society* (New York: New York University Press, 2020).

Honig, Bonnie. *Emergency Politics: Paradox, Law, Democracy* (Princeton: Princeton University Press, 2009).

Honig, Bonnie. *Public Things: Democracy in Disrepair* (New York: Fordham University Press, 2017).

Hoppensted, Max. 'Zu Besuch in Facebooks Neuem Löschzentrum, das gerade den Betrieb aufnimmt'. Vice, 2017. Available at https://www.vice.com/de/article/qv37dv/zu-besuch-in-facebooks-neuem-loschzentrum-das-gerade-den-betrieb-aufnimmt, [cited 27 September 2019].

Horkheimer, Max. *Critique of Instrumental Reason* (London: Verso, 2013).

Hosein, Gus, and Carly Nyst. *Aiding Surveillance. An Exploration of How Development and Humanitarian Aid Initiatives Are Enabling Surveillance in Developing Countries* (London: Privacy International, 2013).

House of Commons. 'Investigatory Powers Bill'. Volume 611, 2016. Available at https://hansard.parliament.uk/Commons/2016-06-07/debates/16060732000001/Investigatory PowersBill, [cited 1 August 2016].

House of Commons Science and Technology Committee. 'Algorithms in Decision-Making. Fourth Report of the Session 2017-2019'. House of Commons, 2018. Available at https://publications.parliament.uk/pa/cm201719/cmselect/cmsctech/351/351.pdf, [cited 20 June 2018].

Hulaud, Stéphane. 'Identification of Taste Attributes from an Audio Signal'. Spotify AB Publisher. United States Patent Office, 2018.

Human Rights Watch. 'Germany: Flawed Social Media Law'. 2018. Available at https://www.hrw.org/news/2018/02/14/germany-flawed-social-media-law, [cited 8 September 2019].

Human Rights Watch. 'UN Shared Rohingya Data without Informed Consent'. 2021. Available at https://www.hrw.org/news/2021/06/15/un-shared-rohingya-data-without-informed-consent, [cited 15 June 2021].

Huysmans, Jef. *The Politics of Insecurity: Fear, Migration and Asylum in the EU* (London: Routledge, 2006).

Huysmans, Jef. 'What's in an Act? On Security Speech Acts and Little Security Nothings'. *Security Dialogue* 42(4–5) (2011): 371–83.

Huysmans, Jef. *Security Unbound: Enacting Democratic Limits* (London: Routledge, 2014).

IBM. 'Everyday Ethics for Artificial Intelligence. A Practical Guide for Designers and Developers'. IBM, 2018. Available at https://www.ibm.com/watson/assets/duo/pdf/everydayethics.pdf, [cited 10 February 2019].

IBM. 'Hybrid Data Management'. n.d. Available at https://www.ibm.com/analytics/data-management, [cited 4 February 2019].

IBM. 'Written Evidence'. House of Commons, 2017. Available at http://data.parliament.uk/WrittenEvidence/CommitteeEvidence.svc/EvidenceDocument/Science%20and%20Technology/Algorithms%20in%20decisionmaking/written/71691.html, [cited 2 June 2019].

ICO. 'Facebook Ireland Ltd. Monetary Penalty Notice'. 2018. Available at https://ico.org.uk/media/2259364/facebook-noi-redacted.pdf, [cited 19 February 2019].

ICO. 'Letter to UK Parliament. ICO Investigation into Use of Personal Information and Political Influence'. 2020. Available at https://ico.org.uk/media/action-weve-taken/2618383/20201002_ico-o-ed-l-rtl-0181_to-julian-knight-mp.pdf, [cited 5 December 2020].

ICO. 'ICO Issues Provisional View to Fine Clearview AI Inc over £17 Million'. 2021. Available at https://ico.org.uk/about-the-ico/news-and-events/news-and-blogs/2021/11/ico-issues-provisional-view-to-fine-clearview-ai-inc-over-17-million/, [cited 30 November 2021].

IEEE. 'Ethically Aligned Design. A Vision for Prioritizing Human Wellbeing with Artificial Intelligence and Autonomous Systems'. IEEE Global Initiative on Ethics of Autonomous and Intelligent Sytems, 2019. Available at https://standards.ieee.org/industry-connections/ec/autonomous-systems.html, [cited 28 May 2019].

ILO. *Digital Refugee Livelihoods and Decent Work. Towards Inclusion in a Fairer Digital Economy*. (Geneva: International Labour Organization 2021).

Information Is Beautiful. 'How Much Do Music Artists Earn Online?'. 2010. Available at https://informationisbeautiful.net/2010/how-much-do-music-artists-earn-online/, [cited 19 July 2021].

Instagram. 'What's the Difference between NetzDG and Instagram's Community Guidelines?'. 2019. Available at https://help.instagram.com/1787585044668150, [cited 18 October 2019].

Institute of Mathematics and its Applications. 'Written Evidence Submitted by the Institute of Mathematics and Its Applications (Alg0028)'. UK House of Commons, Science and Technology Committee, 2017. Available at http://data.parliament.uk/writtenevidence/committeeevidence.svc/evidencedocument/science-and-technology-committee/algorithms-in-decisionmaking/written/68989.pdf, [cited 18 December 2018].

International Committee of the Red Cross (ICRC), and Privacy International. 'The Humanitarian Metadata Problem: "Doing No Harm" in the Digital Era'. 2018.

Introna, Lucas D. 'Algorithms, Governance, and Governmentality: On Governing Academic Writing'. *Science, Technology & Human Values* 41(1) (2015): 17–49.

Irani, Lilly. 'The Cultural Work of Microwork'. *New Media & Society* 17(5) (2015): 720–39.

Irani, Lilly, and M Six Silberman. 'Turkopticon: Interrupting Worker Invisibility in Amazon Mechanical Turk'. Paper presented at the SIGCHI Conference on Human Factors in Computing Systems, Paris, France, 27 April 27–2 May 2013.

Isaac, Mike. 'After Facebook's Scandals, Mark Zuckerberg Says He'll Shift Focus to Private Sharing'. *The New York Times* (6 March 2019).

Isin, Engin F. *Citizens without Frontiers* (London: Bloomsbury, 2012).

Jabri, Vivienne. *The Postcolonial Subject: Claiming Politics/Governing Others in Late Modernity* (London: Routledge, 2012).

Jackiewicz, Agata. 'Outils notionnels pour l'analyse des controverses'. *Questions de communication* 31 (2017).

Jacobs, Adam. 'The Pathologies of Big Data'. *Communications of the ACM* 52(8) (2009): 36–44.

Jacobsen, Katja Lindskov. *The Politics of Humanitarian Technology: Good Intentions, Unintended Consequences and Insecurity* (London: Routledge, 2015).

Janert, Philipp K. *Data Analysis with Open Source Tools* (Cambridge, MA: O'Reilly Media, 2010).

Jaume-Palasi, Lorena, and Matthias Spielkamp. 'Ethics and Algorithmic Processes for Decision Making and Decision Support'. AlgorithmWatch, 2017. Available at https://algorithmwatch.org/en/publication/ethics-and-algorithmic-processes-for-decision-making-and-decision-support/, [cited 3 March 2019].

Jehan, Tristan, Dariusz Dziuk, Gustav Söderström, Mateo Rando, and Nicola Montecchio. 'Identifying Media Content'. Google Patents. United States Patent Office, 2018.

Johnson, Chris. 'From Idea to Execution: Spotify's Discover Weekly'. 2015. Available at https://www.slideshare.net/MrChrisJohnson/from-idea-to-execution-spotifys-discover-weekly/, [cited 27 July 2021].

Jordan, Tim. *The Digital Economy* (Cambridge, UK: Polity, 2019).

Kane, Carolyn L. *High-Tech Trash.* (Berkeley: University of California Press, 2020).

Kaplan, Josiah, and Steve Morgan. 'Predicting Displacement. Using Predictive Analytics to Build a Better Future for Displaced Children'. Save the Children International, 2018. Available at https://resourcecentre.savethechildren.net/node/14290/pdf/predicting_displacement_report_-_save_the_children_mdi.pdf, [cited 8 December 2020].

Kareem v Haspel. 'Memorandum Opinion'. Civil Action No. 17-581, 2019. Available at https://www.casemine.com/judgement/us/5d8cc16c342cca2f5e1c3bdd, [cited 11 November 2019].

Kareem v Haspel. 'Appeal from the United States District Court for the District of Columbia. Opinion for the Court Filed by Circuit Judge Henderson'. United States Court of Appeals, Civil Action No. 19-5328, 2021. Available at https://www.cadc.uscourts.gov/internet/opinions.nsf/0/71B968A8A2A1326E8525865E00542FAA/$file/19-5328-1880258.pdf, [cited 11 November 2019].

Karpf, David. 'On Digital Disinformation and Democratic Myths'. Mediawell, 2019. Available at https://mediawell.ssrc.org/expert-reflections/on-digital-disinformation-and-democratic-myths/, [cited 14 December 2020].

Kates, Graham. '"Far from an Honest Mistake": Facebook Accused of Inflating Ad Data'. CBS News, 2018. Available at https://www.cbsnews.com/news/facebook-committed-fraud-lawsuit-claims/, [cited 18 November 2019].

Katzenbach, Christian, and Lena Ulbricht. 'Algorithmic Governance'. *Internet Policy Review* 8(4) (2019). https://policyreview.info/concepts/algorithmic-governance.

Kaur, Harmanpreet, Harsha Nori, Samuel Jenkins, Rich Caruana, Hanna Wallach, and Jennifer Wortman Vaughan. 'Interpreting Interpretability: Understanding Data Scientists' Use of Interpretability Tools for Machine Learning'. In Proceedings of the 2020 CHI Conference on Human Factors in Computing Systems, 1–14 (Honolulu, HI: Association for Computing Machinery, 2020).

Kelty, Christopher M. 'Hacking the Social?'. In *Inventing the Social*, edited by Noortje Marres, Michael Guggenheim, and Alex Wilkie (Manchester: Mattering Press, 2018).

Kitchin, Rob. 'Big Data, New Epistemologies and Paradigm Shifts'. *Big Data & Society* 1(1) (2014).

Klipp, Liz. 'Prometeo Wins Call for Code 2019 Global Challenge'. 2019. Available at https://developer.ibm.com/callforcode/blogs/call-for-code-2019-finalist-prometeo/, [cited 12 June 2021].

Klosowski, Thorin. 'Personalization Has Failed Us. Curation by Algorithm Hasn't Lived up to Expectations'. *The New York Times* (5 November 2019).

Knight, Will. 'The Dark Secret at the Heart of AI'. *MIT Technology Review*, 2017. Available at https://www.technologyreview.com/s/604087/the-dark-secret-at-the-heart-of-ai/, [cited 30 October 2019].

Knuth, Donald E. 'Computer Programming as an Art. 1974 ACM Turing Award Lecture'. *Communications of the ACM* 17(12) (1974): 667–73.

König, Pascal D. 'Dissecting the Algorithmic Leviathan: On the Socio-Political Anatomy of Algorithmic Governance'. *Philosophy & Technology* 33(3) (2020): 467–85.

Koselleck, Reinhart. *Sediments of Time: On Possible Histories.* Translated by Sean Franzel and Stefan-Ludwig Hoffmann (Stanford, CA: Stanford University Press, 2017).

Koul, Parul, and Chewy Shaw. 'We Built Google. This Is Not the Company We Want to Work For'. *The New York Times* (4 January 2021).

Kozlowska, Hanna. 'The Pivot to Video Was Based on a Lie, Lawsuit Alleges'. 2018. Available at https://qz.com/1427406/advertisers-say-facebook-inflated-video-metrics-even-further/, [cited 25 October 2019].

Krause, Till, and Hannes Grassegger. 'Inside Facebook'. *Süddeutsche Zeitung* (15 December 2016).

Kushner, Scott. 'The Instrumentalised User: Human, Computer, System'. *Internet Histories* 5(2) (2021): 154–70.

Kwet, Michael. 'Digital Colonialism: US Empire and the New Imperialism in the Global South'. *Race & Class* 60(4) (2019): 3–26.

Lafrance, Adrienne. 'Facebook and the New Colonialism'. *The Atlantic* 11 (February 2016).

Lakshanan, Ravie. 'China's New 500-Megapixel "Super Camera" Can Instantly Recognize You in a Crowd'. The next web, 2019. Available at https://thenextweb.com/security/2019/09/30/chinas-new-500-megapixel-super-camera-can-instantly-recognize-you-in-a-crowd/, [cited 20 October 2019].

Lalmas, Mounia. 'Engagement, Metrics and Personalisation: The Good, the Bad and the Ugly'. In Proceedings of the 27th ACM Conference on User Modeling, Adaptation and Personalization (Larnaca, Cyprus: ACM, 2019).

Lanier, Jaron. *Who Owns the Future?* (New York: Simon and Schuster, 2013).

Latour, Bruno. 'Gabriel Tarde and the End of the Social'. In *The Social in Question. New Bearings in History and the Social Sciences*, edited by Patrick Joyce, 117–32 (London: Routledge, 2002).

Latour, Bruno. 'From Realpolitik to Dingpolitik'. In *Making Things Public: Atmospheres of Democracy*, edited by Bruno Latour and Peter Weibel, 4–31 (Cambridge, MA: MIT Press, 2005).

Latour, Bruno. *Reassembling the Social: An Introduction to Actor-Network-Theory* (New York: Oxford University Press, 2005).

Latour, Bruno. 'An Attempt at a "Compositionist Manifesto"'. *New Literary History* 41(3) (2010): 471–90.

Latour, Bruno, Pablo Jensen, Tommaso Venturini, Sébastian Grauwin, and Dominique Boullier. '"The Whole Is Always Smaller Than Its Parts"—A Digital Test of Gabriel Tarde's Monads'. *British Journal of Sociology* 63(4) (2012): 590–615.

Lau, Tim. 'Predictive Policing Explained'. Brennan Center for Justice, 2020. Available at https://www.brennancenter.org/our-work/research-reports/predictive-policing-explained, [cited 4 May 2021].

Laurence, McFalls, and Mariella Pandolfi. 'The Enemy Live: A Genealogy'. In *War, Police and Assemblages of Intervention*, edited by Jan Bachmann, Colleen Bell, and Caroline Holmqvist (London: Routlege, 2014).

Leander, Anna. 'Sticky Security: The Collages of Tracking Device Advertising'. *European Journal of International Security* 4(3) (2019): 322–44.

Lee, Seungha. 'Coming into Focus: China's Facial Recognition Regulations'. Center for Strategic and International Studies, 2020. https://www.csis.org/blogs/trustee-china-hand/coming-focus-chinas-facial-recognition-regulations [cited 28 November 2021].

Lehikoinen, Juha, and Ville Koistinen. 'In Big Data We Trust?'. *Interactions* 21(5) (2014): 38–41.

Lemieux, Cyril. 'À quoi sert l'analyse des controverses ?'. *Mil neuf cent. Revue d'histoire intellectuelle* 25(1) (2007): 191–212.

Liao, Shannon. 'Chinese Facial Recognition System Mistakes a Face on a Bus for a Jaywalker'. The Verge, 2018. Available at https://www.theverge.com/2018/11/22/18107885/china-facial-recognition-mistaken-jaywalker, [cited 23 November 2019].

Lin, Yu-Sheng, Zhe-Yu Liu, Yu-An Chen, Yu-Siang Wang, Hsin-Ying Lee, Yi-Rong Chen, Ya-Liang Chang, and Winston H. Hsu. 2020, 'xCos: An Explainable Cosine Metric for Face Verification Task'. arXiv preprint arXiv:2003.05383.

Liu, Chuncheng. 'Seeing Like a State, Enacting Like an Algorithm: (Re)Assembling Contact Tracing and Risk Assessment During the Covid-19 Pandemic'. *Science, Technology, & Human Values* (2021). doi.org/10.1177/01622439211021916

Liu, Mingyang. '人脸识别黑产:真人认证视频百元一套 [Face Recognition Black Production: A Set of One Hundred Yuan for Real-Person Authentication Video]'. 2021. Available at http://www.bjnews.com.cn/detail/161824564315305.html, [cited 28 July 2021].

Liu, Xing, Jiqiang Liu, Sencun Zhu, Wei Wang, and Xiangliang Zhang. 'Privacy Risk Analysis and Mitigation of Analytics Libraries in the Android Ecosystem'. *IEEE Transactions on Mobile Computing* 19(5) (2019): 1184–99.

Liu, Yuxiu, and Wu Ren. '法学教授的一次维权:人脸识别的风险超出你所想 [a Rights Defense by a Law Professor: The Risks of Face Recognition Are Beyond Your Imagination]'. *The Paper* (21 October 2020).

LLE ONE, LLC, et al. v Facebook, Inc. 'Plaintiffs' Motion for Preliminary Approval and to Direct Notice of Settlement'. United States District Court for the Northern District of California, Case No. 4:16-cv-06232-JSW, 2019. Available at https://assets.documentcloud.org/documents/6455498/Facebooksettlement.pdf, [cited 25 December 2019].

Lodato, Thomas James, and Carl DiSalvo. 'Issue-Oriented Hackathons as Material Participation'. *New Media & Society* 18(4) (2016): 539–57.

Lorenzini, Daniele, and Martina Tazzioli. 'Confessional Subjects and Conducts of Non-Truth: Foucault, Fanon, and the Making of the Subject'. *Theory, Culture & Society* 35(1) (2018): 71–90.

Luchs, Inga. 'Free Basics by Facebook. An Interview with Nishant Shah'. *Spheres: Journal for Digital Cultures* 3 (2016): 1–8.

Lum, Kristian, and William Isaac. 'To Predict and Serve?'. *Significance* 13(5) (2016): 14–19.

Lupton, Deborah. *The Quantified Self* (Cambridge, UK: Polity, 2016).

Lyon, David. *Surveillance after Snowden* (Cambridge, UK: Polity, 2015).

McAfee, Andrew, and Erik Brynjolfsson. *Machine, Platform, Crowd: Harnessing Our Digital Future* (New York: WW Norton & Company, 2017).

McCarthy, Kieren. 'Facebook Puts 1.5B Users on a Boat from Ireland to California'. The Register, 2018. Available at https://www.theregister.co.uk/2018/04/19/facebook_shifts_users/, [cited 7 March 2019].

McCue, Colleen. *Data Mining and Predictive Analysis: Intelligence Gathering and Crime Analysis*, 2nd edition (Oxford: Butterworth-Heinemann, 2015).

McEntire, David A. *Introduction to Homeland Security: Understanding Terrorism with an Emergency Management Perspective*, 2nd edition (Hoboken, NJ: Wiley, 2019).

McGoey, Linsey. *The Unknowers. How Strategic Ignorance Rules the Word* (London: Zed, 2019).

McGranahan, Carole. 'Theorizing Refusal: An Introduction'. *Cultural Anthropology* 31(3) (2016): 319–25.

McIntyre, David P., and Mohan Subramaniam. 'Strategy in Network Industries: A Review and Research Agenda'. *Journal of Management* 35(6) (2009): 1494–1517.

Mackenzie, Adrian. *Machine Learners: Archaeology of a Data Practice* (Cambridge, MA: MIT Press, 2017).

McKinnon, John D. 'Pentagon Weighs Ending Jedi Cloud Project Amid Amazon Court Fight'. *Wall Street Journal* (10 May 2021).

Madianou, Mirca. 'Technocolonialism: Digital Innovation and Data Practices in the Humanitarian Response to Refugee Crises'. *Social Media & Society* 5(3) (2019): 1–13.

Madsen, Anders Koed, Mikkel Flyverbom, Martin Hilbert, and Evelyn Ruppert. 'Big Data: Issues for an International Political Sociology of Data Practices'. *International Political Sociology* 10(3) (2016): 275–96.

Marlow, Cameron Alexander, Dean Eckles, Brian Karrer, John Ugander, Lars Seren Backstrom, and Jon Kleinberg. 'Network-Aware Product Rollout in Online Social Networks', Facebook Inc. Publisher. United States Patent Office, 2013.

Marres, Noortje. *Material Participation: Technology, the Environment and Everyday Publics* (Basingstoke: Palgrave Macmillan, 2012).

Marres, Noortje. 'Why Map Issues? On Controversy Analysis as a Digital Method'. *Science, Technology, & Human Values* 40(5) (2015): 655–86.

Mattingly-Jordan, Sara R. 'Becoming a Leader in Global Ethics. Creating a Collaborative, Inclusive Path for Establishing Ethical Principles for Artificial Intelligence and Autonomous Systems'. IEEE, 2017. Available at https://standards.ieee.org/content/dam/ieee-standards/standards/web/documents/other/becoming_leader_global_ethics.pdf, [cited 20 July 2021].

Mayer-Schönberger, Viktor, and Kenneth Cukier. *Big Data: A Revolution That Will Transform How We Live, Work, and Think* (London: John Murray, 2013).

Mayer-Schönberger, Viktor, and Thomas Ramge. *Reinventing Capitalism in the Age of Big Data* (London: Basic Books, 2018).

Mbembe, Achille. *Politiques de l'inimitié* (Paris: La Découverte, 2016).

Mbembe, Achille. 'The Society of Enmity'. *Radical Philosophy* 2(1) (2016): 23–35.

Mbembe, Achille. *Critique of Black Reason* (Durham, NC: Duke University Press, 2017).

Meier, Patrick. *Digital Humanitarians: How Big Data Is Changing the Face of Humanitarian Response* (Boca Raton: CRC Press, 2015).

Menegus, Brian. 'Thousands of Google Employees Protest Company's Involvement in Pentagon AI Drone Program'. Gizmodo, 2018. Available at https://gizmodo.com/thousands-of-google-employees-protest-companys-involvem-1824988565, [cited 28 January 2019].

Meng, Wei, Ren Ding, Simon P. Chung, Steven Han, and Wenke Lee. 'The Price of Free: Privacy Leakage in Personalized Mobile in-Apps Ads'. In *Proceedings of the Symposium on Network and Distributed System Security* (San Diego, CA: NDSS, 2016).

Merler, Michele, Nalini Ratha, Rogerio S. Feris, and John R. Smith. 'Diversity in Faces'. arXiv preprint arXiv:1901.10436 (2019).

Metcalf, Jacob, Emanuel Moss, and danah boyd. 'Owning Ethics: Corporate Logics, Silicon Valley, and the Institutionalization of Ethics'. *Social Research: An International Quarterly* 86(2) (2019): 449–76.

Meunier, Axel, Donato Ricci, and Jonathan Gray. 'Algorithm Trouble'. In *A New AI Lexicon* (New York: AI Now Institute, 2022). Available at https://medium.com/a-new-ai-lexicon/a-new-ai-lexicon-algorithm-trouble-50312d985216, [cited 17 January 2022].

Mezzadra, Sandro. 'The Proliferation of Borders and the Right to Escape'. In *The Irregularization of Migration in Contemporary Europe: Detention, Deportation, Drowning*, edited by Yolande Jansen, Robin Celikates, and Joost de Bloois, 121–35. (London: Rowman & Littlefield, 2015).

Mezzadra, Sandro, and Brett Neilson. *The Politics of Operations: Excavating Contemporary Capitalism* (Durham, NC: Duke University Press, 2019).

Microsoft. 'Microsoft AI Principles'. 2019. Available at https://www.microsoft.com/en-us/ai/responsible-ai, [cited 30 October 2020].

Miller, Ben. 'Brett Goldstein Leaves Ekistic Ventures for Federal Post'. Government Technology, 2019. Available at https://www.govtech.com/biz/Brett-Goldstein-Leaves-Ekistic-Ventures-for-Federal-Post.html, [cited 30 October 2019].

Miller, Tim. 'Explanation in Artificial Intelligence: Insights from the Social Sciences'. *Artificial Intelligence* 267 (2019): 1–38.

Mitchell, Tom M. *Machine Learning*. (London: McGraw Hill, 1997).

Mittelstadt, Brent Daniel, Patrick Allo, Mariarosaria Taddeo, Sandra Wachter, and Luciano Floridi. 'The Ethics of Algorithms: Mapping the Debate'. *Big Data & Society* 3(2) (2016): 1–21.

Moghadam, Sepi Hejazi. 'Marian Croak's Vision for Responsible AI at Google'. 2021. Available at https://blog.google/technology/ai/marian-croak-responsible-ai/, [cited 30 June 2021].

Mol, Annemarie. *The Body Multiple: Ontology in Medical Practice* (Durham, NC: Duke University Press, 2002).

Morozov, Evgeny. 'Capitalism's New Clothes'. The Baffler, 2019. Available at https://thebaffler.com/latest/capitalisms-new-clothes-morozov, [cited 14 February 2019].

Moulier-Boutang, Yann. *Cognitive Capitalism* (Cambridge, UK: Polity, 2011).

Mozur, Paul. 'One Month, 500,000 Face Scans: How China Is Using A.I. To Profile a Minority'. *The New York Times* (14 April 2019).

Müller, Christopher John. *Prometheanism: Technology, Digital Culture and Human Obsolescence* (London: Rowman & Littlefield, 2016).

Murgia, Madhumita. 'Who's Using Your Face? The Ugly Truth About Facial Recognition'. *Financial Times* (19 April 2019).

Musser, John. 'What Is a Platform?'. 2007. Available at https://www.programmableweb.com/news/what-platform/2007/09/19, [cited 22 October 2019].

Neocleous, Mark. *The Universal Adversary: Security, Capital and "the Enemies of All Mankind"*. (London: Routledge, 2016).

Netflix. 'Engineering Trade-Offs and the Netflix Api Re-Architecture'. Netflix Technology Blog, 2016. Available at https://medium.com/netflix-techblog/engineering-trade-offs-and-the-netflix-api-re-architecture-64f122b277dd, [cited 23 October 2019].

Neumann, Iver. 'Self and Other in International Relations'. *European Journal of International Relations* 2(2) (1996): 139–74.

NeurIPS. 'Reviewer Guidelines'. 2020. Available at https://nips.cc/Conferences/2020/PaperInformation/ReviewerGuidelines, [cited 30 June 2021].

Newfield, Christopher. 'Corporate Open Source. Intellectual Property and the Struggle over Value'. *Radical Philosophy* 181 (Sept/Oct) (2013): 6–11.

Newman, Sam. *Building Microservices: Designing Fine-Grained Systems* (Beijing: O'Reilly, 2015).

Newton, Casey. 'The Trauma Floor. The Secret Lives of Facebook Moderators in America'. The Verge, 2019. Available at https://www.theverge.com/2019/2/25/18229714/cognizant-facebook-content-moderator-interviews-trauma-working-conditions-arizona, [cited 13 October 2019].

Neyland, Daniel. *The Everyday Life of an Algorithm* (Basingstoke: Palgrave Macmillan, 2019).

Ng, Andrew. 'The State of Artificial Intelligence'. YouTube, 2017.

Ng, Andrew. *Machine Learning Yearning*. 2018. Available at https://www.deeplearning.ai/machine-learning-yearning/, [cited 29 November 2019].

Nix, Alexander. 'Oral Evidence: Fake News, HC 363'. House of Commons, 2018. Available at http://data.parliament.uk/writtenevidence/committeeevidence.svc/evidencedocument/digital-culture-media-and-sport-committee/fake-news/oral/79388.pdf, [cited 10 March 2018].

Noble, Safiya Umoja. *Algorithms of Oppression: How Search Engines Reinforce Racism* (New York: New York University Press, 2018).

Norvig, Peter. 'On Chomsky and the Two Cultures of Statistical Learning'. 2012. Available at http://norvig.com/chomsky.html, [cited 29 November 2019].

Nowak, Michael, and Dean Eckles. 'Determining User Personality Characteristics from Social Networking System Communications and Characteristics'. Google Patents. United States Patent Office, 2014.

NSA. 'SKYNET: Applying Advanced Cloud-Based Behavior Analytics'. The Intercept, 2007. Available at https://theintercept.com/document/2015/05/08/skynet-applying-advanced-cloud-based-behavior-analytics/, [cited 3 November 2018].

NSA. 'XKeyScore'. *The Guardian*, 2008. Available at https://www.theguardian.com/world/interactive/2013/jul/31/nsa-xkeyscore-program-full-presentation, [cited 30 June 2020].

NSA. 'New Contact-Chaining Procedures to Allow Better, Faster Analysis'. Snowden Archive, 2011. Available at https://search.edwardsnowden.com/docs/NewContact-ChainingProcedurestoAllowBetterFasterAnalysis2013-09-28nsadocs, [cited 8 November 2016].

NSA. 'SKYNET: Courier Detection Via Machine Learning'. Snowden Archive, 2012. Available at https://search.edwardsnowden.com/docs/SKYNETCourierDetectionviaMachineLearning2015-05-08nsadocs, [cited 29 July 2021].

NSA. 'Data Scientist. Job Description'. 2016. Available at https://www.nsa.gov/psp/applyonline/EMPLOYEE/HRMS/c/HRS_HRAM.HRS_CE.GBL?Page=HRS_CE_JOB_DTL&Action=A&JobOpeningId=1076263&SiteId=1&PostingSeq=1, [cited 16 October 2016].

NSCAI. 'Final Report. National Security Commission on Artificial Intelligence'. National Security Commission on Artificial Intelligence (NSCAI), 2021. Available at https://www.nscai.gov/, [cited 8 February 2021].

OCHA. 'From Digital Promise to Frontline Practice: New and Emerging Technologies in Humanitarian Action'. Geneva: United Nations Office for the Coordination of Humanitarina Affairs (UN OCHA), 2021.

OECD. 'Recommendation of the Council on Artificial Intelligence'. Organisation for Economic Co-operation and Development (OECD), 2019. Available at https://legalinstruments.oecd.org/en/instruments/oecd-legal-0449, [cited 29 July 2021].

Office of Oversight and Investigations. 'A Review of the Data Broker Industry: Collection, Use, and Sale of Consumer Data for Marketing Purposes'. United States Senate Committee on Commerce, Science, and Transportation, 2013.

Ogborn, Miles. *Indian Ink: Script and Print in the Making of the English East India Company*. (Chicago: University of Chicago Press, 2008).

O'Hear, Steve. 'Facebook Is Buying UK's Bloomsbury AI to Ramp up Natural Language Tech in London'. TechCrunch, 2018. Available at https://techcrunch.com/2018/07/02/thebloomsbury/, [cited 27 November 2019].

Olsson, Christian. 'Can't Live with Em, Can't Live without Em: "The Enemy" as Practical Object of Political-Military Controversy in Contemporary Western Wars'. *Critical Military Studies* 5(4) (2019): 359–77.

O'Neil, Cathy. *Weapons of Math Destruction: How Big Data Increases Inequality and Threatens Democracy* (New York: Crown Publishing Group, 2016).

O'Neil Risk Consulting & Algorithmic Auditing. 'It's the Age of the Algorithm and We Have Arrived Unprepared'. 2021. Available at https://orcaarisk.com/, [cited 22 July 2021].

OpenEEW. 'A Low Cost, Open Source, IoT-Based Earthquake Early Warning System'. 2021. Available at https://openeew.com/, [cited 12 June 2021].

Oracle America Inc vs The United States and AWS Inc. 'Pre-Award Bid Protest'. United States Court of Federal Claims, 2018. Available at https://ecf.cofc.uscourts.gov/cgi-bin/show_public_doc?2018cv1880-102-0, [cited 30 July 2021].

Oracle America v Department of Defense and Amazon Web Services. 'Amazon Web Services, Inc's Response to Oracle America, Inc's Motion to Complete and Supplement the Administrative Record and for Leave to Conduct Limited Discovery'. 2019. Available at https://regmedia.co.uk/2019/01/23/190118_aws_submission_jedi_.pdf, [cited 28 January 2019].

Owen, Naomi. 'At-a-Glance: China's Draft Personal Information Protection Law'. 2020. Available at https://gdpr.report/news/2020/10/30/at-a-glance-chinas-draft-personal-information-protection-law/, [cited 8 December 2020].

Oxford English Dictionary. '"Operation"'. In *OED Online* (Oxford: Oxford University Press, 2021).

Palonen, Kari. 'Parliamentary and Electoral Decisions as Political Acts'. In *The Decisionist Imagination: Sovereignty, Social Science and Democracy in the 20th Century*, edited by Daniel Bessner and Nicolas Guilhot, 85–108 (Oxford: Bergahn Book, 2018).

Parker, Geoffrey G, Marshall W Van Alstyne, and Sangeet Paul Choudary. *Platform Revolution: How Networked Markets Are Transforming the Economy and How to Make Them Work for You* (New York: WW Norton, 2016).

Pasick, Adam. 'The Magic That Makes Spotify's Discover Weekly Playlists So Damn Good'. Quartz, 2015. Available at https://qz.com/571007/the-magic-that-makes-spotifys-discover-weekly-playlists-so-damn-good/, [cited 8 December 2020].

Pasquale, Frank. *The Black Box Society* (Cambridge, MA: Harvard University Press, 2015).

Peakin, Will. 'ICO Appoints Researcher to Develop Method for Auditing Algorithms'. FutureScot, 2018. Available at https://futurescot.com/ico-appoints-researcher-to-develop-method-for-auditing-algorithms/, [cited 21 October 2019].

Peck, Jamie, Neil Brenner, and Nik Theodore. 'Actually Existing Neoliberalism'. In *The SAGE Handbook of Neoliberalism*, edited by Damien Cahill, Melinda Cooper, Martijn Konings, and David Primrose, 3-15 (London: SAGE, 2018).

Pedrycz, Witold, and Shyi-Ming Chen. *Information Granularity, Big Data, and Computational Intelligence* (New York: Springer, 2014).

Pentland, Alex (Sandy). *Honest Signals: How They Shape Our World* (Cambridge, MA: MIT Press, 2008).

Pentland, Alex (Sandy). *Social Physics: How Good Ideas Spread—The Lessons from a New Science* (New York: Penguin, 2014).

Perez, Juan. 'Google Wants Your Phonemes'. 2007. Available at https://www.infoworld.com/article/2642023/google-wants-your-phonemes.html, [cited 1 October 2012].

Perry, Walt L, Brian McInnis, Carter C Price, Susan C Smith, and John S Hollywood. *Predictive Policing: The Role of Crime Forecasting in Law Enforcement Operations* (Santa Monica, CA: RAND 2013).

Petzel, Eric. 'Airmapview'. Airbnb, 2015. Available at https://medium.com/airbnb-engineering/airmapview-a-view-abstraction-for-maps-on-android-4b7175a760ac, [cited 2 May 2019].

Phillips, P. Jonathon, and Mark Przybocki. 2020, 'Four Principles of Explainable AI as Applied to Biometrics and Facial Forensic Algorithms'. arXiv preprint arXiv:2002.01014.

Pichai, Sundar. 'AI at Google: Our Principles'. Google, 2018. Available at https://blog.google/technology/ai/ai-principles/, [cited 24 January 2019].

Pielemeier, Jason. 'NetzDG: A Key Test for the Regulation of Tech Companies'. Medium, 2019. Available at https://medium.com/design-and-tech-co/netzdg-a-key-test-for-the-regulation-of-tech-companies-e4ba205b566c, [cited 7 October 2019].

Plantin, Jean-Christophe, Carl Lagoze, Paul N Edwards, and Christian Sandvig. 'Infrastructure Studies Meet Platform Studies in the Age of Google and Facebook'. *New Media & Society* 20(1) (2018): 293–310.

Plantin, Jean-Christophe, Alison Powell, 'Open Maps, Closed Knowledge: What the Platformization of Maps Means for Citizenship and Society'. Paper presented *at IPP2016: The Platform Society* (Oxford: Oxford Internet Institute, 2016).

Plaugic, Lizzie. 'App That Falsely Claimed to Aid Refugees at Sea Pulled from App Store'. 2016. Available at https://www.theverge.com/2016/6/21/11988286/i-sea-app-refugees-ios-fake, [cited 14 October 2017].

Poon, Martha. 'Corporate Capitalism and the Growing Power of Big Data: Review Essay'. *Science, Technology, & Human Values* 41(6) (2016): 1088–1108.

Power, Michael. *The Audit Society: Rituals of Verification* (Oxford: Oxford University Press, 1997).

Power, Michael. 'The Audit Society—Second Thoughts'. *International Journal of Auditing* 4(1) (2000): 111–19.

Prasad, Revati. 'Ascendant India, Digital India: How Net Neutrality Advocates Defeated Facebook's Free Basics'. *Media, Culture & Society* 40(3) (2018): 415–31.

Prasse-Freeman, Elliott. 'Resistance/Refusal: Politics of Manoeuvre under Diffuse Regimes of Governmentality'. *Anthropological Theory* (2020). doi.org/10.1177/1463499620940218

PredPol. 'Geolitica: A New Name, a New Focus'. 2021. Available at https://blog.predpol.com/geolitica-a-new-name-a-new-focus, [cited 4 May 2021].

PRNewswire. 'NJVC Platform as a Service to Include Google Geospatial Services for Ncoic Geospatial Community Cloud Project in Support of Disaster Relief Efforts'. 2013. Available at https://www.giscafe.com/nbc/articles/1/1202884/NJVC-Platform-Service-Include-Google-Geospatial-Services-NCOIC-Geospatial-Community-Cloud-Project-Support-Disaster-Relief-Efforts, [cited 29 July 2021].

Provost, Foster, and Tom Fawcett. *Data Science for Business: What You Need to Know About Data Mining and Data-Analytic Thinking* (Sebastopol, CA: O'Reilly, 2013).

Puente, Mark. 'LAPD Pioneered Predicting Crime with Data. Many Police Don't Think It Works'. *Los Angeles Times* (3 July 2019).

Pugliese, Joseph. 'Death by Metadata: The Bioinformationalisation of Life and the Transliteration of Algorithms to Flesh'. In *Security, Race, Biopower: Essays on Technology and Corporeality*, edited by Holly Randell-Moon and Ryan Tippet, 3–20 (London: Palgrave Macmillan UK, 2016).

Pybus, Jennifer, Mark Coté, and Tobias Blanke. 'Hacking the Social Life of Big Data'. *Big Data & Society* 2(2) (2015): 1–10.

Qaurooni, Danial, and Hamid Ekbia. 'The "Enhanced" Warrior: Drone Warfare and the Problematics of Separation'. *Phenomenology and the Cognitive Sciences* 16(1) (2017): 53–73.

R (Bridges) v CCSWP and SSHD. 'Judgment Approved by the Court for Handing Down'. High Court of Justice, 2019. Available at https://www.judiciary.uk/wp-content/uploads/2019/09/bridges-swp-judgment-Final03-09-19-1.pdf, [cited 24 October 2019].

R (Bridges) v CCSWP and SSHD. 'Judgment in the Court of Appeal (Civil Division)'. 2020. Available at https://www.bailii.org/ew/cases/EWCA/Civ/2020/1058.html, [cited 6 March 2021].

Rahim, Rasha Abdul. 'Why Project Maven Is the Litmus Test for Google's New Principles'. Amnesty International, 2018. Available at https://www.amnesty.org/en/latest/news/2018/06/why-project-maven-is-the-litmus-test-for-googles-new-principles/, [cited 27 January 2019].

Rancière, Jacques. *Disagreement. Politics and Philosophy.* Translated by Julie Rose. (Minneapolis: University of Minnesota Press, 1999).

Rancière, Jacques, and Adnen Jdey. *La méthode de la scène* (Paris: Éditions Lignes, 2018).

Reese, Hope. 'Is "Data Labeling" the New Blue-Collar Job of the AI Era?'. 2016. Available at https://www.techrepublic.com/article/is-data-labeling-the-new-blue-collar-job-of-the-ai-era/, [cited 27 October 2019].

Reisman, Dillon, Jason Schultz, Kate Crawford, and Meredith Whittaker. 'Algorithmic Impact Assessments: A Practical Framework for Public Agency Accountability'. AI Now Institute, 2018. Available at https://ainowinstitute.org/aiareport2018.pdf, [cited 21 October 2019].

Reprieve. 'Two Journalists Ask the US Government to Remove Them from the Kill List'. Reprive, 2018. Available at https://reprieve.org/us/2018/05/03/two-journalists-ask-u-s-government-remove-kill-list/, [cited 5 July 2021].

Resnick, Brian. 'Cambridge Analytica's "Psychographic Microtargeting": What's Bullshit and What's Legit'. *Vox*, 2018. Available at https://www.vox.com/science-and-health/2018/3/23/17152564/cambridge-analytica-psychographic-microtargeting-what, [cited 6 November 2019].

Reuters. 'New Zealand Passport Robot Tells Applicant of Asian Descent to Open Eyes'. 2016. Available at https://www.reuters.com/article/us-newzealand-passport-error-idUSKBN13W0RL, [cited 22 October 2019].

Rider, Karina, and David Murakami Wood. 'Condemned to Connection? Network Communitarianism in Mark Zuckerberg's "Facebook Manifesto"'. *New Media & Society* 21(3) (2019): 639–54.

Rieder, Bernhard. *Engines of Order: A Mechanology of Algorithmic Techniques* (Amsterdam: Amsterdam University Press, 2020).

Rieder, Bernhard, and Guillaume Sire. 'Conflicts of Interest and Incentives to Bias: A Microeconomic Critique of Google's Tangled Position on the Web'. *New Media & Society* 16(2) (2014): 195–211.

Roach, John. 'Microsoft Improves Facial Recognition Technology to Perform Well across All Skin Tones, Genders'. Microsoft, 2018. Available at https://blogs.microsoft.com/ai/gender-skin-tone-facial-recognition-improvement/, [cited 22 March 2020].

Roberts, Dorothy E. 'Book Review: Digitizing the Carceral State'. *Harvard Law Review* 132(6) (2019): 1695–1728.

Roberts, Sarah T. *Behind the Screen: Content Moderation in the Shadows of Social Media* (New Haven: Yale University Press, 2019).

Rogers, Kenneth. *The Attention Complex: Media, Archeology, Method* (Basingstoke: Palgrave Macmilan, 2014).

Rose, Nikolas. 'Government and Control'. *British Journal of Criminology* 40(2) (2000): 321–39.

Rose, Nikolas. 'The Neurochemical Self and Its Anomalies'. In *Risk and Morality*, edited by Richard V. Ericson and Aaron Doyle, 407–37 (Toronto: University of Toronto Press, 2003).

Rosenberg, Matthew, Nicholas Confessore, and Carole Cadwalladr. 'How Trump Consultants Exploited the Facebook Data of Millions'. *The New York Times* (17 March 2018).

Roussi, Antoaneta. 'Resisting the Rise of Facial Recognition'. *Nature* 587 (2020): 350–3.

Rouvroy, Antoinette. 'The End(s) of Critique: Data-Behaviourism vs. Due-Process'. In *Privacy, Due Process and the Computational Turn: The Philosophy of Law Meets the Philosophy of Technology*, edited by Mireille Hildebrandt and Katja de Vries, 143–67 (London: Routledge, 2012).

Rouvroy, Antoinette, and Thomas Berns. 'Gouvernementalité algorithmique et perspectives d'émancipation: Le disparate comme condition d'individuation par la relation?'. *Réseaux* 1(177) (2013): 163–96.

Rudin, Cynthia. 'Stop Explaining Black Box Machine Learning Models for High Stakes Decisions and Use Interpretable Models Instead'. *Nature Machine Intelligence* 1(5) (2019): 206–15.

Russell, Legacy. *Glitch Feminism: A Manifesto* (London: Verso, 2020).

Sanders, Lewis, IV. 'Facebook Funds AI Ethics Center in Munich'. Deutsche Welle, 2019. Available at https://www.dw.com/en/facebook-funds-ai-ethics-center-in-munich/a-47156591, [cited 10 February 2019].

Sandvig, Christian, Kevin Hamilton, Karrie Karahalios, and Cedric Langbort. 'Auditing Algorithms: Research Methods for Detecting Discrimination on Internet Platforms'. Paper presented at *Data and Discrimination: Converting Critical Concerns into Productive Inquiry, a Preconference of the 64th Annual Meeting of the International Communication Association* (Seattle, WA: 2014).

Sandvik, Kristin Bergtora, Katja Lindskov Jacobsen, and Sean Martin McDonald. 'Do No Harm: A Taxonomy of the Challenges of Humanitarian Experimentation'. *International Review of the Red Cross* 99(904) (2017): 319–44.

Saunders, Jessica, Priscillia Hunt, and John S Hollywood. 'Predictions Put into Practice: A Quasi-Experimental Evaluation of Chicago's Predictive Policing Pilot'. *Journal of Experimental Criminology* 12(3) (2016): 347–71.

Schiller, Daniel. *Digital Capitalism: Networking the Global Market System* (Cambridge, MA: MIT Press, 2000).

Schillings, Sonja. *Enemies of All Humankind: Fictions of Legitimate Violence* (Hanover, NH: Dartmouth College Press, 2017).

Schmitt, Carl. *The Concept of the Political*. Translated by George Schwab. (Chicago: University of Chicago Press, 1996).

Schneier, Bruce. 'Why Data Mining Won't Stop Terror'. *Wired*, 2005. Available at https://www.schneier.com/essays/archives/2005/03/why_data_mining_wont.html, [cited 18 February 2019].

Scholtz, Trebor, *Digital Labor: The Internet as Playground and Factory* (London: Routledge, 2013).

Schouten, Peer. 'Security as Controversy: Reassembling Security at Amsterdam Airport'. *Security Dialogue* 45(1) (2014): 23–42.

Schutt, Rachel, and Cathy O'Neil. *Doing Data Science: Straight Talk from the Frontline* (Sebastopol, CA: O'Reilly, 2013).

Science Museum. 'Top Secret. From Ciphers to Cybersecurity'. 2019. Available at https://www.sciencemuseum.org.uk/what-was-on/top-secret, [cited 29 July 2021].

Scola et al. v Facebook Inc. 'Amended Complaint and Demand for Jury Trial'. Civil Action No. *18-civ-05135*: Superior Court of California, County of San Mateo, 2019. Available at https://contentmoderatorsettlement.com/Home/Documents, [cited 29 July 2021].

Scola et al. v Facebook Inc. 'Plaintiffs' Renewed Notice of Motion and Motion for Final Approval of Settlement'. Superior Court of California, County of San Matteo, 2021. Available at https://contentmoderatorsettlement.com/Home/Documents, [cited 28 June 2021].

Scola et al. v Facebook Inc. 'Proposed Settlement'. 2020. Available at https://content moderatorsettlement.com/, [cited 26 July 2021].

Scola et al. v Facebook Inc. 'Settlement Agreement and Release'. 2020. Available at https://contentmoderatorsettlement.com/Content/Documents/Settlement%20Agreement.pdf, [cited 30 November 2020].

Seaver, Nick. 'What Should an Anthropology of Algorithms Do?'. *Cultural Anthropology* 33(3) (2018): 375–85.

Serres, Michel. *Hermès II. L'Interférence* (Paris: Les Editions de Minuit, 1972).

Serres, Michel. *The Parasite* (Baltimore: Johns Hopkins University Press, 1982).

Shanahan, Patrick M. 'Public Declaration and Assertion of Military and State Secrets Privilege by Patrick M. Shanhan, Acting Secretary of Defense'. In *Civil Action No. 1:17-cv-0581 (RMC)*. US District Court for the District of Columbia, 2019.

Shane, Scott, and Daisuke Wakabayashi. '"The Business of War": Google Employees Protest Work for the Pentagon'. The New York Times (4 April 2018).

Sherrets, Doug, Sean Liu, and Brett Rolston Lider. 'User Behavior Indicator'. Google Patents. United States Patent Office, 2014.

Shore, Cris, and Susan Wright. 'Coercive Accountability: The Rise of Audit Culture in Higher Education'. In *Audit Cultures: Anthropological Studies in Accountability, Ethics and the Academy*, edited by Marilyn Strathern, 57–89 (London: Routledge, 2000).

Silver, Ellen. 2018, 'Hard Questions: Who Reviews Objectionable Content on Facebook— and Is the Company Doing Enough to Support Them?'. 2018. Available at https://newsroom.fb.com/news/2018/07/hard-questions-content-reviewers/, [cited 17 May 2020].

Simonite, Tom. 'What Really Happened When Google Ousted Timnit Gebru'. *Wired*, 2021. Available at https://www.wired.com/story/google-timnit-gebru-ai-what-really-happened/, [cited 17 June 2021].

Singh, Angadh, and Carlos Gomez-Uribe. 'Recommending Media Items Based on Take Rate Signals'. Google Patents. United States Patent Office, 2019.

Singleton, Vicky. 'When Contexts Meet: Feminism and Accountability in UK Cattle Farming'. *Science, Technology, & Human Values* 37(4) (2012): 404–33.

Smith, Aaron. 'Gig Work, Online Selling and Home Sharing'. Pew Research Center, 2016. Available at https://www.pewinternet.org/2016/11/17/gig-work-online-selling-and-home-sharing/, [cited 27 November 2019].

Snap Inc. 'Community Guidelines'. 2019. Available at https://www.snap.com/en-US/community-guidelines, [cited 3 October 2019].

Snow, Jacob. 'Amazon's Face Recognition Falsely Matched 28 Members of Congress with Mugshots'. 2018. Available at https://www.aclu.org/blog/privacy-technology/surveillance-technologies/amazons-face-recognition-falsely-matched-28, [cited 17 June 2021].

Solon, Olivia. '"It's Digital Colonialism": How Facebook's Free Internet Service Has Failed Its Users'. *The Guardian* (27 July 2017).

Spotify. 'Letter to Access Now'. 2021. Available at https://www.accessnow.org/cms/assets/uploads/2021/04/Spotify-Letter-to-Access-Now-04-15-2021-.pdf, [cited 11 July 2021].

Squire, Vicki, editor. *The Contested Politics of Mobility: Borderzones and Irregularity* (London: Routledge, 2011).

Srinivasan, Janaki, and Elisa Oreglia. 'The Myths and Moral Economies of Digital ID and Mobile Money in India and Myanmar'. *Engaging Science, Technology, and Society* 6 (2020): 215–36.

Srnicek, Nick. *Platform Capitalism* (Cambridge, UK: Polity, 2017).

Statista. 'Business Data Platform'. 2019. Available at https://www.statista.com/topics/1145/internet-usage-worldwide/, [cited 23 October 2019].

Statt, Nick. 'Google Dissolves AI Ethics Board Just One Week after Forming It. Not a Great Sign'. The Verge, 2019. Available at https://www.theverge.com/2019/4/4/18296113/google-ai-ethics-board-ends-controversy-kay-coles-james-heritage-foundation, [cited 3 June 2019].

Statt, Nick. 'Zuckerberg: "Move Fast and Break Things" Isn't How Facebook Operates Anymore'. 2014. Available at https://www.cnet.com/news/zuckerberg-move-fast-and-break-things-isnt-how-we-operate-anymore/, [cited 14 June 2021].

Stephens-Davidowitz, Seth. *Everybody Lies: Big Data, New Data, and What the Internet Can Tell Us About Who We Really Are* (New York: HarperCollins, 2017).

Stoker-Walker, Chris. 'Twitter's Vast Metadata Haul Is a Privacy Nightmare for Users'. 2018. Available at https://www.wired.co.uk/article/twitter-metadata-user-privacy.

Stoler, Ann Laura. *Duress: Imperial Durabilities in Our Times* (Durham, NC: Duke University Press, 2016).

Stop LAPD Spying Coalition. 'Predictive Policing: Profit-Driven Racist Policing'. 2016. Available at https://stoplapdspying.org/predictive-policing-profit-driven-racist-policing/, [cited 20 May 2021].

Stop LAPD Spying Coalition. 'Stop LAPD Spying Coalition Wins Groundbreaking Public Records Lawsuit'. 2019. Available at https://stoplapdspying.medium.com/stop-lapd-spying-coalition-wins-groundbreaking-public-records-lawsuit-32c3101d4575, [cited 3 May 2021].

Stop LAPD Spying Coalition and Free Radicals. 'The Algorithmic Ecology: An Abolitionist Tool for Organizing against Algorithms'. 2020. Available at https://stoplapdspying.medium.com/the-algorithmic-ecology-an-abolitionist-tool-for-organizing-against-algorithms-14fcbd0e64d0, [cited 20 June 2021].

Strathern, Marilyn. 'Introduction: New Accountabilities'. In *Audit Cultures: Anthropological Studies in Accountability, Ethics and the Academy*, edited by Marilyn Strathern, 1–18 (London: Routledge, 2000).

Stroud, Matt. 'The Minority Report: Chicago's New Police Computer Predicts Crimes, but Is It Racist?'. The Verge, 2014. Available at https://www.theverge.com/2014/2/19/5419854/the-minority-report-this-computer-predicts-crime-but-is-it-racist, [cited 23 October 2019].

Suchman, Lucy, Karolina Follis, and Jutta Weber. 'Tracking and Targeting: Sociotechnologies of (In)security'. *Science, Technology, & Human Values* 42(6) (2017): 983–1002.

Suchman, Lucy, Lilly Irani, Peter Asaro, and et al. 'Open Letter in Support of Google Employees and Tech Workers'. International Commitee for Robot Arms Control, 2018. Available at https://www.icrac.net/open-letter-in-support-of-google-employees-and-tech-workers/, [cited 28 January 2019].

Sullivan, Gavin. *The Law of the List: UN Counterterrorism Sanctions and the Politics of Global Security Law* (Cambridge, UK: Cambridge University Press, 2020).

Sundararajan, Arun. 'Network Effects'. NYU Stern, 2006. Available at http://oz.stern.nyu.edu/io/network.html, [cited 28 October 2019].

Swanson, Christopher, and Johan Oskarsson. 'Parking Suggestions'. Spotify AB Publisher. United States Patent Office, 2018.

Tankovska, H. 'Facebook: Mobile Advertising Revenue Share Q3 2019'. Statista, 2021. Available at https://www.statista.com/statistics/999580/share-of-mobile-facebook-ad-revenue-quarter/, [cited 19 July 2021].

Tegmark, Max. 'Elon Musk Donates $10 M to Keep AI Beneficial'. Future of Life Institute, 2015. Available at https://futureoflife.org/2015/10/12/elon-musk-donates-10m-to-keep-ai-beneficial/, [cited 29 May 2019].

The Economist. 'Digital Verbosity. What's in a Tweet'. *The Economist* (29 September 2011).

The Economist. 'The World's Most Valuable Resource Is No Longer Oil, but Data'. *The Economist* (5 June 2017).

The Economist Intelligence Unit. 'China Regulations: Data Privacy? The First Face-Off'. *The Economist* (9 November 2019).

The Intercept. 'Digint Imbalance'. 2016. Available at https://theintercept.com/document/2016/06/07/digint-imbalance/, [cited 2 August 2016].

The Jargon File. "Luser". n.d. Available at http://catb.org/jargon/html/L/luser.html, [cited 26 July 2021].

The New Inquiry. 'White Collar Crime Risk Zones'. The New Inquiry, 2019. Available at https://whitecollar.thenewinquiry.com/, [cited 29 October 2019].

The Precarity Lab. *Technoprecarious* (London: Goldsmiths University Press, 2020).

Timmermans, Stefan, and Steven Epstein. 'A World of Standards but Not a Standard World: Toward a Sociology of Standards and Standardization'. *Annual Review of Sociology* 36 (2010): 69–89.

Tiwana, Amrit, Benn Konsynski, and Ashley A. Bush. 'Research Commentary—Platform Evolution: Coevolution of Platform Architecture, Governance, and Environmental Dynamics'. *Information Systems Research* 21(4) (2010): 675–87.

UK Home Department. 'Draft Investigatory Powers Bill'. Her Majesty's Stationery Office, 2015. Available at https://www.gov.uk/government/uploads/system/uploads/attachment_data/file/473770/Draft_Investigatory_Powers_Bill.pdf, [cited 7 December 2015].

UNHCR. *Connecting Refugees. How Internet and Mobile Connectivity Can Improve Refugee Well-Being and Transform Humanitarian Action*. Geneva: UNHCR, 2016.

Upchurch, Tom. 'To Work for Society—Data Scientists Need a Hippocratic Oath with Teeth. Interview with Cathy O'Neil'. *Wired*, 2018. Available at https://www.wired.co.uk/article/data-ai-ethics-hippocratic-oath-cathy-o-neil-weapons-of-math-destruction, [cited 1 December 2018].

Van Dijck, José. 'Datafication, Dataism and Dataveillance: Big Data between Scientific Paradigm and Ideology'. *Surveillance & Society* 12(2) (2014): 197–208.

Van Dijck, José, David Nieborg, and Thomas Poell. 'Reframing Platform Power'. *Internet Policy Review* 8(2) (2019). https://policyreview.info/articles/analysis/reframing-platform-power.

Van Dijck, José, Thomas Poell, and Martijn De Waal. *The Platform Society: Public Values in a Connective World* (Oxford: Oxford University Press, 2018).

Van Munster, Rens, and Casper Sylvest. 'Appetite for Destruction: Günther Anders and the Metabolism of Nuclear Techno-Politics'. *Journal of International Political Theory* 15(3) (2019): 332–48.

Varon, Joana, and Paz Peña. 'Building a Feminist Toolkit to Question A.I. Systems'. 2021. Available at https://notmy.ai/2021/05/03/algorithmic-emancipation-building-a-feminist-toolkit-to-question-a-i-systems/, [cited 27 May 2021].

Van Rijsbergen, Keith. *The Geometry of Information Retrieval* (Cambridge, UK: Cambridge University Press, 2004).

Varshney, Kush R. 'Introducing AI Fairness 360'. IBM, 2018. Available at https://www.ibm
.com/blogs/research/2018/09/ai-fairness-360/, [cited 14 November 2019].

Venturini, Tommaso. 'From Fake to Junk News, the Data Politics of Online Virality'. In *Data Politics: Worlds, Subjects, Rights*, edited by Didier Bigo, Engin Isin, and Evelyn Ruppert (London: Routledge, 2019).

Vora, Kalindi. *Life Support: Biocapital and the New History of Outsourced Labor* (Minneapolis: University of Minnesota Press, 2015).

Vora, Kalindi. 'Labor'. In *Gender: Matter*, edited by Stacy Alaimo, 205–22. London: Macmillan, 2017.

Wajcman, Judy. *Technofeminism* (Cambridge, UK: Polity, 2014).

Walker, Richard. 'Germany Warns: AI Arms Race Already Underway'. Deutsche Welle, 2021. Available at https://www.dw.com/en/artificial-intelligence-cyber-warfare-drones-future/a-57769444, [cited 17 June 2021].

Walker, R. B. J. *Inside/Outside: International Relations as Political Theory* (Cambridge, UK: Cambridge University Press, 1993).

Walker, R. B. J. 'The Double Outside of the Modern International'. *Ephemera: Theory and Politics in Organization* 6(1) (2006): 56–69.

Walker, R. B. J. *Out of Line: Essays on the Politics of Boundaries and the Limits of Modern Politics* (London: Routledge, 2015).

Walters, William. *Governmentality: Critical Encounters* (London: Routledge, 2012).

Welch, Chris. 'Spotify Raises Limit for Offline Downloads to 10,000 Songs Per Device'. The Verge, 2018. Available at https://www.theverge.com/2018/9/12/17852304/spotify-offline-download-limit-10000-songs-5-devices, [cited 4 November 2019].

Wessing, Taylor. 'Germany's Network Enforcement Act and Its Impact on Social Networks'. Lexology, 2018. Available at https://www.lexology.com/library/detail.aspx?g=fb107efe-70ae-4e97-9913-5035aeeb518a, [cited 26 September 2019].

Whitman, Brian. 'Demographic and Media Preference Prediction Using Media Content Data Analysis'. Spotify AB Publisher. United States Patent Office, 2019.

Whittaker, Meredith, Kate Crawford, Roel Dobbe, Genevieve Fried, Elizabeth Kaziunas, Varoon Mathur, Sarah Myers West, et al. 'AI Now Report 2018'. AI Now Institute, 2018. Available at https://ainowinstitute.org/AI_Now_2018_Report.pdf, [cited 22 January 2019].

Wilcox, Lauren. 'Embodying Algorithmic War: Gender, Race, and the Posthuman in Drone Warfare'. *Security Dialogue* 48(1) (2017): 11–28.

Wilke, Christiane. 'Seeing and Unmaking Civilians in Afghanistan: Visual Technologies and Contested Professional Visions'. *Science, Technology, & Human Values* 42(6) (2017): 1031–60.

Williford, Jonathan R., Brandon B. May, and Jeffrey Byrne. 'Explainable Face Recognition'. In *Computer Vision—ECCV 2020*, edited by Andrea Vedaldi, Horst Bischof, Thomas Brox, and Jan-Michael Frahm (London: Springer, 2020).

Winfield, Alan F. T., and Marina J Jirotka. 'Ethical Governance Is Essential to Building Trust in Robotics and Artificial Intelligence Systems'. *Philosophical Transactions of the Royal Society A* 376(2133) (2018): 1–13.

Woods, Allan. '"We Were Using Algorithms to Catch and Kill": U.S. Whistle-blower Chelsea Manning Warns Montreal Conference of Perils of Technology, Data Collection'. Toronto Star (24 May 2018).

Wylie, Christopher. *Mindf*ck: Cambridge Analytica and the Plot to Break America* (London: Profile Books, 2019).

Xu, Ke, Vicky Liu, Yan Luo, and Zhijing Yu. 'Analyzing China's PIPL and how it compares to the EU's GDPR'. International Association of Privacy Professionals, 2021. Available at https://iapp.org/news/a/analyzing-chinas-pipl-and-how-it-compares-to-the-eus-gdpr/, [cited 15 November 2021].

Ye, Yuan. 'A Professor, a Zoo, and the Future of Facial Recognition in China'. Sixth Tone, 2021. Available at https://www.sixthtone.com/news/1007300/a-professor%2C-a-zoo%2C-and-the-future-of-facial-recognition-in-china, [cited 17 January 2022].

Yin, Cao. 'Focus Tightens on Facial Recognition'. *China Daily* (18 May 2021).

Yuan, Li. 'How Cheap Labor Drives China's A.I. Ambitions'. *The New York Times* (25 November 2018).

Yujie, Xue. 'Facial-Recognition Smart Lockers Hacked by Fourth-Graders'. Sixth Tone, 2019. Available at https://www.sixthtone.com/news/1004698/facial-recognition-smart-lockers-hacked-by-fourth-graders, [cited 23 November 2019].

Yuval-Davis, Nira, Georgie Wemyss, and Kathryn Cassidy. *Bordering* (Cambridge, UK: Polity, 2019).

Zaidan et al. v Trump et al. 'Complaint. Case No. 1:17-Cv-00581'. United States District Court for the District of Columbia, 2017. Available at https://www.plainsite.org/dockets/34pkvx7dt/district-of-columbia-district-court/zaidan-et-al-v-trump-et-al/, [cited 15 April 2017].

Zaidan et al. v Trump et al. 'Memorandum Opinion'. 2018. Available at https://ecf.dcd.uscourts.gov/cgi-bin/show_public_doc?2017cv0581-13, [cited 20 September 2018].

Zaidan et al. v Trump et al. 'Motion to Dismiss by Central Intelligence Agency, Dan Coats, Department of Defense, Department of Homeland Security, Department of Justice, John F. Kelly, James Mattis, Herbert Raymond Mcmaster, Michael Richard Pompeo, Jefferson Beauregard Sessions, Iii, Donald J. Trump, USA'. 2017. Available at https://www.plainsite.org/dockets/34pkvx7dt/district-of-columbia-district-court/zaidan-v-trump/?, [cited 2 April 2019].

Zaidan et al. v Trump et al. 'Memorandum of Points and Authorities in Support of Defendants' Motion to Dismiss'. United States District Court for the District of Columbia, 2017.

Zehfuss, Maja. *War and the Politics of Ethics* (Oxford: Oxford University Press, 2018).

Zhong, Yiyin. 'Chinese Professor Files Country's First Lawsuit against Use of Facial Recognition Technology in Zoo Row'. *The Telegraph* (5 November 2019).

Zhou, Ding, and Pierre Moreels. 'Inferring User Profile Attributes from Social Information'. Google Patents. United States Patent Office, 2013.

Ziewitz, Malte. 'Governing Algorithms: Myth, Mess, and Methods'. *Science, Technology, & Human Values* 41(1) (2016): 3–16.

Zuboff, Shoshana. *The Age of Surveillance Capitalism: The Fight for a Human Future at the New Frontier of Power* (New York: PublicAffairs, 2018).

Zuckerberg, Mark. 'Free Basics Protects Net Neutrality'. *Times of India* (28 December 2015).

Zuckerberg, Mark. 'Facebook Post'. Facebook, 2018. Available at https://www.facebook.com/zuck/posts/10105865715850211, [cited 6 November 2019].

Index of names

Index of subjects